P9-DWT-041

HITLER'S H✠LY RELICS

*A True Story of Nazi Plunder
and the Race to Recover the Crown Jewels
of the Holy Roman Empire*

Sidney D. Kirkpatrick

Simon & Schuster
New York   London   Toronto   Sydney

Simon & Schuster
1230 Avenue of the Americas
New York, NY 10020

First Simon & Schuster hardcover edition May 2010

SIMON & SCHUSTER and colophon are registered trademarks of Simon & Schuster, Inc.

For information about special discounts for bulk purchases, please contact Simon & Schuster Special Sales at 1-866-506-1949 or business@simonandschuster.com.

The Simon & Schuster Speakers Bureau can bring authors to your live event. For more information or to book an event contact the Simon & Schuster Speakers Bureau at 1-866-248-3049 or visit our website at www.simonspeakers.com.

Designed by Nancy Singer

Manufactured in the United States of America

10 9 8 7 6 5 4 3 2 1

Library of Congress Cataloging-in-Publication Data

Kirkpatrick, Sidney.
　　Hitler's holy relics : a true story of Nazi plunder and the race to recover the crown jewels of the Holy Roman Empire / Sidney D. Kirkpatrick—1st Simon & Schuster hardcover ed.
　　　　p. cm.
　　Includes bibliographical references and index.
　1. Allied forces. Supreme Headquarters. Monuments, Fine Arts and Archives section—History. 2. Horn, Walter William, 1908–1995. 3. Crown jewels—Austria—History—20th century. 4. Art thefts—Germany—History—20th century. 5. World War, 1939–1945—Confiscations and contributions—Germany. 6. World War, 1939–1945—Destruction and pillage—Europe. 8. Art treasures in war—Europe—History—20th century. 9. Cultural property—Protection—Europe—History—20th century. I. Title.
　D810.A7K57 2010
　940.53'1—dc22

　　　　　　　　　　　　　　　　　　　　　　　　　2009052301

ISBN 978-1-4165-9062-0 (hardcover)
ISBN 978-1-4165-9780-3 (ebook)

Photo credits appear on page 318

To Alexander Kirkpatrick

Man thirsts more for glory than for virtue. Armor of an enemy, his broken helmet, the flag ripped from a conquered ship, were treasures valued beyond all human riches. It is to obtain these tokens of glory that generals, be they Roman, Greek or barbarian, brave thousands of perils and endure a thousand exertions.

DECIMUS IUNIUS IUVENALIS,
ROMAN POET OF THE SECOND CENTURY C.E.

CONTENTS

AUTHOR'S NOTE

The true story that follows is based on military records, correspondence, diaries, interviews, archival materials, and the unpublished World War II oral memoirs of University of California, Berkeley, art history professor Walter Horn.

HITLER'S H☒LY RELICS

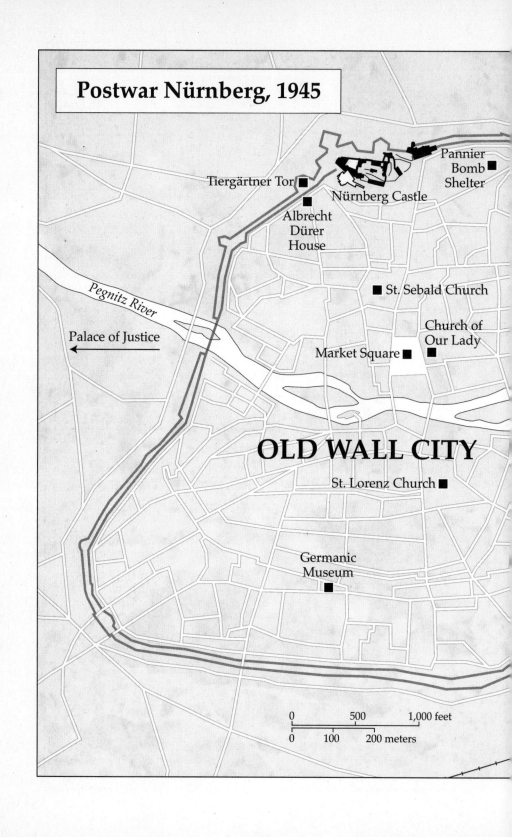

Postwar Nürnberg, 1945

Tiergärtner Tor

Nürnberg Castle

Pannier
Bomb
Shelter

Albrecht
Dürer
House

Pegnitz River

Palace of Justice

St. Sebald Church

Church of
Our Lady

Market Square

OLD WALL CITY

St. Lorenz Church

Germanic
Museum

0   500   1,000 feet

0   100   200 meters

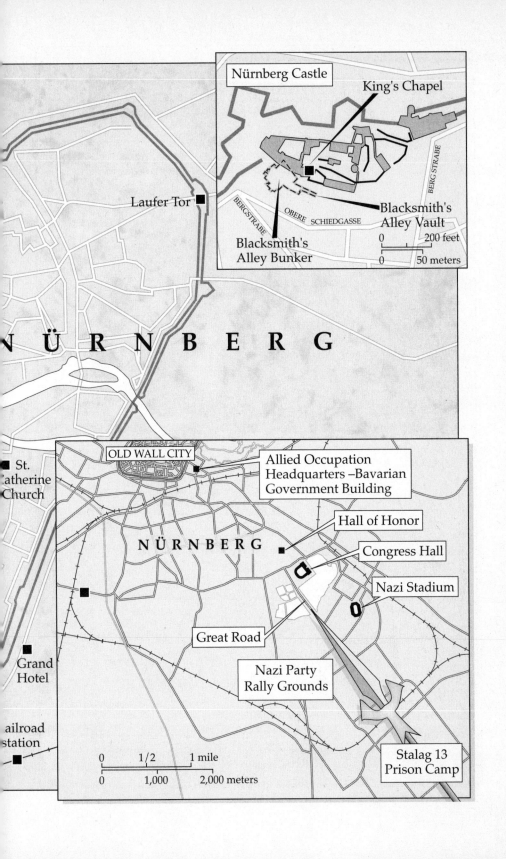

Postwar Germany, 1945

SWEDEN

North Sea

DENMARK

Baltic Sea

AMERICAN ENCLAVE

Hamburg

Elbe R.

Oder R.

POLAND

BRITISH ZONE

Hanover

Berlin

SOVIET ZONE

NETHERLANDS

Weser R.

Externsteine

Wewelsburg

Nordhausen

Rhine R.

Jena

BELGIUM

Namur

G E R M A N Y

Frankfurt

Main R.

Prague

CZECHOSLOVAKIA

LUX.

Heidelberg

Nürnberg

AMERICAN ZONE

Danube R.

FRANCE

FRENCH ZONE

Dachau

Pullach

Munich

SOVIET ZONE

Vienna

AUSTRIA

Zell am See

SWITZERLAND

BRITISH ZONE

ITALY

YUGOSLAVIA

0   50   100 miles

0   100 kilometers

Adriatic Sea

CHAPTER 1

BLACKSMITH'S ALLEY

February 23, 1945

Every morning, like clockwork, Allied bombers would darken the skies over Namur, Belgium. In this last winter of World War II, hundreds and sometimes a thousand planes, flying in vast air armadas known as bomber streams, would thunder overhead for an hour or more at a time, leaving miles-long vapor trails that hung in the air long after the aircraft had vanished and the bombardiers had released their lethal cargo over targets in Germany and Eastern Europe.

The arrival of the bomber streams terrified the captured German soldiers at the U.S. Army detention center in the snow-covered fields on the outskirts of Namur. The prisoners, huddled together and shivering in wire-mesh holding pens, would peer anxiously skyward, dreading the horror about to be unleashed on their friends and families at home. Their American captors would also look up at the planes, but instead of fear, they felt overwhelming admiration for the bomber crews and their firepower. They were the silver hammer that was destroying the Nazi war machine and would soon enable the Allied Army to annihilate Adolf Hitler in his homeland. That the day and night bombing missions targeted not only military objectives but also industrial sites, resulting in the destruction of entire cities, was the price that Germany had to pay for its continued resistance.

First Lieutenant Walter Horn, one of ten German-speaking U.S. Third Army interrogators stationed at Camp Namur, awaited the daily arrival of the bomber squadrons with mixed emotions. Thirty-six years old, with a broad chest and shoulders, dark movie-star looks, and an impatient wife waiting at home in Point Richmond, on the San Francisco Bay, Horn felt tremendous pride in America's ability to build, fuel, maintain, and launch thousands of planes loaded with tens of thousands of bombs, hurtling them hundreds of miles deep into enemy territory. Although he had yet to fire a weapon in combat during two years of service, and his mobile intelligence unit, commanded by General George S. Patton, always remained a comfortable fifty miles behind the front lines, Horn appreciated the daring and courage of the air crews and felt a special kinship with the thousands of others—artillerymen, infantry, medics, cooks, clerks, and quartermasters—who made up the largest, fastest-moving, and best-equipped army that had ever existed.

But the sight of the bomber streams also filled Horn with anxiety. Like the prisoners he interrogated, he had been born, raised, and educated in Germany. He never knew whether one of the bombers would be dropping its payload within range of his family's home in Heidelberg or if, as he looked into the holding pens at the forlorn faces of captured and wounded prisoners, he would one day see the face of his older brother Rudolf.

Lieutenant Horn's orders that winter were to help ascertain whether Hitler would unleash chemical or biological weapons when the Allied Army crossed the Rhine River into the German heartland. It had been rumored that the Germans, in a last desperate attempt to break the vise of the approaching Allied forces, would resort to using such weapons, as they had in the trenches in France twenty-seven years earlier.

Patton's mobile intelligence unit had prepared a detailed questionnaire to ferret out the truth. Interrogators did not ask prisoners directly about weapons stockpiles. Rather, they elicited the information from four out of one hundred fifty seemingly random questions put to the prisoners. The answers would be used to determine if the soldiers had been taught how to use chemical or biological weapons in battle and if, hidden behind enemy lines, shelters were in place to protect the civilian population. Fifteen hundred rank-and-file soldiers, selected from Wehrmacht infantry captured in Belgium after the Battle of the Bulge, had been marched to Namur for this purpose. The interrogation facilities being inadequate, many of the interviews took place out of doors. Horn's office, just beyond the prisoner enclosures, consisted of two empty orange crates, a small desk borrowed from a nearby elementary school, and a stack of questionnaires and pencils.

Horn had already interviewed thirty-five prisoners on February 23, 1945, when a camp guard brought him forty-eight-year-old Private Fritz Hüber from the German 2nd Panzer Division. Lean and haggard, with a narrow face distinguished by an enormous hooked nose, Hüber wore the same ill-fitting uniform in which he had been captured three weeks earlier. Though old by Allied Army standards, Hüber was not an unusual Wehrmacht recruit, as the Germans, after more than five years of continuous warfare, were drafting soldiers as young as sixteen and as old as sixty, mixing them into units of battle-hardened veterans and having them dig trenches, run interference, and haul equipment on their backs or in carts. German manpower, a resource like the diesel fuel to drive their tanks, was now in short supply.

Hüber, recruited in Nürnberg, had received less than a month's training before being marched through the snow into combat in Belgium; he didn't know anything about chemical or biological weapons. Horn checked off the private's answers in rapid succession, obtaining nothing more than "yes," "no," and "I don't know."

The interview completed, Horn was ready to dismiss his prisoner. But as the lieutenant would later note in a detailed account of the interview, he suddenly changed his mind. Looking across the table at the pitiful Private Hüber, hunched over from lack of sleep and clearly suffering from rheumatism in the damp cold, Horn offered Hüber a cigarette and a cup of coffee and asked if there was anything he knew that might interest Army intelligence.

Hüber contorted his face like a schoolboy who had flunked an exam. Tears welled up in his eyes. He wanted to help, to be of service.

The lieutenant had witnessed reactions of this kind before. He saw it nearly every day among prisoners who had lost everything but their lives. Men like Hüber, recruited off the streets by the Gestapo or forcefully removed from their homes and pressed into service for the Fatherland, were neither dedicated nor arrogant Nazis. Many of them had already lost sons, daughters, and wives in the war or had seen their homes and apartment buildings incinerated. They were reluctant warriors. Having given themselves up to the enemy, been stripped of their possessions, and herded like cattle into holding pens, most had lost the last shreds of self-respect. As a final indignity, they now saw and heard the endless streams of bombers overhead and knew that their situation was truly hopeless. Hermann Göring's new and much-vaunted Messerschmitt jet interceptors were nowhere to be seen. If Hitler actually possessed a secret weapon that would turn the tide of the war, as propaganda minister Josef Göbbels had promised the German people, he would have used it by now.

Hüber and his fellow prisoners knew that no one would be coming to their rescue. Yet, despite their utter despair, Horn sensed a strange paradox in them. These footsoldiers, even those who had begun as stalwarts of the Führer's insane dream of world domination, still wanted to be of service, wanted to count for something. They were desperate to be of value, even if it was to the enemy. Private Hüber and countless others like him would be the ones who would one day return home to rebuild their nation.

The prisoner told Horn, apologetically, that he could be of no help.

Horn expected to hear nothing more from him. But as Hüber finished his coffee, and Horn was about to signal to camp guards to lead him back to the prisoner enclosure, the soldier's face suddenly lit up. "Are you interested in art and antiques?" Hüber asked.

Horn smiled broadly. The aging German soldier couldn't have known that in civilian life his interrogator was an art history professor at the University of California at Berkeley or that years earlier, before fleeing Nazi Germany, he had studied art history in Hamburg, Munich, and Berlin, had earned his doctorate under the mentorship of the internationally renowned medieval scholar Erwin Panofsky, and completed postgraduate work with Bernard Berenson in Florence, Italy. There was no subject that Dr. Walter Horn was more interested in discussing than art and antiquities.

"What do you know?" Horn asked.

Hüber sat up stiffly and addressed the lieutenant as if he was being debriefed by a superior in the German Army. "There is a hidden treasure in a bunker underneath the Nürnberg castle. The hiding place is cut into the rock under the sandstone cliff. It's very secret. No one but Reichsführer Himmler, his staff, a few ranking city officials, and workers who labor in the bunker know anything about it."

"Heinrich Himmler, you say? Of the SS?"

Hüber nodded solemnly, adding that the bunker was deep in the castle's bedrock but that its entrance tunnel was from outside, on the street.

Intrigued, Horn asked Hüber to elaborate.

Hüber explained that the entrance was camouflaged to look like the parking garage of an antiques shop off an alley in the old part of the city, with a sign that read *Antiques—New and Old.*

As Horn would later note, Hüber paused as if holding an image of the shop in his mind. The thought seemed to bring a faint smile to his face. He became more relaxed, even upbeat.

The prisoner continued by describing the bunker's layout. He said that the covered car park, with its camouflaged doors, led to a long tunnel that descended some two hundred feet underground. At the end of the tunnel was a four-thousand-square-foot bunker, constructed of reinforced concrete, with five separate storage cells and a bank vault large enough to park a small truck inside. The facility was entirely self-contained. The bunker's guards had their own sleeping quarters, electric generators, fuel, fresh water, food supply, and radio equipment. There were airshafts that opened aboveground and an air-purification system in case the city was fire-bombed.

"If this place is so secret," Horn asked warily, "how did you get to know about it?"

Hüber's face now became animated. "Because our family lives above the antiques shop. My father is in charge of maintaining the ventilation unit that regulates the bunker's temperature and humidity. Mother checks the art and artifacts for possible mold and insect damage. She has to wear special white gloves when entering the storage units. Every now and again, she sprays the facility with pesticide."

Horn listened with growing fascination as Hüber discussed a few of the bunker's elaborate security features. Even the guards protecting the facility could not access the storage units, and no unaccompanied person, except for Himmler and the lord mayor of Nürnberg, Willy Liebel, was ever permitted inside the vault room. Two keys and a five-digit lock combination were necessary to open its foot-thick outer door and a second inner door with steel bars.

"What kind of art is kept inside the bunker?" Horn asked.

Hüber mentioned several of the more than a hundred objects he said were sheltered in the various storage rooms. There were prints and etchings by Albrecht Dürer, sculpture by Adam Kraft and Viet Stoss, medieval codices, maps, Renaissance musical instruments, and Gothic stained-glass windows. Everything was listed in a card catalogue outside the guard's room, in the main hall, and checked periodically by the lord mayor or his secretary.

Impressed, Horn asked what was kept in the vault room.

Hüber was immediately forthcoming. Inside was an array of artifacts packed into wooden shipping crates. In one enormous box containing a glass case were a king's robes, embroidered with pearl-studded pictures of camels and lions. Another box, with the word "Mauritius" stenciled on the side, held an ancient sword. A third box contained a crown covered with uncut sapphires, rubies, and amethysts. Nearby was stored a silver scepter and a golden apple tipped with a jewel-encrusted cross. In its own leather case, resting on a red velvet pillow, was an ancient Roman spear point, which visitors to the vault—among them Himmler himself—referred to as the "Holy Lance."

Horn was both excited and disturbed by Hüber's recitation. He didn't have enough information to identify the origins of the artwork sheltered in the rest of the bunker, but the combination of treasures in the vault belonged to a legendary collection of artifacts that had been detailed in countless medieval paintings and monastic manuscripts.

The king's robes, or imperial vestments, embroidered with the distinctive camels and lions, had been created in the early twelfth century in Palermo, Italy, and had been worn by the great soldier-kings of medieval Europe. The imperial sword—sometimes referred to as the "Mauritius Sword"—was named in honor of a martyred Roman centurion and legendary commander of the Theban Legion. The crown, scepter, and apple-shaped orb had been the property, among others, of King Frederick Barbarossa, the fearsome red-bearded monarch who had once held court in Nürnberg Castle and lost his life during the Third Crusade to the Holy Land. But it was Hüber's mention of the ancient Roman spear point that authoritatively identified the collection. The Holy Lance, known variously as the Longinus lance and Spear of Destiny, was alleged to have been the weapon that pierced the side of Christ at the Crucifixion and had subsequently been carried into battle by Emperors Constantine and Charlemagne.

The objects in the vault were the Crown Jewels of the Holy Roman Empire, the most valuable collection of artifacts in all of Europe. Hitler, in his quest for world domination, had removed them from the royal treasury in Vienna, Austria, and put them briefly on display in Nürnberg. Where he had hidden them after the bombing raids over Germany began, and if the collection was still intact, was a subject of intense speculation among art historians and museum curators the world over.

Horn had no reason to doubt the prisoner's story. Hitler had plundered Europe, stealing all manner of treasure, from Leonardo paintings and Michelangelo sculptures to priceless Russian and Polish icons and medieval monastic manuscripts. Nürnberg, the second-largest city in Bavaria, was a natural place for Hitler to safeguard his plunder. This ancient city, with its massive medieval castle built on a red sandstone mountain, was the Nazi state's symbolic core, sentimentally linked with its perceived mythic past, and the site of enormous staged Nazi Party rallies to glorify the regime's future. Horn himself, over the radio, had heard Hitler, standing at a podium, declare Nürnberg to be "the most German of all German cities" and "the treasure chest of the Nazi Party." Horn had always thought he meant this figuratively. Hüber was telling him otherwise.

The prisoner dutifully wrote down the names of his mother and his father, then drew a map on the back of an Army questionnaire detailing the exact location of the entrance to the underground bunker on a narrow lane that at one end backed against the historic Nürnberg castle and at the other, an open cobblestone square and clusters of medieval buildings that included the former home and art studio of Albrecht Dürer. The address was "52" Upper Black-smith's Alley.

Later that evening, after Horn had returned a stack of question-naires to his commanding officer, he borrowed a typewriter from his friend and fellow German-born interrogator, Master Sergeant Felix Rosenthal, and spent the rest of the night in the officers' mess com-posing a detailed account of his interview. He had every reason to believe that his report would be buried in a slush pile of Army intel-ligence dismissed as unimportant to the war effort, and if for some reason it was passed up the chain of command to General Patton's headquarters, he knew how improbable it would be that a combat operations officer would recognize the recovery of the Crown Jew-els of the Holy Roman Empire as a significant military objective.

In spite of his doubts that his report would climb the chain of command, Horn wrote two drafts, composing his words with the same care and attention to detail as for articles he had published in prominent art history journals before the war. Satisfied with the final result, he sealed his report along with Hüber's hand-drawn map into an envelope and addressed it to Patton's Third Army intel-ligence headquarters in Paris.

CHAPTER 2

MONUMENTS MEN

July 19, 1945

The war in Europe ended less than three months later, on May 8, 1945. Thousands of cities and towns now lay in ruins because of the monstrous power of one man, Adolf Hitler. From the rubble—as the weather warmed and wildflowers bloomed—would come the stench of countless dead men, women, and children. But many of the most horrifying realities of the Nazi killing machine were just coming to light. Even the most battle-hardened combat veterans were stunned and bewildered by the incomprehensible scenes of malnourishment, disease, and wholesale slaughter they saw in the German death camps, where millions of Jews and others deemed undesirable had been starved, tortured, and murdered by the Nazis.

Rather than return home to his teaching post at Berkeley, and against the express wishes of his wife, Horn had joined the campaign to help capture and hold responsible the Reich leadership, which had brought such horror and misery to the world. Accompanied by his friend and fellow interrogator, Felix Rosenthal, he moved with his unit from Belgium through France and across the Rhine River into Germany to Camp Freising, a top-secret U.S. Third Army interrogation center in a small farming village outside Munich. Along the way, he was promoted from interviewing lowly German infantry to interrogating high-ranking Nazis, a task for which he was especially well suited.

The most notorious Nazis he debriefed were Gauleiter Julius Streicher, the regional Nazi Party leader and loathsome publisher of *Der Stürmer,* the Nazi Party's weekly anti-Semitic newspaper, who was arrested while fleeing Bavaria disguised as a house painter; and Himmler's chief of staff, Ernst Kaltenbrunner, head of the Reich Security Main Office, or RSHA, which operated the death camps, who was captured in an isolated mountain chalet while posing as an Austrian physician. Horn's informed and relaxed manner had proved to be his most valuable asset. But it was his uncanny ability to place a particular accent that had earned him modest renown in the intelligence community. In one remarkable interrogation session, Horn had uncovered the true identity of a Gestapo officer by pinpointing where in Berlin he had grown up and gone to school.

As a reward for success, Horn was now working ten-hour days at Camp Freising in a windowless holding cell in a former German Army barracks. The only perk of the job, besides ready access to confidential files and intelligence reports, was not having to sleep on a cot and eat in the officers' mess. Thanks to Rosenthal, whom General Patton had assigned to find a suitable location for the interrogation center, he and Felix were living in the luxurious three-bedroom home of the barracks' former German commandant, which offered hot and cold running water, a dining room, a gourmet kitchen, and a wood-paneled den with its own reference library. He and Rosenthal weren't the most senior officers in the Camp Freising complex, but they had arrived first, before anyone else could lay claim to the best accommodations.

Horn had finished a particularly demanding interview on Thursday, July 19, when he received orders to report to United States Forces European Theater command headquarters in Frankfurt. Rosenthal had only to see the official letterhead of the USFET and Supreme Allied Commander Eisenhower's official stamp at the bottom of the orders to suspect that he was losing Horn to a competing intelligence outfit. But neither of the two interrogators, both deeply involved in compiling dossiers for use in upcoming war-crimes tribunals, connected Horn's orders to the report he had written in Camp Namur.

As Rosenthal would later recall, he and Horn concluded that

another high-ranking Nazi had been apprehended. "Perhaps they've caught Bormann," Horn said, venturing a guess.

Rosenthal admitted that his colleague could be right. Martin Bormann, Hitler's secretary and head of the Party Chancellery, topped the list of missing Nazi officials and was the subject of recent speculation among Freising's intelligence officers. No one knew where Bormann had fled since visiting Hitler's Berlin bunker on the day the Führer killed himself. According to Hitler's chauffeur, Erich Kempa, whom Horn and Rosenthal were currently interrogating, Bormann had escaped on foot into a Berlin subway tunnel with the leader of the Hitler Youth movement, intending to meet up with loyalist troops who would sneak them out of Germany. Many Allied intelligence officers believed that Bormann had subsequently escaped to Brazil by submarine or had joined Himmler's covert resistance army, led by Gestapo chief Heinrich Müller, who was alleged to be operating in the Austrian Alps. If Bormann had indeed been apprehended, Horn—a rising star in the intelligence community—would be the logical choice to debrief him at USFET's Camp King, where the captured Nazi high command was being held.

They would soon find out. Horn promised to keep his friend informed, cleared the trip with his commanding officer, and, early the next morning, hitched a ride on a half-ton Army transport headed to Frankfurt on the autobahn.

Although Horn relished the opportunity to leave the Freising compound, where he felt like a captive, and to visit a city he hadn't seen for a decade, the drive north was no pleasant respite from the reality of postwar Germany. Years earlier, the trip would have been a three- or four-hour cruise past scenic, well-tended farms and pastures. Now the journey consumed half the day, with depressing reminders everywhere of the war's tragedy. Horn's only consolation was that his father, Karl, a Lutheran minister, who had died just as Hitler rose to power, didn't have to experience the utter desolation and despair that gripped the country he had so loved.

Everywhere along the bomb-cratered roadway were the skeletal remains of automobiles, trucks, and treadless tanks. More disconcerting were the parades of former camp inmates and soldiers, and the forlorn processions of displaced others. These refugees of Hitler's war were part of the largest migration in human history:

Russians returning to the east, French to the west, Yugoslavs, Italians, and Austrians headed south, along with homeless Germans going in all directions. The lucky few traveled by car and truck or rode in wagons and carts and on bicycles. The countless others were on foot, with and without shoes, hauling pots, pans, water bottles, and the occasional infant on their backs.

The approach to Frankfurt showed no familiar landmarks, only rows of lonely chimneys. A few scattered buildings remained, but even these were empty shells. The scene inside the city was equally unnerving. Frankfurt's medieval city center, at one time the largest and most opulent in all of Germany, had been leveled. Except for two or three major thoroughfares, its streets lay buried under debris. Trudging through them was the same sea of forsaken and hollow-eyed faces as those on the autobahn, only these were more desperate because they had no place else to go. Either they were already home or they hadn't the strength, the means, or the wisdom to move on.

Paradoxically, the massive Nazi building complex that now housed USFET headquarters, in what was once the city's fashionable west-end district, was untouched by the war. The nine-story sand-colored skyscraper had previously been the world headquarters of I. G. Farben, Germany's largest chemical manufacturer. Here Fritz Termeer, Farben's head of research, had developed the process to turn coal into synthetic oil and rubber and, as Allied intelligence now knew, had formulated Zyklon B, the lethal nerve gas used in Himmler's death camps. That this building had survived when Frankfurt's churches, libraries, museums, and schools had burned was a topic of discussion for the Allies and Germans alike. The scuttlebutt among intelligence officers was that General Eisenhower had ordered the Farben complex spared because he wanted it for his headquarters. Perhaps it was also true that bombers had passed it by because of an adjacent prison camp housing several thousand captured Allied soldiers.

Many visitors to the ultramodern building, with its reflecting pool and landscaped grounds, found the architecture inspiring. To Horn, it was a characterless concrete fortress, representing all that he most detested in the Nazis' sterile and utilitarian architecture. He couldn't, however, fault its technical amenities. After presenting his orders at the command center's reception station, he was led by a white-helmeted military policeman into the main rotunda to elevators that operated on escalator-like conveyor belts. No doors opened or closed. Passengers merely stepped onto the moving platform on one floor and stepped off at any other.

Horn exited on the third floor and followed his escort down a spacious, lofty hallway to a suite of offices. He was not informed of his contact until Lieutenant James Rorimer—oddly attired in combat boots and a formal dress uniform—introduced himself and explained that Horn would be shown into the USFET liaison office of Major Mason Hammond, chief of Monuments, Fine Arts, and Archives.

Lieutenant Horn still didn't know why he had been called to Frankfurt, but the mention of Hammond's name and his supervisory position with the MFAA provided two important clues. He had met Hammond in London two years earlier when they were both on temporary assignment to British intelligence. After a chance encounter on the steps of the British Museum, they discovered that they were both university professors in civilian life. Hammond, the more senior of the two, held a prestigious chair at Harvard University, where he taught Latin and Greek and specialized in Roman history. Horn was just getting started in his career at Berkeley, but his work with Panofsky in Berlin and a two-year fellowship at the German Institute in Florence had impressed Hammond. They had spent a pleasant afternoon strolling the hallowed halls of the British Museum and discussing the finer points of Florentine church architecture. The war hadn't entered their conversation until late in the day, when Hammond invited Horn out for dinner. Hammond, then a captain, had spoken of the possible formation of the MFAA, the Allied military force that would be charged with protecting historic monuments on the battlefield and recovering Nazi plunder. He thought there might come a time, after the Allied invasion, when the MFAA would need someone with Horn's academic and military credentials. Apparently, that time had come.

There were no military salutes. The avuncular forty-two-year-old Hammond welcomed Horn into his office with a warm handshake. He had remembered their afternoon together in London and asked Horn how an article he was writing on the Basilica of San Miniato in Florence was coming along.

Horn admitted that he had carried a draft of the article with him across two continents and seven countries but that he still hadn't submitted it for peer review. He also expressed his uncertainty that it would ever be published. Given the destruction of so many buildings in Italy, San Miniato might no longer exist.

Hammond assured the lieutenant that the basilica was still standing, though a bit worse for wear. He had walked its cloisters six months earlier on an MFAA tour of the city. Florence's magnificent bridges hadn't survived—all but one blown up by the retreating German Army—but the city's principal monuments and churches, including the Duomo, had withstood both Nazi and Allied occupation. Hammond promised to show him photographs, but later. He wanted to know about Horn's interview with Ernst Kaltenbrunner, Himmler's RSHA chief of staff, and the details of a developing scandal in the intelligence community.

Horn shared what he knew. The day after he had interrogated Kaltenbrunner for Third Army G-2—an intelligence unit that operated at corps and divisional level—the prisoner had been questioned by one of Horn's less adept colleagues at USFET, who had failed to secure the interrogation room. Kaltenbrunner had seized a razor that had been carelessly left on a table and slashed his wrist in a suicide attempt. Several other interviews with ranking Nazis had ended in similarly unfortunate ways, foremost among them that of Heinrich Himmler, held by the British, who had swallowed a cyanide capsule.

The lieutenant assured Hammond that although Kaltenbrunner wasn't talking, the RSHA chief would live to stand trial. "Is this why I've been called to Frankfurt?" Horn asked.

Hammond, whose diplomatic skills had earned him the top position at the MFAA, was noncommittal. He explained that until recently, the MFAA hadn't focused its attention on Kaltenbrunner or his immediate superior, Heinrich Himmler. Plundering private and public art collections was primarily the responsibility of Air Marshal Göring, ideologue Alfred Rosenberg, and second-in-command Martin Bormann. Reichsführer Himmler was not known to have kept a private trove of lavish art. Nor did he so overtly participate in the wholesale forced borrowing, illegal gifting, coerced sales, and outright confiscation that created his colleagues' vast collections.

The lion's share of goods that were found in Himmler's private rail car, captured in Dürrnberg, Austria, and in a nearby mine shaft, consisted of books and papers from which the Reichsführer intended someday to write his memoirs.

"Death squads were his chosen vocation," Horn declared, echoing the sentiments of his Third Army G-2 intelligence team.

Hammond accepted what Horn said without comment, reached for a file on the desk, passed it to the lieutenant, and explained that Himmler didn't figure into MFAA investigations until recently, when General Patton had called some of the Reichsführer's nonmilitary activities to his attention.

Horn opened the file. Inside, he was delighted to discover, was his Camp Namur report. His handiwork hadn't languished in a slush pile at intelligence headquarters. "They've found the bunker?" Horn asked.

Hammond said that they had, just where Private Hüber said it would be.

The major briefly described how Horn's report had climbed the ranks to Patton, who was not only a fierce and accomplished warrior but had an unrivaled knowledge of military history. Apparently, the art and artifacts of the ancient soldier-kings of the Holy Roman Empire held a particular fascination for him.

The MFAA chief didn't know many details, only that Patton had forwarded the report to General Alexander Patch of the U.S. Seventh Army, who in turn passed it on to General "Iron Mike" O'Daniel in early April, whose 3rd "Rock of the Marne" Infantry Division, along with General Robert Frederick's 45th "Thunderbird" Division, spearheaded the invasion of Nürnberg.

Hammond confided to Horn that few of his own MFAA requests had been acted upon as quickly or opportunely as the lieutenant's report from Belgium. A Thunderbird commando team had secured the bunker on Hitler's birthday, April 20. Captain John Thompson, the MFAA liaison officer in Nürnberg, had had trouble locating the keys and the lock combination that Private Hüber referred to, but five separate underground storage cells and the main vault were eventually opened and inventoried. Hammond, accompanied by Lieutenant Thomas Carr Howe, had just returned from inspecting the facility.

What they had found, Hammond said, was altogether remarkable.

Each individual storage cell was partitioned so that the air temperature and humidity could be customized to protect the specific type of
art contained within it. There were two sets of boilers, air-conditioning units, and dehumidifiers, should one malfunction. The walls were
insulated with alternate layers of tar and spun glass, and the floors
were a new type of fiber board—a composite made from hardwood
shavings and plaster. The art and artifacts, he admitted, were better
cared for and protected than they would have been in the British
Museum or the Louvre.

Looking down at an open folder in his hands, Hammond mentioned several of the more important antiquities contained inside.
Identification was not a challenge. All of the items, as Hüber had
previously told Horn, were catalogued in a card file in the bunker's
main entrance chamber.

In addition to the Dürer prints Hüber had mentioned was the
world's first pocket watch, created by Nürnberg craftsmen in the
year 1500. Another storage cell contained Martin Behaim's celebrated terrestrial globe, which some scholars believed had influenced the voyages of Columbus and Magellan. A third cell held
the Manesse Codex, a songbook of the celebrated Mastersingers of
Nürnberg, one of the most valuable medieval manuscripts in existence. Horn and his mentor, Erwin Panofsky, had personally examined the manuscript at the University of Heidelberg.

Hammond pointed out that most everything in the bunker was
from German museums, churches, and city collections. This wasn't
Nazi loot plundered from occupied nations. There were, however,
several notable exceptions. An entire storage cell was dedicated to an
altar, carved by renowned sculptor Viet Stoss in the fifteenth century,
which Himmler's SS had removed from the Basilica of the Virgin
Mary in Cracow, Poland. The heavy framework that supported the
altar was still missing, but its panels and gilded figurines—priceless by
any measure—were all together.

As with the codex he had studied in Heidelberg, Horn was intimately familiar with Viet Stoss's Gothic masterpiece. It stood forty-
eight feet high and thirty-two feet long and had been carved early in
the old master's career, when the sculptor lived in what would today
be Poland but was then part of the Holy Roman Empire.

Horn made the first of several observations: every object that

Hammond had mentioned had some connection with Germany's more illustrious ancient past. The Blacksmith's Alley bunker was nothing less than the Third Reich's historic treasure room. And this was what led Horn to jump ahead and ask about the most valuable artifacts, the holy relics that Private Hüber had said were placed in the vault that required two keys and a lock combination to enter.

This collection, too, had been found. The catalogue listed seventeen crates in the vault, all identified as containing the Crown Jewels of the Holy Roman Empire. Hitler had removed them from the royal treasury in the Kunsthistorisches Museum, in Vienna's Hofburg, for display in Nürnberg, and had presumably ordered them hidden in the Blacksmith's Alley bunker once the Allied bombers began raiding the city.

"Is the collection intact?"

"That's the problem," Hammond said. "Two of the seventeen crates are empty, and one crate is missing from the vault altogether."

Hammond showed Horn a typed inventory. Among the thirty-one items still in the vault were the king's robes, various royal ceremonial objects, and a priceless collection of ecumenical relics that belonged to the Holy Roman Emperors. Included among the most valuable items in the vault was the Holy Lance. But missing from the collection were five of the most important treasures: the imperial crown, globe, scepter, and two swords.

"Are you certain they haven't been misplaced or hidden somewhere else in the bunker?" Horn asked.

Hammond was positive. He had ordered an archivist and curator at Nürnberg's Germanic Museum to conduct an investigation.

The major handed Horn a letter stamped with the museum's insignia. At the bottom of the page was the signature of Dr. E. Günter Troche.

The sight of Troche's name came as a delightful surprise to Horn. He and Troche had studied together under Panofsky and at one point roomed together in Berlin. It was doubtful that Hammond could have found a more competent German art historian to examine the bunker.

Horn communicated this to Hammond and expressed his relief that Troche, who hadn't fled Germany as had Horn, had survived the war and was now at Nürnberg's Germanic Museum.

The major was pleased to hear this, because Horn, he said, was being relieved of his duties at Camp Freising and assigned to Nürnberg to investigate the disappearance of the five artifacts. The lieutenant would need every ally he could find. Captain Thompson, the MFAA liaison officer in the city, was in over his head. He didn't speak a word of German or know the first thing about art and antiquities. Moreover, Hammond didn't entirely trust Thompson or his team. He had received several reports from Evelyn Tucker and Edith Standen, MFAA field officers in Bavaria, that security was dangerously lax at many of the Allied facilities where plundered art was being kept.

"Do you think our own men are involved in the disappearance of the treasures?" Horn asked.

Hammond didn't know what to believe but admitted that it was possible. If Tucker's and Standen's reports were accurate, millions of dollars' worth of paintings, jewelry, carpets, and artifacts had vanished into the black market during the Allied invasion and occupation. The jewels on the imperial crown were worth a fortune.

Horn shuddered to think of the priceless treasures being scavenged of their gemstones or, worse still, a five-hundred-year-old scepter melted down for its metals. But such crimes were not unprecedented. The black market thrived throughout occupied Germany. People were doing what they needed to survive, and U.S. occupation officers and GIs alike were happy to look the other way for a cut of the profits. In one G-2 intelligence report Horn had read, a priceless collection of medieval art and manuscripts had disappeared from an Austrian monastery into the hands of a ranking U.S. Army occupation officer. Another American official had been caught shipping Hitler's silverware and gold-plated pistol to his parents' home in Brooklyn, New York.

"Any leads?" Horn asked.

The major said that they had only rumors to go on. Dr. Troche and Captain Thompson, too, were convinced that the Nazis themselves removed or stole the five items before the U.S. Army took possession of the facility. They were running down leads but hadn't made much progress.

Hammond walked to his office window and invited the lieutenant to join him. From where they stood, they could look down into the courtyard in front of General Eisenhower's office. There, in the middle of a reflecting pool, was the famed statue of a water nymph by sculptor Fritz Klimsch. In another setting, the Art Deco masterpiece in the reflecting pool would have made a pastoral scene, but the Nazi architecture, the omnipresent beige cloud of dust blowing up from the ruins, and the rows of chimneys on the roofless buildings beyond ruined the conceit.

Hammond reminded Horn of what he had said in his report from Belgium: the Crown Jewels were Europe's most valuable treasure. As such, Patton wanted to see that the missing items, wherever they might be, whoever may have taken them, were returned to the collection. Eisenhower, too, Hammond said, wanted to see the matter resolved as soon as possible and had given him authority to put Horn in charge of a special MFAA investigative unit, which, for the time being, would consist solely of Horn.

The major gave Horn a set of orders that included travel vouchers, food coupons, MFAA credentials, and authorization for a jeep and a driver from the USFET motor pool. Like Horn's previous orders, these had come from the office of the Supreme Allied Commander, but this time they weren't stamped. They bore Eisenhower's personal signature in his own distinctive bold and flowing hand.

Horn was flattered and delighted. Here was his chance to combine both his skills as an interrogator and his knowledge of art history. And as a new member of the MFAA team, he would also be in very distinguished company. James Rorimer, Hammond's chief aide in Bavaria, came from the Metropolitan Museum in New York. Charles Parkhurst, an MFAA adjunct, was on leave from the National Gallery in Washington, and Harry Grier, another on Hammond's team, was from the Frick. Horn already knew MFAA field officer Thomas Carr Howe, who was director of the Palace of the Legion of Honor fine art museum in San Francisco before the war began. He was perhaps the most important and influential art historian in California and had helped Horn obtain his teaching position at Berkeley.

Hammond acknowledged that virtually all of his top men were museum curators and museum directors. They were people who knew fine art. But they didn't have Horn's experience with Army regulations, procedures, or strategic military interests. Nor did they have the lieutenant's unique perspective on Germany and Germanic art. This was why, the major said, he was assigning the case to him and not to one of his more senior officers. The investigation of the Crown Jewels was a delicate matter, which had to be handled with great care.

The major didn't come right out and say it, but the implication was clear. He needed Horn because he was German, knew German history, and at the same time was not a Nazi. He had proven his allegiance to his adopted nation and had the proper security clearances. He was also an academic like Hammond, with no overt personal or professional bias regarding the conduct of the investigation. In other words, he was not seeking to enhance a particular museum collection in Europe or the United States. The same, Hammond was suggesting, was not necessarily true of others on his staff or higher-ups in USFET command.

Most important, Horn understood what was at stake.

The lieutenant would be joining a relatively small, elite group of MFAA officers who would soon oversee the largest single transfer of public and private art in world history. Just as parents throughout Europe were searching for lost children, the victims of Nazi looting—whether they were individuals, museums, ethnic or religious communities, or entire countries—were looking for their plundered treasures, and Hammond's monuments men were assigned to find and return them. Never before had the victors of war taken on such a responsibility.

Large caches of looted art were already turning up in German castles, warehouses, bunkers, railroad depots, and mine shafts— more than anyone expected or the public was being told. North of Nürnberg, in the Merkers salt mine, and in a nearby mine at Heilbronn, GIs had stumbled upon priceless art collections that included Leonardo paintings and Michelangelo sculptures, along with three hundred tons of pillaged gold bricks and millions of Reichsmarks and U.S. dollars. The Führer's own personal collection, destined for a "super museum" he intended to build in his hometown of Linz, Austria, was discovered in a salt mine in the Austrian alpine village of Altaussee. A large portion of Hermann Göring's vast collection of art pilfered from the Rothschild family in Paris was found in a train car in Berchtesgaden in Bavaria, where Hitler and other Nazi dignitaries had homes. This looted artwork—thousands of masterpieces, exceeding the collections amassed by the Metropolitan Museum of Art in New York, the British Museum in London, and the Louvre in Paris—would soon be on its way to the nations whence the Nazis had stolen them.

The MFAA's mission was to find and protect the cultural heritage of the Allied nations. But it was tasked also with preserving the cultural heritage of Germany. The vanquished were to be protected. This didn't mean that Nazi criminals wouldn't stand trial or that reparations wouldn't be sought. Rather, the Allies, in principle, recognized that if Germany was to rise from the ruins, it not only had to be economically helped, but its cultural patrimony needed to be preserved for future generations. The MFAA was the vehicle to accomplish this.

However, as Horn knew from his work compiling dossiers for upcoming war tribunals, protecting and preserving Germany's cultural patrimony was a politically charged subject at USFET headquarters, and no actual determination had yet been made regarding what constituted war reparations. Museum curators at the Louvre in Paris wanted German art in partial payment for art the Nazis had lost or destroyed. Likewise, the Soviets, and many Allied commanders, too, believed it fair and reasonable that Germany repay war debt in any way it could, including handing over some of its cultural patrimony. Furthermore, there were numerous complications arising from alliances that the Nazi government in Germany made with Italy and Austria—two nations that had provided both men and arms to the Third Reich's war effort. Many U.S. and British commanders shared the French, Belgian, and Soviet view that Hitler's wartime partners didn't deserve repatriation of art and other assets in equal measure to their own.

In this ongoing and volatile debate, with rules not clearly delineated, the Blacksmith's Alley vault was a Pandora's box.

From a historical standpoint, the Crown Jewels belonged to no one nation but to an empire that, like the Third Reich, had crumbled and vanished. They were cherished symbols of the medieval concept of world government that began with the coronation of Charlemagne in the eighth century and ended more than a thousand years later, in the early nineteenth century, when Emperor Francis II abdicated the throne following military defeat by Napoleon Bonaparte. In the early medieval period, the Crown Jewels were the personal property of the emperor and moved with him from city to city throughout an empire that, at its peak, in the twelfth century, encompassed all of modern-day western Europe. In 1424, Emperor Sigismund broke tradition by presenting the collection to the imperial city of Nürnberg, where, by royal decree, it was to be safeguarded for all eternity. The holy relics might well have remained permanently in Nürnberg had the city fathers not moved them into hiding in Vienna, in 1796, to keep them from falling into the hands of Napoleon, who was plundering the Rhineland in his quest for world domination. Now that Hitler had removed the Crown Jewels back to Germany, their traditional home, there was no telling what the conquering Allies might decide to do with them.

Horn didn't cross-examine Hammond to clarify precisely what interest Generals Patton and Eisenhower had in the recovery or restitution of the artifacts in the Nürnberg bunker and whether or not their priorities were the same. Rivalries existed among the Allies as they had among the Nazis. Horn was merely elated to know that two of the Allied command's highest-ranking officers took seriously his concern for the safety of the Crown Jewels, and he was honored that Hammond had confidence in him to accomplish a task he readily admitted was beyond the capabilities of his more distinguished monuments men.

There was just one sticking point. Since Horn's deployment across the Rhine, he hadn't had a single furlough. He was long overdue for a week's leave, which he intended to spend looking for his mother, whom he hadn't seen in seven years.

The last update he had received was from a family friend in Berlin. On the eve of the Allied invasion of Germany, his mother had gone to visit his half-sister in Jena, Germany, southwest of Leipzig, and couldn't now return to the Horn family's home in Heidelberg. Soviet-occupied Jena was no place for two unaccompanied German women, especially not a sixty-nine-year-old widow and an unmarried middle-aged schoolteacher. Even if his brother Rudolf had somehow evaded being put into a POW camp, it was doubtful he or his sister Elsbeth were in any position to bring his mother and half-sister to American-occupied Heidelberg, let alone protect them from poorly disciplined Red Army soldiers and the roving bands of liberated Polish concentration-camp inmates in the Soviet zone.

Horn didn't go into specifics but told Hammond that he was worried for his family, who were split between two occupation zones. "Naturally, I'm concerned for their welfare and would like, with your permission, to see how they're making out before I get started in Nürnberg."

Hammond was sympathetic. He had a family, too—a wife and three young daughters—though they were back in Cambridge. He assured the lieutenant that once his mission was accomplished, there would be time for a reunion. Horn had only three weeks to locate the Crown Jewels before repatriation discussions began in Munich. After that, the entire matter would be out of Hammond's hands.

Horn's enthusiasm at the prospect of serving the MFAA quickly faded. Twenty-one days to find lost treasures in war-torn Germany, even with the help of curator Günter Troche, a fellow art historian whom he hadn't seen for nearly a decade, was a recipe for failure. He had spent longer sketching the interior of the domed chapel at the San Miniato basilica.

"Three weeks?" Horn asked, incredulous.

Hammond was adamant that he conclude his investigation in the time allotted. Patton and Eisenhower wanted to avoid what potentially could become a very embarrassing situation for the U.S. occupation government in Nürnberg. The Polish ambassador had already filed a petition to have the Viet Stoss altar returned to Cracow, and the Austrians were asking the same for the Holy Roman Empire collection. USFET needed to know what had happened in the Nürnberg vault. If any of the treasure were to appear on the black market, if any U.S. servicemen were involved, it could undermine the credibility of the MFAA and, in a larger sense, the very things the occupation government was trying to do in Germany.

The major brought another equally urgent reason to Horn's attention. The treasures of the Holy Roman Empire, as both Horn and Hammond well knew, were symbols of world monarchy. This was why Napoleon had coveted them centuries earlier and was surely why Hitler demanded that they be brought to Germany. The removal of the imperial crown, scepter, orb, and swords from the Blacksmith's Alley bunker, Hammond said, might be part of some neo-Nazi-led resistance plot to embarrass and undermine the Allied occupation. If this were the case, the upcoming Nürnberg war-crimes tribunals would be the obvious and most visible staging ground. Journalists from every nation would be descending upon Nürnberg's Palace of Justice by the end of the next month. The entire world would be watching.

"You think the Crown Jewels could be used as a rallying point for neo-Nazi activities?"

Hammond repeated what he had said earlier: he didn't know. The MFAA's man in Nürnberg, Captain Thompson, was in over his head. Either that, or he was somehow complicit in the theft from the vault.

Horn expressed his surprise that the Counter Intelligence Corps hadn't taken up the matter. As he and the major well knew, the CIC, the component of G-2 military intelligence that normally handled high-profile investigations where sedition, espionage, and occupation resistance movements were suspected, would naturally want to be involved. With covert agents and their own intelligence-gathering network, the CIC—backed up by the Criminal Investigation Division, or CID—was also better equipped to launch field operations than the MFAA or Horn's own Third Army G-2 intelligence unit.

Hammond admitted that the investigation might indeed become a matter for the CIC, the CID, the G-2, and even the FBI. But for the next three weeks, the case belonged to the MFAA, and he meant for it to stay that way. Eisenhower and Patton just wanted the missing items returned to the bunker before RSHA chief Kaltenbrunner or his fellow henchman, Gauleiter Julius Streicher, stood trial in Nürnberg. These were the major's marching orders.

Hammond had now provided two compelling reasons for the lieutenant to get started without delay. Horn added a third.

Beyond whatever political pressures were at play, the lieutenant knew from his war-crimes investigations that trails tended to grow cold quickly in occupied Germany, where there was an almost universal amnesia regarding previous Nazi activities. He also knew from the experience of his displaced mother and half-sister that he was racing not only time but also the ever-changing borders of postwar Germany. From Berlin to Munich, the victors were clumsily redrawing the map of Germany, carving the nation into fiefdoms. In a matter of days or months, intelligence gathered by the French in the north, the Soviets in the east, and the British in the west would not necessarily still be available to the United States in the south. Nor, perhaps, would the spoils of war.

Horn promised to begin immediately. He had only to return to Camp Freising to collect his things.

Hammond left him with another handshake and a thick file folder of military reports on the invasion of Nürnberg. The lieutenant, he said, would find Captain Paul Peterson's account especially interesting. John Thompson would update him on the rest.

Except for this, the major had only one thing to add. As Horn would later that night tell Felix Rosenthal, Hammond said that he shouldn't count on anyone in Nürnberg beside his friend Günter Troche to bend over backward to lend him a hand with his investigation. "Everything is not as it should be at Nürnberg's occupation headquarters," Hammond told him.

CHAPTER 3

CAMP RITCHIE BOYS

July 19, 1945

On that cryptic final remark, Lieutenant Horn left Hammond's office and, with the files tucked under his arm, walked to the motor pool to meet his driver. Eighteen-year-old Private John Dollar, from New York, hadn't experienced combat as had the battered jeep he drove, but he proved adept behind the wheel and claimed to be the only USFET driver who could keep this particular accident-prone vehicle on the road. It had, according to motor pool legend, sustained head-on collisions with a cow in Padua, a stone wall in Reims, and a downed fighter plane in Mannheim.

The promise of a home-cooked meal, a hot bath, and a night in a Nazi commandant's former guest bedroom was all the inducement Dollar needed to cut nearly thirty minutes off Horn's return trip from Frankfurt to Freising. They arrived in the early evening with plenty of time for Horn to notify his commanding officer of his new USFET orders, collect his mail—a single letter from his wife—and join Rosenthal for dinner, a bottle of wine, and their nightly chess match. As Rosenthal donned an apron and busied himself in the kitchen, Horn packed the things he would be taking with him to Nürnberg the next day.

In addition to his toiletries, several changes of clothes, and his books—Horn never went anywhere without his copy of Panofsky's *History of Art*—he packed a footlocker with specialty items that he and Rosenthal kept in a locked closet in the hall. Its contents included luxuries that the two officers had accumulated in England, Belgium, and France over the past two years. The lion's share, however, came with the house, hidden in the attic by the previous Nazi tenant. Besides an album of Marlene Dietrich photographs and a DKW motorcycle stored in the garage, which he and Felix had bought from a farmer in Remagen, the goods in their closet were the most valuable communal property they possessed.

From this stash, Horn selected cartons of cigarettes, boxes of chocolates, nylons, canned meat, and two cases of liquor—the only currency besides U.S. dollars that really mattered in occupied Germany, where a single American cigarette was worth the price of a suburban railway ticket and a pair of nylons could be traded for practically anything from family heirlooms to a night out in Munich.

After Horn had filled the footlocker, Private Dollar helped him carry it to the jeep. As they were loading it into the back, Horn set out the ground rules of what he expected from his driver over the next three weeks. In substance, it was a speech he had given several times before when traveling on field assignments, and everyone who worked closely with the lieutenant had heard at least one version of it.

Horn wasn't going to be a stickler about most USFET rules and regulations. The ones governing fraternization with civilians, which strictly barred American military personnel from conversing with German nationals, whether a stranger on the street or a pretty girl in a bar, were a case in point. Horn couldn't do his job without interacting with the public, and he didn't expect to hold his driver, or anyone else he worked with, strictly accountable for rules that didn't apply to him. Over the coming weeks, Horn would, in fact, encourage Dollar to mingle with the civilians they encountered. In Nürnberg, as elsewhere, it would be a decided advantage having another pair of eyes and ears paying attention.

There was, Horn added, only one caveat. Dollar was not to get high and mighty with the Germans he met. In private and in public, he was to respect everyone with whom he came into contact. By respect, the lieutenant simply meant that Dollar was not to judge people because of where they were born, how they were dressed, and what language they spoke. As Horn would tell many fellow intelligence officers over the years, he wasn't making excuses for what the Nazis did. "You just don't judge someone until you've walked in his boots."

Horn himself, growing up in Heidelberg, had been on the receiving end of many similar lectures delivered by his father, the Lutheran minister. However harsh a taskmaster his father could sometimes be, he had instilled in his son a deep and abiding respect for his fellow man. You didn't have to like everyone you met, but you had to learn to tolerate them.

There were several other points of conduct that Horn deemed unbecoming of an enlisted man, including public drunkenness, slovenly behavior, and Nazi souvenir hunting. However, as with fraternization, there were times when rules could be ignored. Trading the contents of his footlocker for services rendered—technically illegal by Army regulations—was another example. Having goods readily available to distribute in return for information might well make the difference between the success or failure of Horn's investigation.

Dollar was admonished to use his good judgment and to accept the consequences. He was also not to let the footlocker out of his sight. If he had to carry it around with him, then that's what the lieutenant expected him to do. Just as long as it was available when and if they needed it.

Dollar promised to keep Horn's footlocker safe. To show the lieutenant he meant business, he retrieved a length of chain from the jeep's utility compartment, which he used to secure the locker to the stanchion holding the jeep's spare tire.

"Look out for me, and I'll look out for you," was the last thing Horn had to tell him.

Horn's lecture was brief because, as Dollar would inevitably discover for himself, the lieutenant didn't know what they would be doing over the next three weeks. He was sure only that his driver wouldn't just be ferrying him from one Army base to another. They would be mingling with civilians and military alike and developing whatever leads they found. And the interviews Horn would conduct were not likely to occur in the security of a locked cell with an armed MP readily available to keep a suspect in line. If, as Hammond conjectured, a resistance movement might be behind the disappearance of the Crown Jewels from the Nürnberg bunker, there was no telling whom or what they might encounter.

Nothing more needed to be said. He and Dollar were off on a sound footing and would, in the weeks to come, develop a comfortable rapport. Horn took to calling his driver "kid" because Dollar hadn't yet begun shaving, still had acne, and hadn't finished high school. And Dollar called Horn "Professor" because the lieutenant never failed to lecture him on matters related to art, architecture, superior German craftsmanship, and the rewards of a college education.

Minutes after their arrival, Rosenthal—still wearing the apron—served them chicken with roasted potatoes from their own garden, which they polished off with a bottle of Bordeaux, compliments of the former commandant's wine cellar. After they had eaten, Dollar did the dishes, Horn read his mail, and Rosenthal opened another bottle of wine, put their favorite Josephine Baker album on the Victrola, and set up the chess board.

The chess games routinely lasted late into the night. This wasn't because Horn and Rosenthal were well matched or particularly skilled, though they were. The game was an excuse for them to talk and drink and, secondarily, to try to prove one's intellectual superiority over the other. Their rivalry dated back to Camp Ritchie, in Maryland, where they had trained together. Since both of them were German born and highly educated, it was natural that they should bond. But each believed himself to be the better interrogator as well as the superior chess master and took every opportunity to show it.

This was one of the nights they spent more time talking than playing chess. There was Horn's letter from his wife to discuss, along with the details of his new USFET assignment, about which Rosenthal was, as he would later admit, "green with envy." Discussion of his colleague's letter took precedence, as it was foremost on Horn's mind.

The Illinois postmark confirmed that it wasn't welcome news. The former Anne Binkley of Lake Forest always went to visit her parents and brother when they were having marital difficulties, and now that the war was over and Horn had chosen to reenlist rather than return home, her letters were shorter and increasingly laced with veiled threats that she would leave him.

"Not that I can blame her," Horn had told Rosenthal during a previous chess session. "Two years and three months is a long time to wait to resume a marriage that was over before it ever began."

Rosenthal already knew the intimate details, just as he knew the personal and professional challenges that had confronted Horn when he arrived in New York virtually penniless and had gone on to land a teaching position at Berkeley.

Lake Forest's former beauty queen, the future Mrs. Walter Horn, had Betty Grable curves and the sultry allure of Rita Hayworth. Horn didn't exaggerate on this point—he had candid snapshots to prove it. They had married on the spur of the moment, when she was a twenty-year-old fine arts major and he was her thirty-two-year-old art history professor. For the first six months, they had enjoyed an uninhibited physical romance. They made love everywhere—in the backs of cars, in his office at Berkeley, on the Point Richmond beach, and on weeklong camping trips in the High Sierras. Then it had stopped. She found him too remote and cerebral, living too much in his own mind and not sharing his inner life with her.

Anne was right. Walter rarely shared with her what he really felt, for the simple reason that, besides sex, they had nothing in common. Her concept of a dangerous liaison was defying her parents by going to Berkeley and dating an older man—a German, no less. Walter—whose previous lover was a Jewish beauty married to a high-ranking Nazi—had fled his country pursued by the SS, leaving behind everything he couldn't stuff into a single suitcase. The advent of war and its aftermath only heightened their differences.

Walter felt compelled to be a part of the postwar effort, not only to see that his family was safe but because his birth nation, as well as the nation to which he now pledged allegiance, needed him. Anne viewed what he was doing as a distraction from the more important business of raising a family and making a home for themselves, preferably in Lake Forest. She had no interest in where Hitler's secretary Martin Bormann might be hiding, nor did she understand how her husband felt when news reached him that the Nazis had ordered the demolition of an old stone bridge that Heidelberg University students had used to walk to school.

Now she wanted a divorce. That's what she said in her letter, written in her father's study and penned in her fine, almost microscopic calligraphy. She wanted him home. If he couldn't oblige her wishes, she wasn't prepared to wait, and she had hired an attorney to draw up the papers. He could have their home on the beach in Point Richmond, overlooking San Francisco Bay, really no larger than a cottage, and more his than hers because he had purchased the tiny lot before their marriage. Besides, she knew he loved it more than practically anything on earth—more, it seemed, than her.

Horn confided to Rosenthal that he wouldn't try to talk her out of her decision. It was best for both of them. They had no children, and, except for the house, they had no property but his books and her art supplies. Anne was young, bright, and highly desirable. She would pick up and move on, if she hadn't already. And there would be other women for him. It had been that way since he was a teen—so many women, in fact, that he had lost count. But just the same, he would have preferred to end their relationship in person, to put a stamp on the letter, so to speak. He already had enough unrequited loves and unfulfilled dreams to last a lifetime. In love, as in war, nothing ever seemed to happen as planned.

Felix, who had heard much of the story before, took the news in stride and urged his colleague to do the same.

Horn, testing the waters, suggested that he might join Rosenthal in Munich when their tours of duty ended. Now that his marriage was over, remaining in Germany was a distinct possibility. Felix, who was considering staying on in Munich, could certainly use his help and companionship.

Unlike Horn's immediate family, who were still in Germany, Rosenthal's parents and siblings—Munich Jews—had fled the country when Hitler came to power. They had given up their antiquarian bookshop and settled in Italy before moving on to France, England, and finally Berkeley. Their friends who had remained behind hadn't been so fortunate. They had been shipped off to Dachau and hadn't been heard from since.

The Rosenthal family's former Munich home, sold to another German family, had miraculously survived the bombing. It was now sitting vacant in a neighborhood of ruined townhouses across from a public park where Hitler had first rallied support for the fledgling National Socialist German Workers' Party. Felix's dream, after his tour of duty was over, was to refurbish the home and revive the bookstore. Precious leather-bound manuscripts could be purchased for a single stick of margarine, and entire libraries of rare books could be had for what remained of the goods they had locked in their hall closet. Besides, he, like Horn, felt a responsibility as a German to help rebuild his shattered nation.

They made no decision that night about going into business together, or even whether they would remain in the country longer than their tours of duty. Horn might decide to return to Berkeley, and Rosenthal, after considering the hardships of life in a city where Jewish property had been auctioned off to the highest bidder, might decide to join him.

"All things considered, it still would be a good thing to have a Rosenthal back in the Munich telephone directory," Horn told his friend.

There was no more talk of postwar civilian life. After their chess game was under way and Rosenthal, as usual, went on the attack, their discussion turned to the lieutenant's assignment in Nürnberg. As it seemed unlikely to Horn that members of an American occupation team would have purloined a treasure as valuable and difficult to broker on the black market as the missing Crown Jewels, he focused on the logical alternative. He asked how much Rosenthal knew about the alleged neo-Nazi-led resistance movement and wondered if any of its covert agents had taken the Crown Jewels.

Rosenthal had read the same intelligence reports as Horn, but he had one advantage that his colleague did not have. In addition to the G-2 interrogations they had conducted in Freising, Rosenthal had moonlighted for the Counter Intelligence Corps, translating conversations between German prisoners that had been covertly recorded on magnetic tape—an invention that the Germans themselves had brought to the war effort and the CIC had turned against them.

Most intelligence officers were convinced that the Nazis had established an active resistance program in the last year of the war. Martin Bormann had championed the idea, and Himmler's RSHA had put it into operation. Trained resistance fighters were put in place throughout Germany with orders to delay the Allied occupation using sabotage, assassination, and propaganda. However, the resistance fighters had failed to materialize to the extent that they became a serious threat. Those who were captured turned out to be

Hitler Youth, forest rangers, mailmen, and night watchmen, unsuitable for carrying out an effective resistance and incapable of mobilizing a civilian population desirous of ending what had become a nightmare.

G-2 intelligence claimed that Himmler, on orders from Hitler, had disbanded the program on the eve of the Allied invasion, on the grounds that it interfered with the more essential homeland guards, the civilian militias in each city and village who were pledged to fight to the death. The CIC, on the other hand, believed that Himmler hadn't so much dismantled the resistance program as sent its fighters under cover. Their covert task was to infiltrate the military occupation government, collect intelligence on the enemy's means of supply, and encourage the population in boycotts and passive resistance. They weren't to identify themselves as Nazis or neo-Nazis, only loyal Germans aspiring to take back control of their nation. Like still-burning embers beneath the ashes, the heat they created could ignite a nationalist movement to overthrow the occupation government.

Although Rosenthal freely admitted that no highly trained covert operatives had yet been arrested or even identified, he sided with the CIC's intelligence assessment. Himmler might well have put in place a covert army of neo-Nazis, presumably under the direction of Gestapo chief Heinrich Müller, who were secretly operating in cities throughout occupied Germany. There were several known instances of labor boycotts and insurgent efforts aimed at embarrassing the occupation team. And as Horn well knew from his years of studying art history in Heidelberg and Berlin, the Holy Roman Empire Crown Jewels were more than just plunder. They were ancient and distinctly Germanic symbols for world monarchy. In the wrong hands, they could become a potential rallying point for a neo-Nazi movement.

Rosenthal was convinced that Horn would not find the Crown Jewels in Nürnberg. It stood to reason that they were once in the vault under the castle, but his guess was that Himmler had the choice items removed to Austria for safekeeping long before U.S. soldiers invaded the city. "Mark my words," Rosenthal told Horn. "In three weeks, you'll be back in Frankfurt interviewing Kaltenbrunner to find out where Hitler asked Himmler to hide them."

Horn couldn't tell if Rosenthal was merely speculating or knew more about the subject than he was letting on. But the one thing he had learned from experience was to listen to what his colleague had to say.

Probing the deranged mind of Adolf Hitler and the Nazi mind-set, as Rosenthal called it, was his friend's specialty. He was the only intelligence officer in Patton's G-2 unit who had personally met and spoken with Hitler before the war—not once but twice—and though their meetings had been short, Felix had studied Hitler with keen interest then, as he did later. Now back in Germany, Rosenthal was the intelligence officer USFET turned to for help in understanding Hitler, and he had written lengthy, comprehensive, and widely circulated intelligence dossiers on the Führer and his personal idiosyncrasies.

It had been one of Rosenthal's reports that confirmed that Hitler was dead in the bunker in Berlin, just as the Soviets had told the British. Eisenhower and the CIC weren't convinced of Rosenthal's assessment, but Patton and everyone else were. His conclusion drew on the testimony of Erich Kempa, Hitler's chauffeur, who had intimate knowledge of the Führer's undergarments. Under Rosenthal's cross-examination, Kempa revealed that he had darned a hole in the Führer's socks on the night before Hitler's wedding to Eva Braun. It was the same pair Kempa saw on the body that he had helped Martin Bormann carry into the chancellery courtyard and douse with gasoline. Hitler's face was covered with a blanket, but his socks were exposed. Details such as this, from an underling like Kempa, were too unlikely to have been contrived.

"Do you know something about the Crown Jewels that I don't?" Horn asked.

Rosenthal told him about some CIC work he had done several months earlier. There had been talk of the Crown Jewels. He didn't know the specifics but had heard that the Reich treasures, along with Hitler's diaries, were secreted out of Nürnberg and sunk into Lake Zell, in Austria.

Horn dismissed the notion. No Nazis, or anyone of German descent, would risk the loss of the Crown Jewels by dumping them into a lake. An irate, disillusioned officer might drown Hitler's diaries out of spite but not the Holy Roman Empire treasures.

Rosenthal was so certain of his assessment that the Crown Jewels had been sunk into a lake that he was willing to wager his ownership of half their collection of Marlene Dietrich photographs. Besides the DKW motorcycle, it was their most valuable possession. Every soldier in the war wanted Dietrich, regardless of whose side he fought on, and if he couldn't see her in person—as both Horn and Rosenthal had in Munich—photographs would do.

"You're on," Horn said without hesitation.

Rosenthal promised to look into what the CIC might know and, while he was at it, to try to find out what particular personal interest General Patton might have in the contents of the Nürnberg vault. He then sealed their bet with a handshake. They had been wagering this way for the better part of two years, and Rosenthal was ahead by several cases of whiskey, the wind-up Victrola, and the Josephine Baker album. At the rate he was going, Rosenthal would have the Dietrich photos, too, and before their tour of duty was over, everything else in their house, including the cookware in the kitchen, the motorcycle parked in their garage, and perhaps even the snapshots of Horn's soon-to-be-ex-wife.

CHAPTER 4

INVASION OF NÜRNBERG

July 19, 1945

After Rosenthal and Dollar turned in for the night, Horn sat in bed and read the USFET reports that Hammond had given him in Frank-furt. All were similar: firsthand after-action accounts that recapped the battle, the previous April, to capture the heavily defended city of Nürnberg. As Hammond had indicated, the report by Captain Paul Peterson, whose assault team had reached Upper Blacksmith's Alley first, was the most relevant to Horn's investigation.

He opened its pages with an unusual sense of foreboding, his trepidation stemming from his knowledge that Peterson's mission had been determined by what he had written back in Belgium. Horn's report—liberally sprinkled with academic vernacular and his own per-sonal views on the history and importance of the treasures of the Holy Roman Empire—had resulted in a combat team being sent to fight its way through a city under siege. For an academic and an interro-gator, whose previous reports and articles were invariably consigned to an archive—military or otherwise—he felt, for the first time since he had enlisted in the Army, the weight of responsibility that comes with putting other men's lives on the line. That and also what Horn knew from hindsight and what Peterson and his men hadn't known:

the battle for Nürnberg, which would exact a bitter toll of dead and wounded on both sides, was irrelevant to the outcome of the war.

Upward of five thousand troops had been poised to invade Nürnberg on Tuesday morning, April 17, 1945. Peterson, captain of E Company, a 135-man assault team attached to the 2nd Battalion of the 180th Infantry Regiment of the 45th Thunderbird Infantry Division, had been ordered by General Robert Frederick, the ground-forces division commander, to follow Private Hüber's hand-drawn map through the honeycomb of narrow cobbled streets to Blacksmith's Alley. Peterson hadn't been told what was in the bunker, only that it was heavily fortified and that he and his men were to expect strong resistance.

By all accounts, Peterson had full confidence in the men under his command. All were volunteer National Guardsmen and had collectively spent more time in continuous combat under adverse conditions than just about any other company in the war. Together with thirty-eight other veteran front-line infantry companies and backed by two tank divisions, an armored reconnaissance regiment, and thirty thousand men in reserve, they fully expected to overwhelm Nürnberg as they had swept over every obstacle in their three-hundred-mile, monthlong drive into Bavaria.

"Morale is excellent," Peterson reported that morning to his commanding officer, Colonel Eddie Duval. Despite what the captain said, Horn surmised that this wasn't the full truth. According to statements made in the accompanying reports, morale among his men was lower than it had been since they had landed in Sicily with General Patton.

The problem was not combat fatigue, troop turnover, poor rations, inadequate supplies, or inferior leadership, though they had experienced all of those. It was fear of the unknown. E Company's combat experience was on windswept beaches, snow-covered open fields, woods, and small villages, with the occasional foray into towns. They had never before invaded a hostile city the size of Nürnberg, where an estimated seven thousand veteran German infantry and ten thousand conscripted Reich laborers, Hitler Youth, and armed civilians lay in wait behind medieval walls. Nothing was more terrifying to contemplate than combat on narrow, unfamiliar streets amid tall buildings.

E Company's initial foray through Nürnberg's suburbs was on familiar terrain for a clearly observable and worthy objective: liberating a thousand or more British and American servicemen from a mile-square prison camp two hundred yards across an open field from the Nazi Party parade grounds and stadium. Peterson and his men, positioned in foxholes south of the city limits, joined an attack of more than a thousand men spread across three miles of poorly defended countryside. Tanks from the 14th Armored Division cleared the way, and the Thunderbirds charged in behind them.

The battle commenced at precisely 7:00 A.M. with the arrival of two P-51 Mustangs raking enemy positions with .50-caliber machine-gun fire and delivering their first payloads on entrenched German antiaircraft batteries. Behind the planes roared the 45th's howitzers and mortars. The enemy responded in kind. Shells whistled toward the Thunderbirds, blowing craters into the turf in front of them. The last thing Peterson told his men was also the first: "Keep your heads up, your feet moving, and your weapons firing."

E Company's 2nd Platoon drew the first fire. But the incoming rounds were sporadic. The enemy positions atop prison-camp watchtowers were easily identified. Fourth Platoon machine-gunners sprayed the towers with large-caliber rounds, claiming the first known enemy casualties of the invasion. Bombardment from the heavier German guns positioned outside the camp presented even less of a problem. Either Nürnberg's defensive artillery had decided to conserve its ammunition or it was not going to risk jeopardizing the lives of German civilians and Wehrmacht infantry stationed in the prison compound.

The tanks easily flattened the lightly constructed prison camp's barbed-wire fence. Behind them, one U.S. platoon after another poured through the gaps and fanned out into the compound. The shooting ended as abruptly as it had begun ten minutes before. German officers waved white flags from their barracks, and camp inmates cheered wildly from their holding pens. Peterson's men—their boots now muddied and their spirits lifted—enthusiastically fired a salvo of shots into the air as a' victory salute. Reaching their final objective in Nürnberg's inner city—so the men must have now thought—wouldn't be the bloody contest they had imagined.

E Company moved on with the rest of its regiment, leaving rear units with the more troublesome task of processing prisoners and leading camp inmates to safety. In addition to American and British prisoners, the Americans found five thousand Russians who had been captured on the Eastern Front and were suffering from typhus. They were not as easily contained as their fellow inmates, and the liberators narrowly avoided a riot when the Russians saw the change of guard and began pouring out into the campground.

Three hours later, E Company had left the prison camp and was closing in on the adjacent eleven-acre Nazi parade grounds and stadium. Fighting here, as before, was minimal. A few dedicated Nazis were reported to have held out in Hitler's Hall of Honor, but a hundred or more others, huddled beneath the stadium's concrete stands, freely gave themselves up. For the first time since the war had begun, Peterson and his men saw German soldiers breaking down and sobbing. Like Private Hüber in Belgium, the Germans were experiencing a mental disconnection. Never in their wildest nightmares had they imagined that enemy tanks could so easily roll into the same stadium where Hitler had incited his countrymen with visions of world domination.

E Company did not rest. Less than thirty minutes after an unnamed Thunderbird lowered the Third Reich's blood-red flag, Peterson rallied his men and sent them charging to the Nazi Party's Congress Hall, a mammoth four-story, partially completed structure bounded on two sides by a large lake and defended by antitank artillery and enemy infantry positioned behind massive granite building blocks and construction equipment.

After reconnoitering with Colonel Duval, Peterson sent the 2nd Platoon around the left side of the lake while he and the rest of E Company hunkered down along a narrow concrete causeway. In situations like this, the remedy was always the same: call in more firepower.

Minutes later, a hundred rounds of heavy shells whistled low over their heads and exploded into the enemy positions. The German defenders not killed in the initial bombardment retreated inside the building when U.S. infantry joined the fray. Three of Peterson's men were wounded, and a 2nd Platoon sergeant, catapulted into the air by the explosion of a German shell, landed flat on his back, raised his head, and died before he could cry out for a medic.

There was no time to remove the body as the rest of the men blasted their way into the building. Once they had assembled in the lobby, Duval ordered platoon commanders to separate their units into five-man fire teams. Beginning on the top floor, they worked their way downward, clearing one room after another. As Horn knew from his boot-camp training at Fort Benning, there were procedures for this. If the men came to a closed door, they were to announce their presence and give anyone inside a chance to surrender. If no one opened the door, one soldier would kick it open, another would lob a grenade inside and wait for the explosion, and the others would enter shooting. E Company's men, however, dispensed with protocol. They simply kicked open the closed doors and entered firing—a practice for which E Company was severely reprimanded.

Peterson promised to rein in his men, but Duval didn't give him the opportunity to make good on his pledge until the next day. The invasion was delayed by heavy resistance to the east, where a thousand 3rd Infantry Division troops, already in the city, were fighting to take the railroad station and train yards.

Back in action on their second day, Peterson's men experienced the kind of fighting they would encounter on their drive into the inner city: no frontal charge behind tanks but house-to-house combat on narrow, rubble-filled streets against infantry, isolated pockets of Hitler Youth, and civilians, firing on them from every conceivable nook and cranny. To add to the savagery, U.S. medics, easily identifiable by the red crosses on their helmets, suffered indiscriminate fire, which hampered and sometimes prevented them from reaching their wounded. By now, the enemy was using civilians to gather intelligence. An old man or a child would walk up to the corner near the invaders' front line, stand for a few moments, and then dart away. Shortly thereafter, artillery rockets would smash into American positions. After four E Company men were wounded this way, Peterson received orders passed down from headquarters that future "observers" were to be fired upon.

The men spent the rest of the morning clearing building after building on their block-by-block drive toward the castle, the highest point in the city. In an effort to stay off the streets, they used grenades to clear the nearest structure, then ran inside for cover. They would then blast a hole through the wall into the adjoining building, creating an opening large enough to climb through into their next position. In this way, platoon leaders didn't expose their men to street fire until they came to the end of the block.

The casualty toll escalated when platoon leader Ray Fee's legs were shot from under him as he was trying to clear enemy snipers from an overturned street car. Fee was reportedly throwing a white phosphorus grenade when the enemy opened fire. The grenade dropped back down onto him, burning a hole into his chest. Peterson assigned a tech sergeant to lead Fee's platoon, but the sergeant's challenges were exacerbated by several wounded men and the loss of his platoon's map to the Nazi bunker, which had burned along with Fee.

The fatigued and famished GIs pressed on through the rest of the day. Anticipating that they would soon be relieved, Peterson radioed in their progress and expressed his hopes that they would be put into reserve. Instead, he received orders to forge ahead without delay to his objective. Antiaircraft searchlights would be brought up from the rear to illuminate the medieval inner city.

E Company fought its way northward, passing the smoking façade of the now roofless Saint Lorenz Church and crossing an arched stone bridge spanning the Pegnitz—the shallow, muddy river that runs like a canal through the middle of Nürnberg. At every block, amid the ghostly halos cast by the floodlights and the acrid, eye-watering smoke from the burning buildings, Peterson's men encountered more resistance. The Nazis, it seemed, had never intended to protect the stadium and parade grounds but had concentrated their entire defense in the inner city, just where Peterson and his men were tasked to go.

Now the carefully laid-out plans for the men to stick together went astray. As they moved forward through the shadows, the 2nd Platoon was pinned down in a firefight around a collapsed apartment building. Nothing in the reports explained why no one came to its rescue, but one could assume that no one dared to step into the rain of oncoming fire. The ground around the 2nd Platoon had erupted in a barrage of bullets, shells, and the dust of shattering masonry. Communications with it ceased altogether.

After checking with battalion headquarters by radio, Colonel Duval ordered tanks to destroy any building that even remotely might conceal artillery. The cost to the civilian population and the remaining historic structures was devastating, but General Frederick believed he had no choice. By this time—according to the reports— he had intercepted communications from Nürnberg's defense min- ister, Karl Holz, directing the city's remaining civilian and military forces from an underground command post at Gestapo headquar- ters, southwest of the train station. Holz had informed Hitler that "the city would stand until the last man" and that "nothing of value would find its way into enemy hands."

The arrival at dawn of a second Thunderbird company hastened the search for the missing platoon. At last, the platoon leader and several of his men were found dead in the rubble of a fallen build- ing, their bodies riddled with wounds. All that could be said for the company's thirty-hour ordeal was its arrival, at long last, into Nürn- berg's old inner city. It was due a day of rest, which Duval approved.

Peterson and his platoon leaders spent their third day discussing the lessons they had learned and deciding how to capture the bunker. Unexpected help arrived in the form of an unlikely new E Company recruit, Lieutenant James Low, of Johannesburg, South Africa. The lieutenant, an infantryman, had been freed from the prison camp lib- erated on the first day of the assault. He had somehow browbeaten Duval into approving his on-the-spot enlistment into the U.S. Army. Having spent the last three years as a forced laborer in the city, he spoke some German, was intimately familiar with the layout of the inner city, and knew its major defensive positions.

Low's presence helped to rally the men as they returned to ac- tion at 7:00 A.M. on Friday, April 20, Hitler's fifty-sixth birthday. Their plan was to fight their way north, using the old city walls to avoid being flanked. They had less than a hundred yards to go, a mere fraction of the distance they had already come.

The men crept forward. The enemy resisted from inside over- turned vehicles, basement crawl spaces, the shattered skeletons of gutted buildings, and, in one case, an underground sewage pipe. Later in the day, a woman with a rocket launcher took out a tank of the 14th Armored Division.

The pockets of resistance dwindled as the assault team contin- ued inching north. No longer was there the roar of artillery, only the crackle of burning buildings and the occasional collapse of a wall.

Lone civilians darted past them, running south. The entire population of the old inner city, it seemed, had suddenly decided to surrender, including a troupe of Hitler Youth led by a German infantry officer waving a white flag.

Relief from the incoming fire was short-lived. The civilians and isolated pockets of enemy snipers had left old Nürnberg for a reason. They knew what battalion command did not: the remnants of the elite German 22nd Regiment had chosen to make their final stand in a rabbit warren of narrow cobblestone alleys and crumbling buildings at the foot of the castle.

Peterson's plan was to meet two companies of the 3rd Infantry Division in an open triangle of cobblestones in front of Tiergärtner Tor, an ancient tower portal guarding the northernmost gate into old Nürnberg. But as his men stepped tentatively out into the open, the enemy rained fire down on them from two still-standing buildings at the entrance to Blacksmith's Alley. E Company dropped behind the rubble, pinned to the ground. It was less than twenty yards from its objective, but the effort it would take to close the distance must have seemed formidable.

Platoon leaders parleyed by radio before calling Duval for help. The problem with bombarding the enemy position from the air was the danger of hitting their own men. Forward elements of both infantry divisions, inexorably encircling the medieval city and castle, were within thirty yards of each other. Duval instead dispatched a tank, which arrived within the hour.

How the tank crew maneuvered through the narrow streets was a testament to its commander's tenacity. But he faced his most serious challenge upon arrival at the foot of the castle. He couldn't risk rolling out into the courtyard beneath the castle's ramparts. Nor could the tank punch through the thick city walls and come at the enemy from behind. He was boxed in. The quick-thinking commander turned his tank, pushed its muzzle through a Gothic window in one of the ancient buildings, and fired fifteen rounds directly into Blacksmith's Alley.

The destruction was overwhelming. Every street was blocked with debris, and most of the buildings had been reduced to rubble. But the battle was won. Enemy fire ceased. The entire city, Peterson reported, was eerily quiet.

At 4:00 P.M., after the men had shaken the dust off their helmets and caught their breath, the hunt for the bunker began. The difficulty was self-evident: finding anything under the rubble, even a street number, was virtually impossible.

Reading the reports, Horn noted significant uncertainty about who actually discovered the Blacksmith's Alley tunnel's partially buried entrance. More than one account credited Lieutenant Low, who had taken over Peterson's 1st Platoon. Another praised an unidentified private, and a third celebrated the courage of the 3rd Division infantry who captured the castle. The confusion about who made the discovery and what happened next was natural, given the chaos of the last hours of battle and the discovery, to everyone's surprise, of not one but three bunkers, each larger than the last. Just south of the Blacksmith's Alley facility were two others connected by underground tunnels leading into other parts of the city. The latter two bunkers also contained communications and medical equipment, stores of ammunition, and caches of artwork. At approximately 4:40 P.M., soldiers were entering all three underground shelters.

The facility under the Hüber family's house was the only major underground complex in the inner city not interconnected by a web of other passages leading aboveground. Its entrance, almost totally blocked by the fallen rubble, was large enough for only one soldier at a time to squeeze through.

The safest approach would have been for Peterson's men to roll a few grenades into the opening or, at the very least, enter firing. But Duval had admonished E Company not to use explosives to secure the site, and no one could be sure, as the men peered into the tunnel entrance, that they had indeed found what they were looking for. There were several promising cavelike crevices among the collapsed buildings. Each had to be probed before the men moved on to the next.

Lieutenant Low and several volunteers entered one such tunnel. Despite the heavy shelling that had caused the destruction overhead, they found the passage clear of debris and well lit. The air was clean and fresh. From somewhere ahead of the men came the hum of machinery, the whirring of a fan, and the crackle of a radio.

No enemy was in sight, only the long, downward-sloping tunnel, like a mine shaft, leading ever deeper underground. Horn imagined what it must have been like: backs pressed against the smoothly chiseled rock walls, the men quietly inching downward, careful not to set off trip wires for booby traps, and ready to fire at the slightest provocation.

Low and his men walked ninety feet to where the tunnel leveled off. Here they came to a service door on the right, the humming they were hearing now louder, obviously coming from inside. They correctly identified this as a utility room. Nearby were a toilet, a sink, and a shower. Just beyond these rooms, the tunnel intersected a larger chamber lined with brick, giving onto a smaller room without doors, where the radio played, and a long hallway with rows of locked compartments. A map on the wall, written in German, provided a key to the site plan. Adjacent to it was a card catalogue, similar to what one would expect to see in a library.

No firefight took place. Despite the evidence that the facility had recently been occupied—the crackling radio, the humming diesel generators, and the cool stream of air from the ventilation ducts—there wasn't a German guard or civilian to be seen. To the men's relief, E Company had the entire facility to itself.

Duval, accompanied by Peterson, was reported to have entered the tunnel a few minutes later. An exploration of the complex revealed several side passages, blocked by massive steel doors with dial locking mechanisms. At the far end of the main corridor was an even more substantial door, like that on a bank vault. It, too, was sealed shut.

Peterson didn't know what was inside, why the facility had apparently been evacuated by the Nazis, or why Army intelligence had identified the bunker as a military objective in the first place. He could only hope, however, that securing it was worthwhile. As he would note in the conclusion of his report, E Company had lost more than twenty men dead or wounded over the past four days to capture it.

CHAPTER 5

THOR'S HAMMER

July 20, 1945

Human beings are not the only casualties of war. Along with bodies come the desecration and sometimes wholesale destruction of homes, schools, libraries, churches, museums, and the public parks, monuments, art, and architecture that are the accumulated cultural legacy one generation passes to the next. Lieutenant Horn, in civilian life, made this cultural landscape his life's study. As a child, he had played in the crumbled ruins of a Roman amphitheater, and as a young college student, he had helped sift through the debris of the previous world war to restore a mosaic tile floor in the courtyard of a medieval French cloister. As a soldier, he had seen the fire-scorched belfries in Belgium and Brussels. But never before had he experienced cultural loss in such a visceral way as he did on the afternoon of Friday, July 20, when his jeep crested the thickly forested Franconian Hills and he saw what remained of Nürnberg.

The city—where adolescent children had welcomed Hitler's motorcade with posies of alpine flowers, where red-cheeked Hitler Youth presented themselves for review, and where the Führer himself, standing atop a raised dais in the Nazi Hall of Honor, told hysterically cheering crowds that Germany would rule the world—was now a heap of rubble. The truly epic calamity was that the same city that had opened its arms to Hitler and the hundreds of thousands of Germans attending the Nazi Party rallies each year was also where tinkers invented the pocket watch, where astronomers created the first celestial maps of the universe, where publishers printed the first illustrated history of the world, where craftsmen manufactured the first lead pencils, and where confectioners perfected the gingerbread cookie. This proud history was buried along with the rest.

Horn had driven through Frankfurt and thought he knew what to expect in Nürnberg from reading Captain Peterson's after-action report. But no report could prepare him for the gut-wrenching impact of actually seeing the panorama of destruction. Bombing and shelling had reduced the city to a ruin of craters, burned-out buildings, and masses of charred brick. Frankfurt, Hamburg, and Dresden had also been flattened, but those cities were distinctly more metropolitan than bucolic Nürnberg, which was comfortably nestled in a lush valley of rolling meadows and pastures. The sight of the city from the green hills above, with their tall jack pines and clear mountain streams, was all the more surreal, as if an enormous meteor had fallen from the heavens to blight a pastoral and unspoiled landscape—or Thor, leaning out of a cloud, had smitten the earth with his mighty hammer. Indeed, this had been the effect. The four-day campaign to liberate Nürnberg had laid waste to large sections of the city, but the more substantial destruction had occurred while Horn was in Belgium and Patton's army was preparing to cross the Rhine River, when more than eight hundred Allied bombers in eleven separate missions had poured fourteen thousand tons of high explosives into an area no larger than a London suburb.

The scattered remains became more distinct as Dollar drove Horn past the sprawling Nazi parade grounds in the city's southern outskirts. Horn prided himself on never having attended one of the party rallies held there each September, but he had seen the massive Nazi building and landscape projects in various stages of construction on family visits to relatives in nearby Fürth. Nürnberg was where architect Albert Speer, in his twisted vision of heaven on earth, created his sprawling "temples" dedicated to the majesty and glory of the Third Reich. Hitler himself had paid the city his highest compliment. The Führer had declared that while Berlin was the

Nazi Party's brain and Munich—where the movement began—its heart, Nürnberg was its soul.

Horn and Dollar passed by the parade grounds, transformed into a massive labor camp and army supply depot, and drove on toward the city itself, threading their way between teams of POWs clearing debris from what had once been neighborhoods of row houses, the bullet-riddled façades, caved-in roofs, and shattered walls looking like so many smashed dollhouses. Motoring closer to the medieval inner city—where Thor's hammer had struck more authoritatively—the centuries-old gabled homes of the burghers had collapsed inward and, with them, the sculptures and reliefs that identified the city fathers and their trades. The new markers along the route, posted for the benefit of the children, old women, and laborers—all there seemed to be in Germany since the war had ended—were wooden signboards covered with fading snapshots of missing persons and typed lists of family and friends searching for loved ones.

Old Nürnberg had been reconfigured thanks to the piles of rubble that made all but a few streets impassable. Despite the carnage, some landmarks remained to help Horn find his bearings. The meandering Pegnitz River divided the city into two equal halves. Looming overhead, to the far north, was the old castle, the one sure compass point since the days when wandering troubadours entertained lords and ladies and Tyrolean huntsmen delivered beef for the castle stew pots. The vast mountain of stone blocks that made up the old fortress remained unscathed, lacking only the timber roofs and storybook spires.

Horn didn't venture far into the old city that morning. His destination was a wide boulevard just outside the old city walls. Fighting here had been intense, but many of the large buildings remained intact. At the far western end of the curving boulevard was Fürther Strasse, with its Palace of Justice and accompanying prison, where the upcoming war-crimes tribunals were to be held. To the east, on Bahnof Strasse, were the Nazi Party Building and the Deutscher Hof Hotel, where Hitler stayed when visiting the city. Hermann Göring preferred the adjacent Party Guest House, as it was air-conditioned. Except for the railroad station—now a twisted mass of steel beams melted and meshed with locomotives—these buildings, many still missing windows, had been salvaged for use by the occupation government.

Private Dollar dropped Horn at the Bavarian Government Building, a low-slung structure of red Prussian stone, which served as occupation headquarters for Governor Delbert Fuller, the U.S.-appointed chief administrator of the city. Even without the flags and military police out front, they couldn't miss finding the right address. A quarter-mile-long line of civilians led from the cobbled street to its front doors.

Horn incorrectly assumed that a special event was taking place at occupation headquarters. Perhaps this was the day each month when food-ration coupons were distributed or employment listings were posted. An MP at the entrance disabused Horn of that notion. The civilians had been waiting for days and weeks for help locating missing or arrested family members, searching for places to live, food subsidies, or merely permission to leave the city. It was what they did every day, Horn was told. Pushing his way through the line and into the building, Horn didn't dare offer advice or let on that he spoke German, lest there be a stampede.

As Major Hammond had told the lieutenant in Frankfurt, and Horn now saw for himself, all was not as it should be at occupation headquarters. Nürnberg's civilians had come to the right place to air their grievances and request help, but the doors to the occupation offices they sought—whether it was Lieutenant Arthur Forbes's Ministry of Economic Development or Captain Richard Mershon's Civil Affairs Commission—were closed. Even the guards in the hallway didn't know when they would open. The MP in front of the Monuments, Fine Arts, and Archives office simply referred Horn to the Grand Hotel, across the street from the train station. His advice was for Horn to check what was commonly referred to as the "snake pit," in the hotel's former ballroom, which was serving as the officers' club.

How the "snake pit" earned its name was apparent the moment Horn presented his credentials at the door and stepped inside a dark, cavernous, and smoke-filled room. Although it was still morning—just past 10:00—the place was packed with military and civilians alike on bar stools in front of an empty stage and at tables dotted through the room. A pianist was tapping out Broadway show tunes. Few officers wore anything close to a full dress uniform, and the civilians, mostly men in seedy brown suits and women in faded day dresses, moved about like courtiers.

Regulations had relaxed since the war's end, but this put an entirely new face on accepted Army protocol. General Patton, as much a stickler for the rules of nonfraternization as he was for spit and polish, would surely have ordered its closure without a second thought. He might well have stepped inside, seen what was taking place, and drawn his ivory-handled six-shooters.

Judging by telephones on some of the tables and the ranks of the officers using them, Horn suspected that not only was MFAA Captain John Thompson among the early-morning drinkers, but so was the entire fifteen-officer occupation team. Horn confirmed as much when he was directed to a lean, middle-aged captain with jet-black hair and a ring of stubble around his chin, sitting with two civilians at a far table. A thick stack of U.S. Army requisition forms and file folders in front of the three men conveyed the disheartening truth. The real business of Nürnberg's occupation didn't take place at command headquarters but here in the "snake pit."

Horn dutifully stepped forward, saluted, introduced himself, and passed Thompson the orders he had received in Frankfurt.

Thompson summarily took the documents from him, but the first words out of the captain's mouth had less to do with the purpose of Horn's investigation than with the lieutenant's ethnicity. As Horn would later relate the story to Rosenthal, the captain called him a "kraut" or made an equally derogatory statement to that effect.

Horn's accent had elicited many crude remarks since he joined the Army, but this had invariably been from battle-weary foot soldiers letting off steam. The higher up the military command, the fewer problems German-Americans encountered. At the highest levels, it actually worked in their favor, as Eisenhower and many of the upper-echelon commanders were of German descent, and Patton himself, though of Scottish lineage, made no secret that he preferred the company of Germans to his British, French, and Soviet allies.

"I'm from Heidelberg," Horn said, delivering his stock response, speaking loudly so as to be heard over the din in the room. "And I hate the Nazis as much as the next man."

Horn's meeting with Thompson hadn't gotten off to a good

start and continued to deteriorate as the captain wondered aloud why Hammond had selected him—a mere lieutenant—to head a special MFAA investigative unit. According to Horn, Thompson was either unfamiliar with how G-2 military intelligence had tipped invading forces off to the existence of the bunker, or he simply wasn't aware of how the "Horn Report" had been named.

Having looked over Horn's orders, Thompson repeated what he had apparently told Major Hammond, that it was pointless to send someone to Nürnberg to investigate the disappearance of the artifacts from the Nazi bunker. If the entire collection of Holy Roman Empire treasures had ever actually been in the vault—and Thompson was not entirely convinced that this was the case—the missing items were removed by the Nazis before the U.S. Army invaded the city. Horn would be better off looking for them in Munich or Berlin.

Horn admitted that he had heard the same rumor, except that he had been told that they were sunk into Lake Zell, in Austria. He might well find himself dredging the lake or, conversely, poring over Himmler's papers in Dürrnberg, but this didn't preclude conducting a thorough investigation in Nürnberg. Horn intended to talk to the soldiers who first entered the bunker, along with everyone— German nationals and U.S. servicemen alike—who had been inside.

Thompson offered no encouragement. As far as he was concerned, Horn was wasting his time. Captain Peterson and the other soldiers who first entered the Blacksmith's Alley facility had long ago been transferred out of the city. The last he had heard, E Company was in Dachau, soon to leave for Austria. The Germans who built and operated the bunker were either dead or marched out of town to work camps. If the Nazis had kept lists of bunker personnel, Thompson hadn't seen any.

"Just the same," Horn came back. "I'll need to know everyone who has been inside the facility since the occupation forces arrived. Major Hammond told me that you would help me get started. How soon can I get into the bunker?"

Thompson was noncommittal, except to say that he would try to arrange a tour the following week. This was a Saturday, and Horn had twenty days left to find the artifacts or file a report that he had failed; the delay might shave four days off his investigation.

Despite Horn's respectful but insistent protests that he be permitted into the bunker without delay, the captain was unmoved. He gave the lieutenant a curt nod, which Horn interpreted as his cue to leave the way he had come. And having dismissed him, Thompson turned his attention back to his drinking companions.

Horn hadn't expected to be welcomed in Nürnberg with open arms. After all, he was an MFAA field officer with authority to investigate civilian and military personnel alike, regardless of rank. He couldn't necessarily compel a captain to cooperate, but he could make life difficult for him. The question Horn asked himself, and noted in subsequent conversations with other MFAA officers, was whether the captain was brushing him off because he had something to hide or merely because, as Thompson himself had said, the lieutenant's investigation was a lost cause.

Horn didn't jump to any premature conclusions. However, he couldn't help but suspect some form of malfeasance on the captain's part, which, in Horn's experience, was to be expected from an occupation officer. Outside of whatever MFAA liaison duties were assigned to Thompson, the captain was a member of a ruling elite notorious for its incompetence. With rare exceptions, they were not soldiers who had been through boot camp, served their country in combat, or risen up through the ranks by virtue of their leadership skills. They were political appointees, prized for their ability to sell war bonds and perform behind a desk. The extent of their training consisted of a year of political indoctrination at the University of Virginia. A man like Thompson, Horn supposed, in addition to not speaking the language, had probably never set foot out of the United States before his assignment to Nürnberg. It was doubtful he had a clue to the value or importance of the treasures in the vault and likely resented someone, especially a German with a doctoral degree, who did.

There seemed little point in Horn explaining what he had previously said in his report: the Crown Jewels were priceless one-of-a-kind artifacts that had been passed on from one ruler to the next without interruption for nearly a thousand years, worshipped as holy relics by peasant and nobility alike, and, in the hands of Hitler, could well have been as formidable a psychological weapon in winning the trust of fellow Germans as the V-2 rockets had been in spreading fear and dissention among the British. Horn didn't play that card. It was too abstract a concept for an administrator whose knowledge of German history was confined to State Department handbooks.

Horn retrieved the orders Hammond had given him. Perhaps the captain, in his haste, hadn't seen who had signed them. To be certain that Thompson understood whom Horn was reporting to and the importance his superiors placed on his mission, he flipped to the last page and said that Eisenhower expected a full report, sooner rather than later, and that Horn intended to write one, with or without the captain's help.

Horn now had the captain's attention. Without further delay, Thompson dismissed his two drinking companions and invited Horn to take a seat. Either Thompson had been trying to measure the degree of Horn's resolve in the matter, or perhaps, as Horn would later conclude, he was taking the path of least resistance. For the next twenty minutes, the captain would rattle on about the challenges that his occupation team faced in Nürnberg and why Horn's investigation, however well intentioned, was futile.

The root of the problem, Thompson made clear, was that all of the residents of Nürnberg were hard-core Nazis. They had brought invasion and the ensuing destruction on themselves, and the occupation team was left to pick up the pieces. Horn had heard the story before—every occupation officer in Germany had a similar one—but what Thompson had to tell Horn was unique in that conditions in Nürnberg were actually substantively worse than in any other city in the entire American occupation zone.

According to Thompson, Generals John O'Daniel and Robert Frederick, who led the invasion into Nürnberg, had given residents ample opportunity to surrender. Thousands of leaflets were dropped over the city, urging everyone to raise white flags. There was no reason not to. Three-quarters of the country had already fallen, and with the Russians battling their way into Berlin, the Führer had already retreated into his bunker. But the townspeople had chosen to fight it out. Nürnberg never surrendered in the way other cities had. O'Daniel simply declared the city defeated after the last Germans were killed, went into hiding, or put down their arms. But this, Thompson said, was just the beginning of the U.S. fight to take the city.

There were fifteen occupation officers and ten enlisted men

assigned to administer and bring peace to Nürnberg. But this was impossible, Thompson said, because everyone was a Nazi. The city's entire police force had joined the fight to defend Nürnberg from the Allied army. The few policemen still alive after the invasion had to be sent to the detention centers or marched out of town to work camps, which left the city's street-car conductors doing the job of the police. But since German civilians under the rules of occupation couldn't be issued arms, they could do no more than direct traffic.

Lack of police, Thompson pointed out, would not have been a serious issue if not for the several thousand Reich laborers liberated from the prison camp, who, understandably, went looking for revenge on their former captors. This and the presence of a vast supply of abandoned weaponry in the streets made for a volatile situation. Everything from handguns to rocket launchers was strewn throughout the city, and there was no one to retrieve them from the rubble because the police were gone and the U.S. Army, except for two companies of war-weary soldiers, had moved on to conquer the rest of Germany.

Thompson continued to paint an unremittingly bleak picture. Allied Command was not prepared to feed and house the entire population of a city that had been self-sufficient until a few months before. Aid packages arrived, but instead of food and medical supplies, the first provisions to reach Nürnberg were Ping-Pong paddles, baseballs, and textbooks—that which Allied Command, in its wisdom, thought would restore democracy, freedom of speech, and racial tolerance. Even the maps issued to occupation officers were practically useless, as they had been printed for use in World War I, before the Nazi parade grounds even existed.

That was just the start. Food-distribution centers and medical clinics were slow to open, and when emergency supplies finally arrived, the transport trucks couldn't maneuver over the rubble. This led to the birth of a bustling black market, which, Thompson fully admitted, was the only functioning market in the city. Rising inflation and the desperate needs of residents made a can of powdered milk, a container of canned meat, or a bar of soap cost the equivalent of a full day's wages. A vial of penicillin to combat typhus, which had spread from the prison camp, was worth a week's wages. But since occupation dollars had not yet been distributed and there was no readily available legal currency, food and medical supplies were bartered for weapons and whatever possessions residents still owned or could steal. To make things worse, three weeks into the occupation, government employees, protesting the enforcement of stringent occupation regulations forbidding administrators from hiring anyone with Nazi affiliation, declared a citywide strike. And this was before the situation got totally out of control.

Faced with an impending humanitarian disaster, Governor Fuller disregarded Allied Command's explicit directive not to employ or enlist former Nazis Party members in the reclamation effort. Thompson said that Fuller didn't know what else to do. In less damaged cities, or where the Nazi presence was not as pronounced, he might have successfully removed or excluded former Nazis. In Nürnberg, however, every ranking city employee was a party member, and the most skilled and experienced among them, those whom Fuller and his colleagues depended on to resume vital city services, were dedicated Nazis. Although obvious war criminals and Nazi party leaders were not officially permitted to resume their senior positions in various government services, Fuller let them be hired as adjuncts in lesser positions, under the supervision of civilians USFET deemed more suitable for employment. Thus, two months into the occupation, Nürnberg's former fire chief became a paid "consultant" to his secretary, and the city's "retired" postal inspector officially worked as an assistant to a mail carrier. Their duties remained the same, and in many cases they sat at the same desks in their former offices. Only their rank and official status changed.

Thompson, without coming out and directly stating the obvious, made it clear to Horn why civilians were unofficially mingling with military personnel at the officers' club rather than meeting at occupation headquarters, where military protocol required a documented record of what transpired. The civilians in the officers' club were private contractors providing essential services to the city. They did what the military government couldn't legally do, because they weren't technically bound by the same regulations or subject to the same oversight. The corps of contractors was led by a member of Nürnberg's new ruling elite, Heinz Levié, who had no previous Nazi affiliation. Four months before the invasion of Nürnberg, he was an inmate of the concentration camp in Mauthausen. Now, in addition to being the club's piano player, he was the most important civilian in the city. Hundreds and perhaps even thousands of former Nazis were employed by him. No major building project, Thompson said, could get under way without him.

Horn was a sympathetic listener. That's what he did as an interrogator, and he was happy to let Thompson emote. But the real question, to his mind, was not how many times General O'Daniel gave the people of Nürnberg a chance to surrender or the details of the unhappy marriage between occupier and occupied. The greater question was how toy makers, confectioners, and other Nürnberg civilians had been so thoroughly co-opted by Hitler and his henchmen that they were willing to destroy themselves and their city for Hitler's madness. And that, Horn suspected, had less to do with weaponry than it did with the stadium and parade grounds—and perhaps, too, the treasures of the Holy Roman Empire.

"I've been assigned to find the Crown Jewels," Horn told the captain. "The sooner I get started, the better. If it means negotiating with civilian contractors, putting out the word on the black market, or interrogating former Nazis, then that's what I'll do."

Thompson once again dismissed the notion as unrealistic. Horn obviously still didn't understand the situation in Nürnberg. Investigating what had happened in the bunker—if there was actually anything to be investigated—was next to impossible. Everyone who knew anything was dead. Any documents, which may or may not have existed, were buried under tons of rubble.

As if Horn needed more convincing, Thompson showed him MFAA files on the table in front of him. Every day, he said, new orders arrived from Frankfurt. But what was requested of him bore little resemblance to the reality on the ground. He had been assigned to protect sixty-five listed artistic monuments, in addition to the various bunkers and bomb shelters that were also his responsibility. But thirty-two of these structures on his list no longer existed. They were piles of rubble. Another eighteen were so badly damaged that they ought to be bulldozed. But he couldn't do that, because the MFAA had declared that they were national treasures and must be preserved. It was dangerous, he said, to step inside the buildings. The rest probably could and should be saved. But how was he to do that when Army regulations prevented him from hiring former Nazis to get the work done? Thompson had no choice, he declared, but to sit on his hands until USFET bureaucrats gave him the ways and means to accomplish his mission. He couldn't turn to a middleman like Heinz Levié for help, because the MFAA didn't have the funds that the Ministry of Economic Development or the Civil Affairs Commission had to spend. Thompson's team was at the bottom of the pecking order.

There was money pouring into the city, Thompson readily admitted, but most was going to renovate the Palace of Justice, its accompanying prison, and the Grand Hotel, in anticipation of the war-crimes tribunals. USFET wanted a showcase so the world could see that the United States was in charge of the city, except that from Thompson's perspective, the United States wasn't in charge. The Palace of Justice would be ready in time for the tribunals, and there would be adequate hotel space, but the rest of the city was coming apart at the seams. People were starving. In addition to this, there was an epidemic of typhus spread from the prison camp. Packs of wild dogs roamed the streets at night. Then there were underground paramilitary Jewish vengeance groups, armed Reich laborers, black marketers, and the Nazis, now out of uniform but present nonetheless.

Thompson's most pressing concern, he said, was the nearly ten thousand homeless people still living in bomb shelters and bunkers. USFET had ordered the shelters to be vacated and the doors sealed. But what was he to do? Toss another several thousand women and children into the streets? To be raped? To be robbed?

Thompson's message was clear. He didn't think that finding the missing artifacts—saving what he termed German art for Germans— was an order worthy of his attention. Enough lives had already been lost in the battle to capture the city. There were far more important things that took priority over the lieutenant's investigation.

Horn, against his better judgment, was actually beginning to like Thompson. Not that the feeling was mutual or that he would ever envision a day when they would sit back over a bottle of wine and reminisce about the war; it was just that Horn saw Thompson for what he was: a mid-level paper pusher with a modest education and plenty of flag-waving patriotism, perhaps too old for or incapable of combat service, who chose occupation duty because he imagined that he would be welcomed into Germany like a conquering hero. Coming to a place like Nürnberg for such a man must have been like being hit by a truck.

Still, this was no excuse for Thompson to bury his head in a liquor bottle at the officers' club, to absent himself from headquarters because he had nothing to tell the people who counted on him for help, or to turn the real work of running the city over to civilian contractors looking to make a dollar, to ruffians looking to take vengeance, to former Nazis now out of uniform. This would never solve the city's problems or discover who took the missing Crown Jewels.

After further discussion and a bit of cajoling, Thompson agreed to meet Horn the next morning in the bunker. Meanwhile, he would have his adjunct, Lieutenant Klise, find Horn a room at the Grand Hotel. Private Dollar could bunk with the 2nd Cavalry at the Merrell Barracks, over by the parade grounds.

"Now, is there anything else?" Thompson asked, impatient to be done with him.

Horn could think of several things, but for the time being, access to the bunker was enough. As an afterthought, however, he asked where he could find Governor Fuller, as he was obligated to check in with the occupation team's commanding officer.

The captain motioned across the room to an elderly man in a wrinkled uniform seated beside the piano player. He encouraged Horn to introduce himself. "But it's not going to do you any good," Thompson added. "He's been relieved of duty. For hiring former Nazis."

CHAPTER 6

PANDORA'S BOX

July 21, 1945

Nürnberg's timekeeper was gone.

Like an injured child without his two front teeth, the fire-scorched western face of the Church of Our Lady was missing its famous clock and life-sized mechanical figurines of Holy Roman Empire royalty. For more than four hundred years, the Männlein-laufen had counted out the hours above the historic market square in the heart of the old inner city. Every day at noon, to the musical accompaniment of a rotary-driven glockenspiel, delicately carved page boys, drummers, and trumpeters heralded the arrival of seven princes, dukes, and bishops. The royal procession then emerged from a hidden niche behind the clock to swear allegiance to a figurine of Emperor Charles IV, seated on a gilded throne, wearing a polychrome crown, and fittingly attired in the colorful robes and imperial regalia of the Holy Roman Empire.

The Männleinlaufen and its polychrome Crown Jewels had been removed to safety before bombs blew the roof off the church and fire destroyed the adjacent buildings. As Horn stood in the market square looking up at the hole in the wall where it had been, he recalled his childhood delight and surprise when he had first strolled through the idyllic cobbled square, heard the trumpeters, and looked up at the clock to see the colorful medieval tableau come to life. But this day, he hadn't visited the square to reminisce about his youth and the facsimile Crown Jewels. He had stopped en route to Blacksmith's Alley to see where, centuries before the authentic Holy Roman Empire treasures had been removed to Austria, they had been publicly displayed in Nürnberg. It was here, in medieval times, on the cobbled market square, in the shadow of the old stone castle, that the associations among the Crown Jewels, the monarchy, and the German people had been forged.

Panofsky, Horn's mentor, would surely have pointed out that the ancient square in which he now stood had once been the city's Jewish ghetto. It had been cleared by town fathers in the fourteenth century when Nürnberg's commercial interests expanded beyond the castle. At the end of the fifteenth century, Jews had been murdered or run out of Nürnberg. Adjacent to the site of a former synagogue, where the Roman Catholic church now stood, crowds had gathered in the square each year on the second Friday after Easter to view the imperial treasure displayed on a specially constructed shrine and stage. Pilgrims believed that correct performance of a sacred devotional ritual would reduce their stay in purgatory by thirty-eight years. Since the church had assured them that their purgatory might last two thousand years, thirty-eight years less of torment for an hour or two of devotion was a bargain. Like the indulgences that were once sold at the Church of Our Lady, the imperial insignia of the Holy Roman Empire was big business. Thousands of Germans—royalty, knights, and serfs alike—and pilgrims from as far away as Spain and Portugal participated in the weeklong, elaborately staged civic spectacles.

The veneration of the treasures and the persecution of the city's Jews had seen a resurgence in the Nazi era. Nürnberg's Jewish population was deported to concentration camps, the clock and facsimile Crown Jewels—fallen into disrepair—were restored to their former splendor atop the Männleinlaufen, the imperial treasures were repatriated from Vienna and put back on display, and the historic market square was renamed Adolf Hitler Platz. In books, magazines, and even children's stories, the city was compared to the Grimm Brothers' fairy tale "Sleeping Beauty," in which Nürnberg—the sleeping princess—had been a beautiful and vibrant metropolis forced into an anguished slumber by evil Jews during the nineteenth century. Hitler, as the new fable went, woke her with his heroic deeds, and the city emerged from its long slumber once again to become a vibrant beauty. He, the Führer, was *der Starke von Oben*, the "strong one from above."

Now there had been another changing of the guard. The city was in ruins. The Männleinlaufen was gone, five of the most important real Crown Jewels were missing from the Holy Roman Empire collection, a Jewish inmate from Mauthausen was the city's leading building contractor, and the square had been rechristened General Mike O'Daniel Plaza.

Into this purgatory—for this was indeed how residents surely viewed the twilight in which they now lived—Horn had been sent to reclaim the imperial treasures on behalf of the conquering army, as Napoleon had dispatched soldiers to try to claim them centuries earlier. No matter that the French had failed to recover the Crown Jewels because Nürnberg's city fathers had hidden them in Vienna or that the odds against finding them were similarly stacked against General Eisenhower's emissary.

Horn couldn't help but marvel that the ghosts of the past continued to haunt the present. Just as the removal of Nürnberg's timekeeper represented the loss of a significant mental anchor for residents of the city, creating a void in which townspeople felt unbalanced and out of sync, the removal of the Holy Roman Empire treasures from public display must also have left a void difficult to fill. The art historian in Dr. Walter Horn wondered whether veneration of these treasures would be substantively different now that one monarchy had been replaced by another and if the events of the war forever altered the meaning and significance city residents had invested in the imperial regalia. The soldier in him, however, focused on the more immediate task at hand: finding the genuine articles.

The lieutenant didn't give in to the temptation to step inside the burned-out Church of Our Lady or to see what remained of the nearby Protestant church, Saint Sebald, where Pachelbel had played. Neither did he visit the gutted remains of the city hall, where lyric poet Hans Sachs and the Mastersingers had performed, or the roofless Nürnberg State Theater, where Richard Wagner had conducted.

All that remained of the Heilig Geist Spital, or Hospital Church of the Holy Ghost, where the Crown Jewels were stored for more than three centuries, was a polygonal ridge-turret perched precariously on the southern arm of the Pegnitz River.

Horn's only stop before leaving the historic square was to the sixty-foot-high Schöner Brunnen, the magnificent fountain that also displayed stone-carved figures of the Holy Roman Empire's princes, dukes, and bishops, along with a host of angels and biblical figures who blessed them. Unlike the Männleinlaufen, it could not be safely moved into storage. The city fathers had protected the fountain by constructing a massive concrete shell around it. As Horn stood watching, a crew of prison-camp laborers with telltale numbers stenciled on their uniforms were busy chipping away at the superstructure to reveal, piece by piece, the stonework beneath. According to the soldier supervising the workers, Governor Fuller had ordered the fountain's shelter removed so that Nürnberg's latest visitors—judges and their staffs called to the upcoming war-crimes tribunals—would have something besides courtrooms, jail cells, and rubble to see.

Horn walked on, finally meeting his first familiar face in the city, Albrecht Dürer. The bronze statue of the city's most famous resident was pockmarked by bullets, but it still stood, a lone sentinel poking its head above the debris just north of the square. Dürer's house, around the corner in front of Tiergärtner Tor, had not fared as well. The walls of the half-timbered structure had withstood the bombing, but the roof, windows, and doors were gone. The building could be rebuilt as long as Thompson, in a rush to move on with reclamation, didn't have it bulldozed. Horn made a mental note to remind the captain that every missing brick, doorjamb, and leaded windowpane should be collected and salvaged. Ignore the sightseeing judges and jurists come to try the Nazi criminals. Like the ticking clock and the fountain beneath the cement shell, Dürer's house had to be preserved if Nürnberg's residents were ever to hold their heads up again.

The entrance to the bunker was half a block away. There was no evidence of the garage door that had shielded the tunnel from prying eyes when the Hüber family occupied the upstairs and little evidence that a building had ever occupied the space. All Horn could see from the street was a pair of metal doors, compliments of the U.S. Army, between two large mountains of rubble. The sign that had once stood out front, *Antiques—New and Old,* was gone, as were the Nazi guards, who must have found the designation as whimsical as Private Hüber and his family did.

Nearby, on either side of the doors, teams of contract laborers were hard at work sorting intact stonework and building blocks for later reclamation. The rest of the debris was being carted down the street in wheelbarrows and dumped into flatbed gondolas, where it would be rolled out of the city on a crudely constructed rail system. Just as the ancient castle walls had enclosed the old city, a massive new landfill was rising to enclose occupation-era Nürnberg.

The doors to the tunnel entrance were open. Inside, beyond a loading dock, was the long, downwardly sloping tunnel that Peterson and his men had explored. The entrance, now cleared of rubble, was guarded by two soldiers with machine guns. A group of other infantrymen milled about the loading dock—a sure sign that Thompson had lived up to his word and was expecting him inside. Horn introduced himself and waited while one of the guards disappeared down the tunnel to fetch him.

Horn wasted no time beginning his examination of the facility. His first observation was that it hadn't originally been a bunker. The rough-hewn stone had been chipped away using hand tools, and the gradual downward slope and arched ceiling of the tunnel leading to the chambers beneath were a necessity for laborers rolling casks and wheelbarrows.

"It was a beer cellar," he told Thompson when he arrived at the entrance a few moments later.

Horn's observation didn't impress the captain. As the lieutenant would do throughout his investigation, he would have to explain the history behind the history of what Thompson was looking at for it to have meaning or hold his attention.

Horn explained that the Nazis had merely converted the cellar to meet their needs. Such a space under the castle was unexceptional, as nearly every family in old Nürnberg had its own beer cellar, and Nürnberg's burghers had extensive cellars not only for storing beer but also for brewing hops. There were actually times in Nürnberg's history when the law required all property owners to keep such facilities. Understandably so: German beer—brewed with antibacterial hops—was not as easily contaminated as the water supply. When the city was fending off invaders, its entire population—human and beast—subsisted on beer.

Furthermore, given the tunnel's location directly under the castle, Horn suspected that the Nazi bunker might once have been the royal brewery. He hadn't seen enough of the facility to be certain, but he would venture a guess that Thompson's men would find a viaduct leading to the castle well, along with a passage into one of the castle's many subterranean chambers. Among the largest of these chambers was the castle grainery, where food could be stored for centuries. This was, according to legend, no exaggeration. Emperor Charles V was alleged to have had a loaf of bread baked from grain that had been in storage for 180 years.

Thompson dismissed the possibility of a hidden passage. If there was another entrance or exit, he and his men would have found it.

Having made this pronouncement, the captain showed Horn into the bunker complex. The air, as Peterson had noted in his report, was clean and cool. The ventilation system was still operating. Except for English graffiti on one wall—no doubt scrawled by a bored GI tasked with protecting the site—there was no sign of damage.

The captain assured Horn that the facility was the safest place in the city. He had men stationed inside and at the tunnel entrance on around-the-clock guard duty. No one could go in or out without his knowing about it.

Horn followed the captain past the latrine and shower to the main corridor, where he made his second observation. Not only was the tunnel the entrance to a beer cellar, but it likely had been the royal brewery, given its high ceilings and spacious interior. The brew kettles would have been in the main corridor, and the rooms where the beer kegs would have been stacked had been converted into art-storage cells.

Horn pointed out the salient features. The Nazi improvements were a brick and cement shell constructed inside the larger existing chamber. The red sandstone's porosity and the naturally cool and damp environment necessitated insulation and the climate-control apparatus. An environment ideal for brewing hops was unsuitable for art.

The complex was indeed impressive. Besides two coal furnaces and separate chambers housing the heating and ventilation units, there were the guards' sleeping quarters, a single room with two bunk beds, table, chairs, bookshelf, and a picture hook on the wall where a framed photograph of the Führer must have hung.

Thompson didn't know what, if anything, had been found in the guards' quarters when the bunker was opened. If documents had been there, they might well have been claimed as souvenirs by the same unnamed GI who had scrawled the graffiti. Horn thought there was no point in discussing the matter with Thompson, because whatever had been taken, the captain assured him, had been removed before he and his occupation team had secured the facility.

The captain attempted to hurry Horn along the corridor. The lieutenant, however, was not going to be rushed through the facility. He took his time to examine and note what he found at each step of the way.

The most ingenious engineering had gone into the air ducts leading aboveground. As Horn had previously learned from Private Hüber, they could be sealed in the event of a fire-bombing or poison-gas attack. Hüber had described in addition special bomb traps built into the ducts, which would protect the bunker from grenades or other explosives dropped down the shafts.

To Thompson's annoyance, Horn inspected each shaft before moving on to the furnace room, which contained three-hundred-gallon fuel tanks. As he had suspected, the source of water to feed the cooling system came from an ancient viaduct in the wall, no doubt attached to the castle well.

More significant—and cause for concern—was what appeared to be an escape hatch Horn found in the exhaust chimney of the bunker's emergency power generator. He couldn't tell where the hatch led because its metal door—barely wide enough for a man to squeeze through—was rusted shut. Horn wondered if it had been this way when Peterson and his men had ventured into the bunker. He jotted down a reminder in a slim black pocket notebook to have Private Dollar try to pry the hatch free and see where it led.

Embarrassed that the lieutenant had so easily made a discovery overlooked by his men, Thompson reassured him that although someone could conceivably have gained access to the bunker from above using this hatch, an intruder would have been confronted by the guards inside, and moreover, the storage units and vaults themselves were kept locked at all times.

There was no apparent damage of any kind to the main corridor and access rooms. This raised a question that had been on Horn's mind since he had read Peterson's after-action report. Why had the Nazis, after having gone to such lengths to build the vault and install such elaborate security features, left the facility unguarded during the final hours of the invasion? Private Hüber had told him that a company of SS guards had been stationed in the bunker, and Peterson's report clearly indicated that the generators and ventilation system were running when his team had entered the facility. Where had the guards gone, and when? Had they taken with them the missing Crown Jewels?

Thompson didn't know or wouldn't say. All he had heard from the civilians he had interviewed was that the bunker had been a closely guarded secret. The SS guards, whomever they answered to, were presumably now part of the ever-expanding landfill on the city's outskirts or in one of the POW camps.

Horn, for the time being, didn't pursue the matter and instead turned his attention to the storage units. Five in all, they were blocked by eight-foot-tall steel doors, each with its own locking mechanism and thick enough to withstand shock waves from an explosion.

As Horn stood waiting for Thompson to open them, the captain did an about-face and walked toward the main vault, where several MPs stood with one of the civilians Horn had seen with Thompson at the officers' club. A small man in his late fifties or early sixties, he was dressed in the same soiled suit from the day before.

Thompson introduced Horn to Albert Dreykorn, secretary of the city's historical committee, who had been working with Thompson and his occupation team to help jump-start the reclamation process.

Dreykorn nodded solemnly but didn't reach out to shake Horn's hand.

The captain said no more about Dreykorn, leaving Horn with the impression that he was the captain's guest, come to view the facility. It was not until the small man produced a set of keys that Horn realized he had a more important supervisory role in the captain's monuments operations.

"I'll open the vault now," Dreykorn said in broken English.

Horn was dumbstruck. Not only was the captain apparently not in possession of the keys to open the vault, but the possessor of the keys was a German national, perhaps even one of the former Nazis unofficially on the occupation force's payroll.

Rather than call Thompson's attention to this obvious breach of security, Horn decided to wait until they were alone to voice his concerns. "I want to see the other storage units first, not just the main vault," Horn said in German and then in English.

Thompson acceded to Horn's wishes, but not without expressing his irritation at having to extend the inspection beyond the vault from which the treasures had been presumably removed.

Dreykorn similarly appeared annoyed at the prospect of Horn making any more than a cursory inspection of the bunker. He clearly had previously shown visitors through the facility and saw no point in having to do so again, especially for a junior officer. He reluctantly turned the dial-locking mechanism on the first storage cell and then rolled back its massive steel doors.

The room was packed floor to ceiling with art objects. Horn's initial interest was less in the treasures themselves than in the chamber's construction. As Major Hammond had noted back in Frankfurt, the first layer was a thick sheet of spun fiberglass, a state-of-the-art material used for thermal insulation. Beneath this was a thick layer of waterproof tar painted over brick. Although Horn couldn't easily probe far with his penknife, he likely would find yet another layer of tar beneath the brick, and then cement. The floor and ceiling were treated similarly, minus the spun glass. In its place was a layer of composition board. All in all, it was indeed an impressive construction.

Horn perused the contents of each cell. Among the most valuable objects was the "Angel's Greeting," by Viet Stoss, Nürnberg's celebrated woodcarver, bridge builder, stonemason, and bronze caster. The massive moon-shaped carving, depicting the Virgin Mary and Archangel Gabriel at the annunciation, had hung in the choir of Nürnberg's Church of Saint Lorenz.

Nearby, another storage unit was packed floor to ceiling with stained-glass windows from the same church. The card-catalogue inventory in the bunker's entrance hallway indicated that the windows dated to the last quarter of the fourteenth century, after the completion of the high Gothic choir. One particular window from this collection, illustrating scenes from the book of Exodus, was designed by Michael Wolgemut, the famed student of Albrecht Dürer.

The art historian in Horn once again trumped the soldier. He ran his hand over the finely grained wood of a medieval lute, paused to examine the intricate detail on a Carolingian ivory, noted the handsome relief work on the limestone tomb effigy of a knight and the delicate brushwork on an illustrated manuscript from a monastic book of hours, and saw his own reflection in a burnished gold and silver goblet.

As Major Hammond said, and Thompson now drew to his attention, this was German art from German museums.

Dreykorn chimed in to confirm what the captain had said. By tradition and by royal proclamation, these treasures had been the property of Nürnberg for more than seven hundred years.

Horn didn't comment. Although Dreykorn was probably right about the other objects Horn examined, not everything in the bunker was the property of the city before Hitler arrived on the scene. The truth was in the next storage room: the panels and figurines from the Viet Stoss altar stolen from the cathedral church of Saint Mary in Cracow.

Nürnberg had indeed been the birthplace of the controversial Viet Stoss. The artist was branded on both cheeks after being convicted of forgery there in the early fifteenth century. However, the altar had been commissioned and carved in Cracow, where the sculptor had lived for nearly two decades before returning to his birth city. The Polish authorities and the Vatican had lodged formal complaints about the Nazi theft of the revered masterpiece from Cracow but couldn't stop its removal. In the larger scheme of things, its disappearance was a trifle in comparison with the greater human atrocities taking place throughout Nazi-occupied Poland.

Then there was the Holy Roman Empire treasure—the most valuable items in the entire bunker—that had been removed by the Nazis from Vienna and had temporarily been put on display in Nürnberg.

Horn went to see this collection next. Dreykorn led the way to the vault, which stood at the farthest end of the bunker.

A numeric code opened the foot-thick steel door, and two keys accessed a smaller inner door made of solid steel bars. Dreykorn, to Horn's surprise, had the five-digit lock combination as well as both keys.

After the heavy door was swung open, Horn politely asked Dreykorn to remain outside. The little man was taken aback by what he obviously deemed to be a decision that was not Horn's to make. Access to the vault, Dreykorn claimed, was at the discretion of the city's historical committee. Rules must be followed.

Thompson turned to Horn as if the lieutenant himself was unreasonable in demanding that Dreykorn wait outside the vault, but, seeing Horn's resolve as he stood blocking the entranceway, he handled the matter to Horn's satisfaction. Dreykorn could stand guard outside the vault to see that nothing was removed.

Thus mollified, Dreykorn waited in the corridor while Horn, followed by Thompson, entered the vault. Inside, packed in neat rows, floor to ceiling, were wooden shipping crates. A narrow aisle, just wide enough for one person to maneuver, ran from front to back. The only things out of place were two empty crates at the far end of the room and, nearby, a small pile of loose packing material strewn on the floor.

"Don't mind Dreykorn," Thompson said after they were alone in the vault. "He is a bit protective of this stuff."

Horn could see why. The other chambers were full of treasures, too, but this room was different. Approximately thirty to thirty-five feet long and half as wide—like the safety-deposit room in one of the large city banks—it contained the most ancient and valuable artworks and artifacts in Europe. Art historians in Paris and London might not have agreed, claiming that their museums, in aggregate, had more varied and valuable collections, but none could argue that the treasures the Nazis hoarded here, measured by square foot and pound for pound, had their equal in historic and monetary value anywhere else in Europe.

Horn opened and examined the contents of each crate. As Hammond had said and Dr. Troche, from Nürnberg's Germanic Museum, had confirmed in the inventory he had prepared for the MFAA, all were numbered and labeled, identifying their contents, points of origin, and the dates they arrived in the bunker.

Inside the largest crates, in glass cases, were the embroidered silk coronation mantle, imperial undergarments, royal slippers, gloves, stockings, and vestments. The cloth was so subtle and the colors so vibrant that Horn had the impression they were reproductions—only the stitching, beadwork, and precious stones assured him that they were the actual coronation clothing of the ancient soldier-kings. The next-largest crates contained relics and ecumenical treasures, individually wrapped in spun glass and protected in separate leather, wood, and metal boxes. The most significant artifacts here were two large crosses of very ancient vintage—one made of wood and the other of gold and silver and studded with gemstones. Two smaller crates contained, among other items, three pairs of spurs, two gold arm bracelets, and a ring. A lesser but still substantial crate contained the Holy Lance, or Spear of Destiny.

If the Nazi inventory was correct—and Horn had no reason to doubt its accuracy—all five of the missing treasures had been part of the larger collection that was moved into the vault. As Dr. Troche had noted in his report to Hammond, the imperial crown was listed as having been stored in the now-empty crate 15, the scepter and orb in crate 10, and the two swords in the missing crate 11. Strangely—or perhaps on purpose—these items had been taken, while the Holy Lance, which Horn presumed to have been as valuable as the two swords, the orb, and the scepter, had been left behind. This was as great a mystery to Horn as the fact that the facility, built to withstand Allied bombs, had been left unguarded in the last desperate hours of the invasion.

From what Horn could deduce from the manner in which the two empty crates had been opened—the top panels were pried off and left on the floor beside the loose packing material—the same care and attention that had gone into transporting and storing the treasures were not taken in their removal. The thief or thieves had been in a hurry. As the crown, orb, and scepter were relatively small, Horn presumed that they had been transferred into crate 11 with the swords, which was then removed from the bunker. But when had they been taken, and by whom? There wasn't a single clue.

Horn could draw no further insights from the vault. Having thoroughly examined the empty boxes, he turned his attention to the matter of security. Captain Peterson's after-action report indicated that he and E Company, along with others, had entered the bunker complex but had not opened the various storage cells. Inspection of the storage cells and vault had apparently taken place sometime later, after the occupation team arrived and the main body of U.S. forces had left the city. Hammond, in Frankfurt, had referred to some kind of delay.

"How did your team gain access to the vault?" Horn asked.

"Dreykorn, of course," Thompson said easily. "He opened the vault about a month or so after General Frederick's men pulled out."

By way of further explanation, the captain said that he hadn't the time or wherewithal to open it when he and his occupation team arrived in Nürnberg on April 21, the day after the fighting had ended. Given the desperate conditions in the city, he decided that the treasures presumed to be hidden inside were safer there than they would be anywhere else. Dealing with the logistical problems of establishing medical and food-distribution centers and the civil unrest as residents adjusted to the occupation, it was several weeks before Thompson had actually tried to gain access. By this time, military intelligence had identified the now-deceased likely possessors of the keys and the lock combination, Mayor Willy Liebel and Defense Minister Karl Holz.

Liebel was believed to have died by his own hand in his office, shot once in the head with a large-caliber weapon found beside his body. Since the corpse's face was mangled and its pockets empty, initial identification was difficult, but a distinctive ring on the little finger and a monogrammed pocket handkerchief finally verified that the victim was Mayor Liebel.

Holz's body was found in the courtyard outside Gestapo headquarters. A preliminary investigation concluded that he and one of Himmler's SS officers had barricaded themselves in Holz's office as infantry stormed the building. Shots were exchanged through the locked door, and the SS officer was killed. Holz escaped through a shell hole in the wall and dropped to the ground outside. An American soldier spotted him racing across the courtyard and shot him in the neck. He bled to death before anyone could come to his aid.

Thompson said that he and his men had turned the city inside out but found no keys or lock combination. Any paperwork associated with the bunker was burned before they arrived.

Judging from the captain's previous oversight of the hidden escape hatch, Horn didn't take what he said as the gospel truth. Operating an installation the size of the bunker complex would have generated reams of paperwork. At the very least, the Nazi hierarchy, notorious for documentation, would have kept duplicates of work orders and lists of personnel.

Thompson continued his story as Horn took notes. With his investigation stymied, Governor Fuller pressing him for upbeat, positive news to offset press coverage of the deteriorating situation in Nürnberg, and anticipating the imminent arrival of MFAA chief Mason Hammond from Frankfurt, Thompson had decided the time had finally come to open the vault. The reinforced concrete was impervious to picks and sledgehammers, and its door was judged to be too thick to burn through, so he called in demolition experts. Dreykorn arrived while Thompson was inside the bunker discussing how much ordnance might be necessary to remove the vault door.

It was at this point in Horn's conversation with Thompson that the captain revealed what he should have told the lieutenant from the start. Albert Dreykorn, who had opened the vault for Thompson, was none other than Mayor Liebel's former personal secretary. Not only were Horn's suspicions correct that Dreykorn was a former Nazi, but he was secretary to the city's most important official, a man who was regarded as a personal friend of Adolf Hitler. Dreykorn himself may have fielded calls between Liebel and the Führer.

In defense of his decision to trust Dreykorn, or perhaps simply to reassure Horn that supervision of the vault was a high priority for him, Thompson reminded the lieutenant of the things he had explained the day before at the officers' club. Everyone in Nürnberg was a former Nazi. His occupation team needed them to keep the city running. Who better to protect German art than Germans?

Horn pressed Thompson for more details. "Did Dreykorn volunteer his services?"

Thompson admitted that Dreykorn had approached him, not the other way around. He had simply told the captain that explosives wouldn't be necessary to open the vault.

Horn didn't stop Thompson to point out that Dreykorn, by the captain's own admission, had arrived at precisely the right moment to prevent the forcible entry by U.S. soldiers into the vault. For all Thompson really knew, Liebel's former secretary might have had the facility under surveillance since Peterson and E Company arrived on the scene. The pervasive use of Germans as secretaries to the occupation teams might also have explained the "coincidence." Dreykorn might have found out through the civilian intelligence grapevine about Thompson's intentions regarding the vault even before Governor Fuller and the other occupation officers were informed.

"Dreykorn provided you with the keys and the combination?" Horn asked.

Thompson explained that Dreykorn had felt certain that Liebel and Holz, before the invasion, had passed the keys and the lock combination to three trusted members of the Nürnberg city council. With Dreykorn's intercession, two of the councilmen, Heinz Schmeissner and Dr. Konrad Fries, would come forward with the keys. The third councilman, Julius Lincke, who possessed the lock combination, hadn't been heard from since the invasion and was presumed dead. This, however, didn't present an obstacle, as Liebel had also trusted Dreykorn with the lock combination.

Pulling the complete story out of Thompson was not easy, either because the captain was embarrassed to reveal the truth or simply because, as Horn later learned, a behind-the-scenes deal had been struck, and the captain and his team didn't want it on the official record. The two still-active councilmen were members of the former Nürnberg elite who, like the postmaster and the fire chief, had agreed to assume their former city government positions at the behest of the desperate and overwhelmed occupation team. In addition to providing help to Thompson's occupation-team colleagues, they were appointed by the captain to his own Monuments and Fine Arts–sponsored City Historical Committee, of which Dreykorn was acting secretary.

The excuse councilmen Schmeissner and Fries gave Thompson for not having stepped forward sooner was their previous Nazi affiliation and fear that they would be prosecuted. Dreykorn acted as a go-between.

Horn marveled at the deals that had been cut for the sake of expediency. Even Hammond probably didn't know the full extent of Nürnberg's disorder. Not only were civilian contractors doing the work of the occupation team, but Nazi foxes were guarding the art-treasures henhouse.

"Did Dreykorn tell you anything about who may have removed the Crown Jewels?" Horn asked.

Thompson admitted what Horn had already guessed. Dreykorn and the two councilmen on the historical committee were the source of the rumors that the Nazi high command had removed the treasures before the U.S. forces arrived. The only people who might have known for certain, according to Dreykorn and the councilmen, were Liebel and Holz, who—as Thompson had pointed out—were both dead.

Horn wrote Dreykorn's name along with those of Liebel's city councilmen into his notebook, then turned his attention back to the vault to make certain that no clues had been overlooked. He would interrogate Dreykorn, Schmeissner, and Fries on his own, without Thompson looking over his shoulder.

While Horn continued to investigate the vault room, Thompson did several things that infuriated the lieutenant. As Horn later recounted to Rosenthal, the captain had the audacity to light a cigarette. A gentle reprimand from Horn prompted him to stamp it out reluctantly. Minutes later, a second reproof was necessary when the captain began carelessly rooting though a crate containing the coronation garments—items he contemptuously regarded as a dead king's cape, underwear, and booties. Heedless of Horn's protests, the captain next turned his attention to an adjacent crate with the collection of delicately wrapped ecumenical objects in their own leather cases and jeweled boxes.

The crate Thompson picked through was filled with arguably the most valuable collection of holy relics outside the Vatican. Among the ecclesiastical treasures the Nazis had sheltered was a reliquary containing a sliver purported to be from the True Cross, a burse or relic box with soil soaked with the blood of the martyr Saint Stephen, a tiny casket with threads from the robe worn by the apostle John, links from a chain that shackled Saint Paul, and an ostensory, or holy container, with a bone of legendary Theban legionnaire Mauritius, otherwise known as Saint Maurice.

Thompson expressed his surprise that the SS would have gone

to such trouble to build a vault to protect church property, let alone a collection of religious artifacts that couldn't possibly be authentic. After all, Hitler and his cronies were pagans. Nuns had been raped and churches burned when the Nazis invaded Russia and the Balkans.

Horn wasn't a particularly religious man, although he had been trained to be one. Yet he stiffened when he saw the cavalier manner in which Thompson was handling the artifacts and bristled at the mistaken notion that the Nazi elite and their foot soldiers considered themselves godless heathens. Horn couldn't blame the captain for doubting the authenticity of the artifacts, however. During medieval times, holy relics were produced on demand. Every church and cathedral had them.

It wasn't that Horn believed these pieces of bone and fabric to be genuine, though they might be. These objects deserved respect and vigilant care, if only because they had been venerated since Roman times, before Michelangelo, the Magna Carta, and Columbus. And contradictory though it seemed to Thompson, these ancient pan-Germanic treasures were as much a part of Nazi identity as the cobbled streets surrounding Nürnberg's market square and the elaborate ceremonies staged in the Party rally grounds. Along with the crown, scepter, orb, and swords, they were sacred treasures of the Holy Roman Empire—what Hitler called the First Reich and what more recently he and his inner circle considered treasures of Germany's new "Third" and equally "Holy Reich."

The words *holy* and *Reich* didn't belong together. At least, no respectable Christians dared pair them. The macabre discoveries made at Dachau were surely proof of the Nazis' evil and demonic obsessions. But there was more to the story of how and why the ecclesiastical treasures came to be in the bunker than Thompson was aware, just as there was greater significance to the disappearance of the Crown Jewels than the loss of gold, silver, and gemstones.

Horn was tempted to launch into a discourse that his fellow officer sorely needed to hear and the lieutenant was fully prepared to deliver, about what Hitler had done to win the enthusiastic cooperation of millions of Catholic and Protestant Germans. Trickery, propaganda, intimidation, and murder all played significant roles in the creation of the Third Reich, as did the untenable economic conditions after World War I. But Thompson was wrong in assuming that the atrocities committed against the Jews and the persecution of the Roman Catholic Church were acts of people who considered themselves pagans. Hymnals and rosaries had been found along with children's toys in the gated compounds where death-camp clerks and crematorium supervisors had lived with their families. Hitler's *Mein Kampf* had been edited by a Catholic priest, and Julius Streicher, in addition to his work as the Reich's leading anti-Semitic propagandist, once taught in a Nürnberg elementary school and was the author of children's storybooks filled with fanciful accounts of German history and the lives of Christian martyrs.

The Führer's ideologues sought not to do away with God but to champion their own twisted notions of Aryan Christianity, Germanic history, and rulership. Lines couldn't be drawn separating the ecclesiastical treasures from the regalia of the emperor. This "stuff," as Thompson so blithely referred to the contents of the vault, was all sacred symbols of Reich continuity and the dynastic succession of the Holy Roman Emperors.

Now was not the time to discuss it. Horn saved his lecture for later that night. As a launching point, he would choose the object that was the most celebrated of all the Passion relics and was central to understanding the greater significance of the entire collection of the Holy Roman artifacts, that which Private Hüber himself had called to Horn's attention and which Thompson, foraging into another crate, removed from inside a delicately carved box. The captain hefted the twenty-inch-long steel spear point purported to have pierced the side of Christ. Lifting the weapon from its velvet pillow, he pointed it at Horn as he would a bayonet.

"It can't be real, can it?" Thompson asked.

Horn had never seen the legendary Longinus lance in person and certainly had never dreamed that he would ever handle it himself. He did so now, carefully removing it from Thompson's hand and replacing it in its box. As Horn would later describe the experience to his students at Berkeley, the Holy Lance was heavier than he had imagined, and its weight, and the knowledge of what it purported to be and why Hitler may have coveted it, made him tremble.

CHAPTER 7

SPEAR OF DESTINY

July 21, 1945

That night after dinner, Horn guided Thompson through two thousand years of Christian mysticism and pan-Germanic superstition. His impromptu lecture might not improve relations between the two men or facilitate the recovery of the missing Crown Jewels— a task that now seemed unachievable given the state of affairs in occupied Nürnberg—but it would help the captain understand why Hitler, like Napoleon before him, coveted the Holy Roman Empire treasures in the first place.

Horn delivered his lecture from an armchair in a quiet vestibule in the hotel lounge. Thompson's preferred haunt in the officers' club, with its din of late-night revelers and civilian contractors, was decidedly not a suitable forum to discuss medieval ritual and the veneration of holy relics. Moreover, Private Dollar, who asked to sit in on the lecture after his return from a failed attempt to free the bunker's escape hatch, didn't have the rank to venture beyond the hotel lobby.

Eventually, they were joined by several of Thompson's friends and other military personnel who were staying at the hotel or had stopped by on their way through the lobby. That Thompson's colleagues felt compelled to stay and listen rather than take their usual places at the piano bar was a gratifying indicator to Horn that his words were not falling on deaf ears and that in his own modest way, he was helping his fellow servicemen to better understand the cultural landscape of the city they sought to govern. U.S. dollars and good intentions weren't enough to win the hearts and minds of a population whose concept of empire and monarchy reached back eight hundred years before the *Mayflower* arrived at Plymouth Rock.

The lieutenant addressed his audience as he would students who didn't know enough about a subject to ask the right questions. He couldn't fault their ignorance of the dynastic succession of the Holy Roman Emperors any more than Panofsky would have called one of his German students to task for not knowing that the Detroit Tigers were a baseball team. Most Americans had little grasp of world history.

If Horn was to accomplish anything that evening, it was to help his listeners bridge a significant cultural divide. While schoolchildren on both sides of the Atlantic learned history from textbooks and museum field trips, in Germany and the rest of Europe, history was more intimately woven into the fabric of daily existence. They had grown up in the shadow of Roman aqueducts, walked roads that had been trod for thousands of years, and attended churches that were built before the age of literacy, when worshippers learned scripture from artists' depictions in stone, wood, and stained glass. Many of these same churches were erected on the sites of earlier pagan temples. Just as ancient timbers and stone were recycled, pagan beliefs and rituals informed Christian liturgy and tradition.

There was no such thing as "new" construction in quite the same way as there was in the "new world." Nürnberg Castle, for example, wasn't actually one castle but three different overlapping structures built around what might have been a fortified Roman watchtower. Before that, it could well have been home to Germanic tribesmen who practiced paganism, as carvings on one of the castle's tower walls indicated. Similarly, the Third Reich could not be understood as an ideological and political movement unaffected by what preceded it. Horn's lecture topic, the Holy Lance, was the perfect vehicle by which to tell the broader story of how one empire's treasures became holy talismans for the next.

The lieutenant didn't need notes. In addition to his own doctorate in art history, his father and grandfather had both been Lutheran ministers, his older brother Rudolf a respected Germanic history professor at the University of Heidelberg, and his brother-in-law Erich Maschke chair of the archaeology department at the University of Leipzig. Conversations around the dinner table often devolved into arguments as both his brother and his brother-in-law became card-carrying Nazis, but despite party affiliations and the looming threat of world war, everyone in the family had a deep appreciation for the legends and lore of the Holy Lance. They understood the object's aura of holiness and how, down through the centuries, its iconic power flowed like a river from biblical times to the present.

Horn began his presentation as he would, years later, begin a similar lecture at Berkeley. "The question isn't whether or not the Longinus lance in the Nazi bunker is the one that actually pierced Jesus," Horn said. "Maybe a time will come when it can be studied and determined decisively if the spear is real or not. The important point is that generations of German Christians venerated it as the genuine article, as many still do today."

That veneration, Horn explained, was linked to the most significant moment of the Christ story: when Jesus—bleeding and battered, with a wreath of thorns wrapped around his head—was nailed to the cross. Because that happened on the Friday before Passover, and Jewish law forbade execution on holy days, Jesus' body had to be removed for burial by sunset. To be certain that Jesus was dead, a Roman soldier, standing at the foot of the cross, drove his spear deep into Jesus' right side, from which flowed blood and water.

Horn pointed out that the Bible in John 19:34 does not identify the soldier who wielded what became known as the Holy Lance. The name of Longinus first appeared in a collection of early Christian texts known as the Apocrypha, where he was described as a centurion who had served his legion faithfully before poor eyesight ended his battlefield career.

Out of respect for his loyal service, Pontius Pilate gave Longinus less demanding assignments on Mount Calvary, which included his participation in Jesus' crucifixion. As described in the Bible and expanded upon in the Apocrypha, when Longinus withdrew his spear from Jesus' right side, blood and water poured down the lance's shaft and into the centurion's eyes, cleansing him of sin and restoring his vision. Inspired by Jesus' dignity and courage in his final hours and transformed by the miraculous healing, Longinus knelt before the cross, begged forgiveness, and loudly proclaimed Christ's divinity.

Longinus left Mount Calvary a changed man. Never again would he serve Pontius Pilate and the Roman legions. After quitting the army, he sought the company of Jesus' followers. Unlike most of the disciples, Longinus was a Roman citizen and could travel freely. For the next twenty-eight years, spear in hand, he walked the dusty roads of the Roman Empire, testifying that Jesus was the Messiah, thereby spreading the news to the Western world. He finally fell afoul of Roman law and endured scourges designed to make him deny his faith. Torturers removed his teeth and tongue and finally severed his head. Yet according to tradition, his testimony could not be silenced. Centuries later, the martyred Longinus was declared a saint.

Horn pointed out that the importance of the Longinus story did not rest solely on New Testament scripture and the Apocrypha. Jesus' claim to being the Messiah was dependent on the centurion's fulfillment of the Old Testament prophecy that "a bone of him shall not be broken" and that "they shall look on him whom they have pierced."

Nothing Horn had yet said veered far from the Longinus story as it appeared in *Butler's Lives of the Saints,* an accepted reference text that art historians and theologians on both sides of the Atlantic consulted. It was what the lieutenant said next that would disturb his listeners.

"Tradition suggests that Longinus was an Aryan, descended from one of the Germanic tribes conquered by the Romans. Christ's executioner, an Aryan soldier, might well have been the first Christian, as Christianity didn't exist until Christ died on the cross and Longinus fulfilled ancient prophecy."

Horn had now captured everyone's attention with a distinctly Germanic interpretation of the story that was popular in pulpits in Nürnberg before and after Martin Luther. This interpretation had a unique appeal for Christians desirous of removing Judaism from the Christ story and focusing on the means by which Christ became the

Messiah and Christianity spread through the Roman Empire. It was only through struggle and bloodshed—when the Aryan Longinus was bathed in the Messiah's blood—that purification and redemption could take place.

In the eyes of some German theologians, Horn explained, it was significant that an Aryan soldier played the pivotal role in the Crucifixion, that this same soldier carried the message of Christianity into what became Europe, and that Longinus, later declared a martyr, inspired generations of soldier-kings and Holy Roman Emperors who fought on the same battlefields as combatants did in the war that had just ended.

Horn was tempted to present the Nazis' own revisionist interpretation of the Passion of Christ, in which Jesus, too, was an Aryan, and Longinus had come to save the Prophet from the Jews who persecuted him. But this was not the focus of his present lecture. He provided no further commentary on the centurion. It was the Holy Lance that would forever eclipse the man behind the legend and would ultimately become the supreme "blood relic" of the Holy Roman Empire.

Having piqued his audience's interest, Horn transitioned from biblical times to the first historically reliable reference to the Longinus lance, which placed it in the hands of another Roman legionnaire, Mauritius, commander of the Theban Legion, whose legendary courage on the battlefield was matched only by the ardor of its faith in Christ.

"Never mind how Mauritius obtained the lance," Horn said. "Medieval chroniclers only say that it was in his possession in the third century, when Roman Emperor Maximian, a pagan, ordered the Theban Legion to put down a rebel insurgency among the Aryan tribes in Gaul."

Upon reaching the battleground in the foothills of the Alps, Mauritius and his legionnaires discovered that the enemy insurgents were Christians like themselves. Having been taught to abhor pagan ceremonies as they were still commonly practiced throughout much of the Roman Empire and prepared to suffer extreme penalties rather than kill fellow Christians, the Theban legionnaires refused to join the battle.

Enraged that Mauritius should defy the direct order of his

Roman superior, Emperor Maximian ordered a "decimation," in which every tenth man was selected from the ranks and beheaded. The only way the Theban legionnaires could save themselves was to renounce Christ, proclaim Maximian's divinity, and make offerings to the Roman gods. Rather than give up their faith, as Maximian anticipated, each selected legionnaire knelt and prayed and then willingly offered his neck to his executioner in Christ's name.

In typical medieval hyperbole—worth noting, Horn explained, because of the legend that would attach itself to the Holy Lance—Longinus's ghost appeared before the legionnaires and invited each to join his Christian army in the afterlife. As heads fell, numerous miracles were reported. A fallen Theban soldier rose from the ground and carried his own head to the top of a hill, where he knelt, prayed, and at last lay down. As the survivors of the first round of executions persisted in declaring their faith, the butchery continued until the nearby Rhine River flowed with the blood of six thousand martyrs.

The cult of the martyred Theban Legion would spread throughout a divided Roman Empire with tales of how the similarly executed Mauritius defied the might of Roman authority and stood before his men brandishing the Longinus lance, reminding them of the one who had been crucified on Mount Calvary.

Horn next explained how the lance eventually became the property of Maximianus Herculius, the third-century coruler of the divided Roman Empire, whose daughter Fausta married Constantine, the Roman king who would become the world's first Christian emperor. Then, as later, the transfer of the lance—as part of Fausta's dowry—was not without fatal consequence for its former possessors: Maximianus was said to have committed suicide when he was implicated in a plot to assassinate the young Constantine, and Fausta was later executed by her husband when she, too, became embroiled in a royal murder plot involving Constantine's son Crispus.

Constantine, Horn said, survived the court intrigue and went on to consolidate the empire. His victory at Milvian Bridge, outside Rome, proved to be the single most important event to date in the spread of Christianity. As chroniclers of the story would write, on the night before the epic battle, Constantine had a vision of a flaming cross in the sky and Greek letters emblazoned on the clouds, which indicated that he and his men would be victorious.

By the end of the first quarter of the fourth century, Constantine was sole master of the Roman Empire. Most notably, he declared Rome to be a Christian city and summoned the First Ecumenical Council of the Church, convened in Nicaea. The Holy Lance was on public display throughout the proceeding, and while disputes raged over what texts would become Christian canon, the emperor was said to have sat quietly on a dais holding his "holy talisman of power and revelation" to his chest.

Constantine's mother, Empress Helena, famed for her piety, promoted the symbolic use of Christ's cross to represent the Messiah's conquest over death, but the Holy Lance, in the hands of her son and future kings, came to represent Christian conquest over pagans—most notably Jews. Popular legend asserted that whoever possessed the lance and understood its power held the destiny of mankind in his hands.

The lance's next claimant, Emperor Theodosius, the son of a Roman general, won fame for his victories against the Goths. Under his reign, the last vestiges of paganism were removed from the Roman Empire, and Christianity, in the form of Nicene orthodoxy, was declared the state religion. Extremist Christians toppled sculptures of pagan idols, possibly including the *Venus de Milo*, which lost its arms. The Rome of Augustus and Tiberius was gone forever. The eternal fire in the Temple of Vesta in the Roman Forum was extinguished and the vestal virgins disbanded. But from the foundations of these pagan temples would rise great cathedrals, Vatican City, and the fortress that would become Nürnberg Castle.

In the ongoing struggle for Nicene orthodoxy at the end of the fourth century, Theodosius would massacre many thousands of non-Nicene Christian men, women, and children. In atonement for what the Church deemed to be his excessive behavior, he would perform three months' penance and place the Holy Lance on public display in a cathedral he built for it in Milan. Here, for the first recorded instance in history, the lance attracted thousands of viewers and was incorporated into the Holy Day Eucharist. The lance was used to cut the bread and was then dipped in the chalice of wine. Held aloft, soaked with consecrated Eucharistic wine, the Holy Lance became the "bleeding lance" of the Longinus sacrament, a ceremony that would be practiced in some church traditions into modern times.

Following Theodosius's death at the end of the fourth century, the lance was removed to Rome to protect it from Alaric, the Visigoth king. A ferocious fighter and natural leader, Alaric conceived a daring plan to invade Italy and sack Rome. After a series of indecisive battles with Roman legions and several attempts to negotiate a peaceful settlement, he underwent a supernatural experience, recorded for posterity by the Roman poet Claudian: "Break off all delays, Alaric," an unearthly voice instructed him. "This very year thou shalt force the Alpine barrier of Italy and thou shalt penetrate the city."

A year later, Alaric and his men stormed into Rome and ransacked private houses and public buildings. In the midst of the pillage, Alaric dressed himself in splendid robes and sat on the throne with a golden crown on his head and the Holy Lance in his hand.

Not all possessors of the lance were recognized as rightful rulers of the lands they conquered. The continued dissolution of the tottering Roman Empire over the next century would be filled with unconfirmed and spurious accounts of who had the lance and what powers it conveyed upon its owner.

Among the most colorful of the alleged lance possessors was Attila, who cut his swath of destruction across Europe following his fifth-century accession as king of the Huns. His route of conquest came to a halt at the gates of Rome. Chroniclers of his day wrote that Attila was dissuaded from sacking the city by Pope Leo I, who offered him a vast treasure, which was said to have included the lance. Before Attila marched his men back to northern Italy, he was alleged to have paused at Rome's gates, drawn the Holy Lance from his saddlebag, and hurled it at the feet of the Roman soldiers.

Justinian, ruler of a divided kingdom in the early sixth century, was intent on restoring the former grandeur of the Roman Empire. In addition to codifying the constitutions and statutes, he went to war on several fronts and eventually reconquered North Africa, Sicily, northern Italy, and Spain. His fortifications along the western and southeastern frontiers, Horn noted, were still visible. General Patton himself had pointed them out on the western frontier as he and his men drove to the German border.

Citing Justinian's biographer Procopius, Horn described how the emperor collected and disseminated legends of the Holy Lance so that Jesus' sufferings "could be kept before the mind of the people" and "the spearman's lance would be known to all." How it would be known, however, was the greater question.

Although Justinian was undeniably a man of great purpose and energy, he had no qualms about using the most savage methods to impose his rule on the rebellious pagan corners of his empire. In one of his first acts, he used his possession of the lance in defense of his abolition of the Academy of Plato in Athens and the murder of more than thirty-five thousand Jews. His savagery, Horn declared, was not soon forgotten. Christians themselves in the next century considered the lance a symbol unfit for their Church. The Holy Grail instead became the iconic symbol of the medieval Church, while the Holy Lance and the accompanying Crown Jewels would come to represent God's appointed earthly monarch, the Holy Roman Emperor.

Horn moved his story ahead by three centuries, from Roman times to Emperor Charlemagne, whose fierce adherence to family and the chivalric code personified the greatness of a medieval Christian king. He was claimed by the Catholic Church as a saint, by the French as their greatest king, by the Italians as their emperor, and by the Germans as father of their nation. Among his many achievements were introducing trial by jury, reforming weights and measures, and minting coinage. He also took great interest in theology, collected and ordered the copying of thousands of religious texts, reorganized the Church, and prompted monastic reform.

To Charlemagne, Horn explained, the lance was not only a symbol and source of power for Christian conquest but a holy object endowing its owner with divine right to rule. Just as the sword of a king placed on the shoulder of a soldier conveyed knighthood, the Holy Lance placed on the shoulder of a pious prince made him king. The sufferings of Jesus were symbolically "shouldered" by the new king, who would gladly shed his blood for the redemption of sinners and be an instrument of vengeance against those hostile to Christ.

Charlemagne's biographer claimed that the emperor carried the Holy Lance with him on every one of the forty-seven campaigns that made him the first effective ruler since the fall of the Roman Empire. He supposedly always kept the spear within arm's reach, right up to the day when he accidentally let it fall from his hands while returning from a victorious campaign. His loyal subjects believed this to be an augury of tragedy to come. They were right. It was his final campaign.

Charlemagne's heritors—his three sons—were not as successful in their efforts to consolidate and reform Christian nations. Over the next century, the empire fell to pieces. Henry I, generally considered the first king of a distinctly German or pan-Germanic state, what Hitler referred to as the First Reich, was said to have carried the spear into battle before passing it to his son, Otto I.

Like Charlemagne and Henry I before him, Otto used the lance to establish his legitimacy as emperor. When not being carried into battle, it was placed on an altar in the opulent cathedral he built in Magdeburg, Germany, along with other imperial relics and treasures. Foremost among them was the crown, which was not round in shape, like more modern crowns, but octagonal, with eight hinged plates, rounded off at the top, and surmounted with a gold cross. Added to the crown were the orb and scepter, symbolic of worldwide Christian rulership, and two swords. At coronation ceremonies, the imperial sword, or sword of Mauritius, was always carried ahead of the king, pointed upward. It could be distinguished from the ceremonial sword—which the king used to bestow knighthood on loyal subjects—by its pommel, with an imperial eagle, and the crossbar inscribed with the words *Christus vincit, Christus regnat, Christus imperat,* or "Christ triumphs, Christ rules, Christ commands."

As sacred as these and other of the Crown Jewels were to what would become the Germanic monarchy, it was still the Holy Lance that fired the imagination of medieval chroniclers. A popular tenth-century story, shared by Horn, told of a plot hatched on Christmas in 941 to send two assassins to kill Otto in Magdeburg Cathedral before he could be crowned the Holy Roman Emperor. Intuiting that he was in danger, Otto allegedly seized the spear from the altar and used it to defend himself. The would-be assassins were soon captured by royal guards and presumably executed.

Henceforth, Emperor Otto, crowned in 951, would add significantly to the Holy Lance's purposes. In addition to being an important relic of the greater coronation regalia, it was incorporated into a baptismal blood ceremony for the Teutonic Knights, a medieval Germanic brotherhood of soldier-priests dedicated to protecting the emperor and guarding the Crown Jewels. Pagan ceremonies, which to varying degrees informed the Longinus legend, included the notion that blood was the vehicle of "vital energy" and that the person who poured it upon his body and moistened his tongue with it would become endowed with the courage and strength of the slaughtered, whether man or beast, Jew or Gentile.

From Otto I's death to Henry IV's accession in the early eleventh century, the spearhead, shorn of its wooden shaft, was on continuous display with curious augmenting features. To the blade was added a Holy Nail said to have come from the True Cross. While a craftsman was cutting a narrow slot into the blade to insert the nail—or on some unspecified earlier occasion—the lance was accidentally broken in half. Craftsmen did not try to mend the two halves but instead tied two thin knife blades to either side of the fracture. Around these blades they wrapped a silver and then a gold band. Once the bands were in place, there was no way to tell that the lance had been broken. Rather than explain the damage and subsequent repairs, Emperor Henry IV claimed that the bands had been attached to show how deeply the spear point had plunged into Jesus' body. This is why, Horn explained, the object in the Blacksmith's Alley bunker appeared as it did, with the gold sheath around its middle portion. At Henry's coronation, the additions, or improvements, enhanced by the king's claim that the lance's power—now with the Holy Nail—had been doubled, created a sensation.

Ownership of the lance and regalia, however, did not secure Henry's reign. Three children feuded for his throne so violently and protractedly that Henry, fearing for his life, gave the lance to his more faithful daughter, Agnes. From her hands, it passed, as a result of her marriage, to her grandson Frederick I, named Barbarossa, or "Red Beard," who was a frequent visitor to the Nürnberg Castle.

King Frederick's life proved one long, unyielding struggle with problems at home in Germany, civil unrest in Lombardy, and disputes with Pope Alexander III in Rome. He undertook six expeditions to Italy and joined the unsuccessful Second Crusade, during which his relations with the Roman Catholic Church deteriorated. Frederick was summarily excommunicated. In response, he declared his support for the antipope Victor IV and sought to remove the seat of the Church to Nürnberg, an effort that culminated in the early twelfth century with several bloody battles and Frederick's defeat.

Ironically, Horn pointed out, Frederick's defeat proved more valuable to him than his previous military successes. The emperor confessed his errors and, with the lance in his hand, knelt and kissed the feet of the pope. With the pontiff's blessing, Frederick once again presided over a united empire. As penitence for his previous insolence, he joined the Third Crusade, marking the first return of the lance to the place of its hallowing more than a thousand years earlier.

Tragedy befell Frederick on the crusade. On June 10, 1190, as his army approached a small bridge, he was said to have galloped ahead to join his son across the river, leading the advance guard, and plunged his horse over the side into the water. Mount and rider were swept away. Frederick's heavy armor left him helpless, and he drowned. According to popular legend, the lance fell from his hand into the water at the moment of his death.

The Holy Lance disappeared for the next one hundred fifty years, but its legend was celebrated in the great medieval epic poem *Parzival*, by the German knight Wolfram von Eschenbach. In it, the "bleeding spear" would be forever intertwined with the "holy chalice" and give rise to myths and legends that dominated sacred and popular literature and would later inspire Richard Wagner, Hitler's favorite composer, to write the opera *Parsifal*.

Fourteenth-century emperor Charles IV, whose modeled figurine sat atop the throne on the massive Männleinlaufen of Nürnberg's Church of Our Lady, much admired Eschenbach's poem and sought to find similar adornments to add luster to his royal court. Desperate to possess both the Holy Grail and the Holy Lance, he dispatched couriers across his kingdom on a chivalric quest to find them. When their first attempt failed, he encouraged his knights to go farther afield. They did not find the Holy Grail, but they did find the Holy Lance, or at least a Roman spear point, which he displayed in Nürnberg. Charles's physical possession of the holy object apparently convinced the populace of his qualifications to rule. It had become, by this time, less a symbol of Christian authority than a means of transference, or *translatio imperii*, from one Holy Roman Emperor to the next.

Regardless of whether it was the same as that previously venerated in Milan, Charles IV's lance remained the sacred possession of
subsequent monarchs for five centuries. Further, Charles IV's son,
Emperor Sigismund, in an attempt to end the ever-recurring quar-
rels over ownership of the Crown Jewels, had the lance and the
other imperial regalia assembled into one large collection and delivered to Nürnberg. By imperial decree, the collection would no
longer reside with the emperor for safekeeping but would remain
permanently in Nürnberg and leave the city for use only during the
coronation. Also by royal decree, the treasures were to be presented
once a year for public viewing.

The display ceremony, known as the Feast of the Holy Lance,
would begin with a triumphal parade to the market square, after
which the treasures would be placed on a raised platform above a
scaffold. First would come the showing of relics related to Christ's
birth, then the imperial insignia—crown, orb and scepter, and
swords—and finally the Passion or blood relics, culminating in the
unveiling of the Holy Lance.

Nürnberg was the best choice to safeguard the treasures for
several reasons, Horn explained. Most important, Nürnberg had
the distinction of being an "imperial city" independent of any in-
termediary feudal lord or vassal. In other words, its castle was the
property of the Holy Roman Emperor, and the city was governed
by councilmen who swore their allegiance directly to him. It was
this city council and its Teutonic Knights—not the clergy and lesser
royalty of the empire—whose task it was to protect and display the
treasures.

Horn moved on, drawing attention to the fact that custody of
the treasure greatly contributed to the city's prestige as the unoffi-
cial capital of the Holy Roman Empire. In actuality, Horn explained,
no capital existed, as the empire was a loose-knit confederation of
city-states and other kinds of territories: counties, lordships, duch-
ies, principalities, prince-bishoprics, baronies, margraviates, and
landgraviates. Its emperor traveled from city to city and was voted
into office by a consensus of participating dukes, bishops, and other
nobility, known as electors.

The relic's supposed mystical powers were as real for townspeople as for visiting royalty. In what was regarded as one of the

most fantastic events in Nürnberg's history, residents beheld what sixteenth-century chroniclers called a "frightful spectacle" and a "dreadful apparition." In a Nostradamus-like vision of the Apocalypse, the skies over Nürnberg Castle filled with strange barrel-shaped objects, which flew through the air and exploded into red, black, and orange fireballs. At the conclusion of what clerics declared was a "celestial battle," the heavens cleared, and there arose, for all to see, a ghostly image of the Longinus lance.

In all likelihood, what they had seen was a meteor shower. The Renaissance mind-set, however, took this as a divine manifestation, a premonition of disaster. And perhaps it was, given the bombing that engulfed the city 384 years later.

The cult of the Holy Lance remained an active and powerful force in Nürnberg throughout the decline and eventual dissolution of the Holy Roman Empire. Even after the Protestant Reformation and the Thirty Years' War, when the Roman Catholic Church was under siege throughout Germany, no less a spiritual authority than the revered German mystic Anna Katherine Emmerich conferred her blessing on the relic. An Augustinian nun widely regarded for her ability to peer into the ancient past and preview the future, Emmerich was asked by Nürnberg's city fathers to verify that the spear was authentic, that it had pierced the body of Christ.

To the astonishment of clergy and a distinguished jury of councilmen gathered around the revered nun, she touched the tip of the spear point, fell into a state of ecstasy, and manifested a stigmata. Witnessed by all, a wound miraculously appeared on the lower right side of her chest, from which flowed blood and water.

Pilgrims still came from far and near to view the Holy Lance and other Crown Jewels. Isabella of Spain sent an emissary to bring a swatch of muslin to Nürnberg to be pierced by the spear point so that she could wear it close to her heart. Count Ferdinand of Austria had the weapon dipped in a keg of wine, convinced that by drinking the contents, he would be endowed with the blood of Christ.

The Longinus cult was still flourishing when Napoleon Bonaparte arrived on the scene in the waning years of the eighteenth century. The last of the would-be Holy Roman Emperors and the greatest plunderer of all time, Napoleon desired the ancient symbols of imperial power for his own. Fearful that the all-conquering Corsican intended to claim Nürnberg's lance and imperial regalia, the city council moved them into hiding in Regensburg. The mission was entrusted to Regensburg's imperial envoy, Baron von Hugel, who eventually transferred the collection to Vienna, promising to return it to Nürnberg when Napoleon was defeated.

Peace was finally restored in the early years of the nineteenth century, but Germany itself was now divided, and the Holy Roman Empire, for all practical purposes, no longer existed. Baron von Hugel took advantage of the legal confusion over who, if anyone, rightfully owned the treasures and sold them to the Habsburgs, the imperial family who had ruled Austria for nearly four hundred years. Nürnberg's city council demanded their return, but Austrian authorities refused. Right of possession and superior military strength trumped the ancient decrees and customs of the long-deceased soldier-king who had given them to Nürnberg.

In the hands of the Austrians, the lance and other Crown Jewels were still valuable treasures, but not as they had once been. No longer was the lance considered a sacred symbol of world conquest and divine rule. Removed from its cult following in Nürnberg, and with Reich Chancellor Bismarck in Berlin attempting to modernize Germany, there was little interest in exploring the lance's deeper spiritual mysteries and superstitions. The lance and imperial regalia were eventually moved from the Habsburgs' treasury into the Kunsthistorisches Museum. And there in Austria, in Vienna's Hofburg, the treasures might have remained, if not for the attentions shown to them by a twenty-three-year-old art student with grand ambitions but little talent.

Thompson, Dollar, and the various officers listening to Horn didn't need to be told the name of that student. Adolf Hitler would write about the collapse of Germany's "Second Reich" and his formative years in Vienna in the pages of *Mein Kampf.* "In this period there took shape within me the world vision and philosophy which became the granite foundation of all my acts," Hitler wrote. "The ancient insignia of imperial glory held in Vienna seemed to be working its past magic."

CHAPTER 8

HIMMLER'S SCHOLARS

July 22, 1945

Early the next morning, Horn walked to the Germanic Museum to visit Günter Troche. Finding his friend didn't prove as difficult as he'd supposed. The former Carthusian monastery and cloister that housed the museum was a fire-scorched shell in south Nürnberg, but it was business as usual in its warehouse, located in a former fire station around the corner.

Thirty-six-year-old Troche was standing in the middle of the street, directing a fleet of trucks queuing for the loading dock. He was much thinner than when Horn had seen him in Berlin eight years earlier, and his dark, neatly clipped hair had gone prematurely white. Still, he appeared the same energetic museum curator of his early days, equally at ease among artists, truckers, and cargo handlers. He wore a clean white smock, held a clipboard in one hand, and waved a traffic baton with the other. From a lanyard around his neck dangled a whistle, which he intermittently blew to catch the attention of idling liverymen.

Like his fellow curators busily inspecting cargo, Troche was in high spirits. Despite the loss of the museum's exhibition space, its vast collection of German art and antiquities—from medieval suits of armor to eighteenth-century brass door knockers and butter churns—had survived the bombing and subsequent invasion. After three years in various storage rooms outside the city—in barns, church basements, and castle dungeons—the collection was coming home. The return of the museum's remaining treasures, now under Allied authority and housed in the Blacksmith's Alley bunker and several other underground facilities, was expected before the end of the year.

Troche was justifiably enthusiastic. As he and the other curators were to explain to Horn that morning, all 2 million items in their prewar repository were accounted for. The only losses were several hundred paintings and antiques that made up the city government collection, not technically part of the Germanic Museum collection, which former city defense minister Karl Holz had demanded remain on the walls of Nürnberg's administrative offices. To remove this art, Holz had declared, was treasonous, a suggestion that the Nazi regime could not adequately protect the city from attack.

The result was self-evident. The city government art not burned or bombed had been looted during the invasion. This was a great loss, indeed, but insignificant compared to the dispersal and destruction of German art in the Berlin and Munich museums. The loss of art and antiquities in those cities now made the Germanic Museum's holdings the premier collection in the nation. And with U.S. dollars being funneled into the museum's coffers in anticipation of the arrival of thousands of visitors to the war-crimes tribunals, the museum was certain to open its doors soon.

The almost joyful optimism among the curators was a refreshing change from the oppressive gloom that permeated the rest of the city. Horn couldn't help but share their excitement when he finally caught Troche's attention, walked out into the middle of the road, and wrapped him in a heartfelt and well-received embrace.

Troche handed his baton to a colleague and led Horn into the warehouse, which was filled nearly to overflowing. He collected a few books and files from his desk and steered Horn out of the room to where they could speak privately.

They walked through the charred remains of the museum on their way to the former monastery's cloister. Given the boarded-up and roofless exhibition rooms they passed along the way, Horn was delighted to find the cloister, with its quadrangle enclosed by a vaulted arcade, in nearly pristine condition. The debris from burning timbers had been removed, and the centuries-old stone fountain in the middle of the enclosure had been scrubbed clean and filled with water. It was an odd thing, Horn would later muse. Everywhere around them were reminders of the sophistication and culture that had created this peaceful oasis, while just outside was a mountain of charred brick and rubble.

The debris would soon be gone, Troche assured him. And if he had his way, the museum would rise like a phoenix. In addition to re-creating the old exhibition spaces, the curator envisioned building an entirely new structure for contemporary German art—not Nazi art, Troche was quick to point out, but new German art.

Troche rattled off names of men and women whom he and Horn had known from their school days, when Berlin had eclipsed Paris as the destination of choice for the Expressionist movement in fine art and film. As Horn well knew, there had been a mass exodus of creative talent as Germany mobilized for war. Troche was certain the artists would return and was committed to seeing that Jews and Gentiles alike would have gallery space in the Germanic Museum to display their work.

Horn had every reason to believe Troche. If any curator in Germany could get the job done, and if anyone had the most reason to do it, that man was Troche. His and Horn's paths had separated before the declaration of war, but they shared a similar desire to help repair the damage and injustice done by the Nazis. The important difference was that Troche was a perpetrator of the injustice. As he confessed to Horn that morning, he felt great personal responsibility to try to right the many wrongs. He was doing so the way he knew best, by helping to create a museum that would reflect and celebrate cultural diversity.

Fate had now thrown the two men together to return the missing Crown Jewels. Despite their desire to get started, they stole three-quarters of an hour to reminisce about old times and to ponder what might have been had Horn remained in Germany and Troche left for America.

They had first met in Berlin in the early 1930s, when they were students of Panofsky. Like Horn, Troche was a rising star in the academic firmament, and though he was slightly younger than Horn—

just starting his doctoral dissertation as Horn was finishing—they had gone on many field trips together, studied the same museum collections, sat front-row center in the university auditorium when visiting scholars came to lecture, and had briefly lived together in a rooming house.

Berlin before the war had been exhilarating for both men. Few people who had not experienced it for themselves could fully understand the hothouse environment that it had been or comprehend the incredible creative and sexual freedom that drove the city's students to extremes of excellence and excess. The best minds of the twentieth century—scientists, mathematicians, and engineers, artists and art historians—came together in coffee shops, beer halls, and university common rooms to argue the great issues of the day. Berlin's students and professors led the world in virtually every field and, along with the city's other residents, were the most literate and educated population in the world. This had unfortunately worked to the Nazis' advantage, for people worldwide understood the Germans to be highly cultured and sophisticated. Even those who would later be taken to the concentration camps often willingly surrendered to the Nazis because they thought the Germans incapable of the kinds of atrocities they would ultimately suffer.

Despite the growing undercurrents of anti-Semitism, Jews were at the forefront of the arts and sciences. In addition to winning the lion's share of Nobel Prizes in the decade leading up to the war, Jews hosted the most celebrated dinner parties, operated the fashionable galleries, and were also the popular opera conductors and cabaret entertainers.

Horn and Troche had thrived in that environment, fully engaging themselves and enjoying the intellectual and sexual freedom. Many a night they spent studying in the library before going out to clubs until the early hours. Besides their mutual love of art history and their sporting prowess—Horn was a javelin champion, and Troche excelled in track and field—they both had Jewish lovers. In Horn's case, it was Gretl, a woman ten years his senior and married to a Nazi industrialist. Troche's lover was Jan, an immensely talented male Jewish artist and art critic.

Panofsky, himself a Jew, had warned them to watch what they said and did as the mood of the nation shifted from lesser forms of discrimination to outright intolerance and physical abuse. He urged them to leave the country as he himself was preparing to do. Horn heeded Panofsky's advice, taking a job at the German Institute in Florence. Troche stayed behind and became an archivist in the curatorial department at Berlin's National Gallery.

Horn's three and a half years in Italy, from 1934 to 1938, were an extension of the carefree lifestyle he had enjoyed in Berlin, but his friendships expanded to include a more international and well-heeled circle of art lovers. Instead of visiting coffee houses and nightclubs, he joined a salon of art historians, dealers, museum curators, and expatriate artists that revolved around critic and collector Bernard Berenson, the undisputed god of the post-WWI art world.

At Berenson's forty-acre villa, I Tatti, in the foothills outside Florence, Horn was introduced to a constant stream of European and American intellectuals at courtly teas and candlelit dinners: British art dealer Joseph Duveen, collector Isabella Stewart Gardner, Metropolitan Museum of Art director Alfred Hamilton Barr, Paul Sachs of Harvard, and Worth Ryder from Berkeley. It didn't matter that Horn had only recently received his degree, had published just a single journal article, and was living on a modest stipend from the German Institute. He was treated as one of the inner circle and invited on summer trips with Berenson to Madrid and Paris and winter jaunts to the Alps.

Back in Germany, the hammer was falling. Troche's lover and several hundred activists were in the midst of pushing legislation through the Reichstag to overthrow the law that made sex between men illegal. It was a hopeless endeavor; the new Nazi leadership was rabidly homophobic. Hitler himself had declared homosexuality to be "degenerate behavior" that posed a threat to the "masculine character" of the nation. Names of known homosexuals were being collected, as were those of Jews, Jehovah's Witnesses, and a growing list of other "undesirables."

Horn received his first wake-up call when he briefly returned home to bury his father in 1934. Along with his older brother Rudolf and his future brother-in-law Erich, he joined a street rally celebrating the recently installed new Reich chancellor. Making light of the cheering crowds, Horn thrust his arms up with everyone else. Instead of shouting "Heil Hitler," he mockingly intoned "Drei liter." In the tumult of the noisy crowd, the common refrain for "three liters" of beer couldn't be differentiated from what everyone else was shouting. It was only after Hitler's motorcade had passed that his brother pulled him aside and pointed out the danger he had barely skirted. Those who didn't raise their hands in salute or, worse, raised them with a fist instead of the outstretched fingers were removed from the crowd by storm troopers and had their hands smashed. Horn was upset and angered by what he saw but downright bewildered when Erich, about to marry Horn's sister Elsbeth, reprimanded him for his lack of respect and "Jew-loving" ways.

Horn did have a long history of love affairs with Jews. Before Gretl, there was a woman who joined him on overnight hikes in the Alps and, in his more distant youth, a girl in Heidelberg who had saved him from drowning. He had never thought of the women in his life as belonging to a race separate from his own.

A year later, on another trip from Florence, Horn heard Troche describe the terror that now swept the nation. His lover Jan was a public enemy on two counts: his Jewish descent and his homosexuality. Troche had managed to steer clear of trouble himself, but Jan had been arrested and sent to Dachau, which at that time was exclusively used to house political prisoners and petty criminals. Horn, fearing that Gretl might also be in danger, unsuccessfully pleaded with her to leave the country before she, too, was arrested. Gretl didn't believe she would be affected—she had lived in Germany her entire life and had the protection of her Nazi husband.

The political complexion of Germany was changing in other disturbing ways as well. Just as Hitler sought to reshape concepts of the state's national interests and obligations, artists and art historians were pressured to fall into line with everyone else. Nowhere was this more evident than in the premiere of the first exhibit of official Nazi art in July 1937. At its opening, Hitler decried modern art as the creation of "smearers and blotters," which had been foisted upon the public by Jews who had exploited their hold over the press. All art historians and museum curators were now on notice. Just as Hitler had his own concept of art, and hence what should be collected and preserved, he clearly delineated what must be destroyed or removed from public viewing. The latter included any work that could not be easily understood or required what Hitler termed "pompous literary commentary," an offensive description for exactly what Horn and Troche were trained to do.

Horn returned to Italy, where he anticipated riding out the Nazi storm in the comfort of Berenson's villa. But he was not out of reach of the long arm of Heinrich Himmler, whose Gestapo and SS were as interested in quashing dissent at home and abroad, along with rounding up scholars to justify their activities. In January 1938, news reached Horn through a friend in the interior minister's office that an SS officer was on his way to the German Institute with instructions to "supervise" the further education of Horn and his expatriate colleagues. "He is one of Himmler's attack dogs," Horn's friend said of the officer. "Better watch what you say."

Political indoctrination was the least of Horn's concerns. He needed to find out if Gretl's Nazi husband had put Horn on some kind of list or if one of the many derogatory comments Horn had made about the Nazis had been reported. Perhaps Panofsky's outspoken criticism of the regime and subsequent departure for the United States had cast suspicion on his favorite student. Or was the SS officer's trip to Florence more benign? Horn's brother Rudolf, five years his senior, had told him that the Nazis were actively seeking scholars of German and pan-Germanic history. "Aryan Studies" had become the most popular new major at the University of Heidelberg, where he taught and where Horn one day intended to teach.

Horn hatched a plan to ferret out the truth. For help, he enlisted a Swedish colleague studying at the German Institute. Divorced, with a small child, she was, as Horn and several of his friends knew from firsthand experience, "generous" with her physical affections. "Not what one would call monogamous," was how Horn later described her to Rosenthal and eventually to Troche. The plan was for her to seduce the officer and discover his intentions. She agreed to act as Horn's spy on the sole condition that she find the SS officer attractive. To Horn's immense relief, the officer looked quite handsome stepping off the train in Florence in a well-tailored black uniform with its distinctive Death's Head insignia.

A dinner party was thrown in the officer's honor that same night. Afterward, when Horn and the others left, his spy stayed behind to help the German visitor become acquainted with social life in Florence. Everything went as planned. The next morning, at a streetside café, Horn's spy told him that the officer had been sent to Florence on a recruiting mission. Horn's name was at the top of his list. Recruits, however, were not to be given a choice about whether to return to Germany to serve their country.

That very day, February 7, 1938, Horn spent all but his last fifty dollars on a steerage-class ticket on a transatlantic steamer sailing from Genoa. Although the ship was bound for Cuba and not the United States, Horn wasn't about to cavil. He made his farewells, packed his things, and headed to the train station. The only person who came to see him off was the last man on earth he wanted to see. Minutes before the train was scheduled to leave the station, the SS officer, in full dress uniform and carrying a holstered pistol, sat down in the seat next to him.

Horn was so frightened that the blood began to drain from his face.

"You think I don't know what you're up to," the officer said. "But you see, I do."

Horn pretended that he was merely visiting Genoa on a short sightseeing trip. The officer was not fooled. He knew about the steerage-class ticket to Cuba. He also knew details of Horn's personal life—that he could trace his lineage back five generations in Germany, that he had been under consideration for the Olympic javelin team, that he played the violin, however poorly, that he spoke five languages, and that he had a doctorate in art history and a minor in pan-Germanic prehistory.

"I had hoped to find a place for you in the new world order," the officer told him. "But it's too late for that now."

Horn was certain that the SS officer was about to reach for his pistol. But instead, he extended his hand and wished Horn a safe journey. He was, he said, envious. "Just don't try to come home," he added. "It wouldn't look good for either of us."

That was the last conversation Horn had before stepping on-board the steamship bound for Havana. Even after the ship weighed anchor, he dreaded that the Nazi secret police would suddenly materialize and yank him off the boat.

"After that, things were a lot less complicated for me," Horn told Troche. "The United States is an easy place to get settled. I'm now a professor at the University of California at Berkeley, and have a house overlooking San Francisco's Golden Gate Bridge."

It wasn't as easy for Horn in the United States as he described to his former schoolmate. He had arrived in New York with six dollars left in his pocket, the address of a colleague in Greenwich Village, and a pocket diary containing a list of people he had met at Berenson's villa.

The first year, he survived by working as a guest lecturer in art history, which wasn't necessarily an easy thing considering that English wasn't his native language. His income was so meager that he sometimes walked out of a lecture hall in one city with only enough money for train fare to the next college or museum where he was engaged to speak. Once, after delivering a talk at the Cleveland Museum of Art, he hitched a ride back to New York with a well-to-do museum patron. They stopped for lunch along the way at a large mansion in Hyde Park. Horn spent a thoroughly enjoyable afternoon chatting with his hostess and her luncheon companion, not realizing until after he left that he had dined with Eleanor Roosevelt, the First Lady of the United States, and her friend Brooke Astor, one of the wealthiest women in the world.

Horn recounted other adventures, such as meeting a cowboy on a train trip through Arizona on his way to a lecture at the University of California at Berkeley. The cowboy, Horn delightedly told Troche, hadn't boarded at a station. He had galloped his horse alongside the passenger car and jumped aboard.

The lecture in Berkeley had gone especially well, and Horn was offered a full-time position developing the school's first art history program. That's when he bought the property in Point Richmond, married Anne Binkley, and obtained his citizenship.

He would never forget attending his first faculty meeting, for it was the first truly democratic experience of his life. In German academia, as in so many other aspects of German society, decisions always came from the top. You either toed the line or stepped out of line. As Horn would later describe the experience in his oral memoirs, "the faculty at Berkeley made decisions together—men and women in free deliberation, without fear of expressing dissent. I fell in love with America on that day and haven't looked back since."

Just as Horn had soft-pedaled some of the difficulties of adjusting to his life in America—learning to deliver a coherent and compelling lecture in a foreign language was but one challenge, Anne Binkley another—he didn't convey the anguish he felt for his friends and family back home. He received only sporadic letters, and nothing from Gretl.

Then came the war in Europe. Horn had been an adolescent during the previous war and knew the hunger and deprivation that had been its consequence. His parents, unable to feed him, had sent him to live on a farming commune in Sweden run by fellow Lutherans. His much-beloved uncle, who had been like a second father to him, had died horribly from an infected gunshot wound, and other relatives were left maimed. Now another world war was under way. To make matters worse, his family was not only refusing to leave Germany and join him in the United States, but his brother Rudolf and brother-in-law Erich, professors at major universities, were active in the Nazi Party and steering their impressionable young students to follow the Führer's call to arms.

The United States was slow to join the war effort. But when it did, Horn met the call.

Intelligence work was out of the question. A recent arrival in the United States and the owner of oceanfront property on a bluff that could be used to signal enemy ships, he was put on a blacklist of potential German spy operatives. To show his allegiance to his adopted nation, and in spite of the potential for meeting former friends in combat, he volunteered for the infantry.

Horn earned his credentials as a marksman at Camp Roberts in California's Salinas Valley. Just as he was about to ship out, he came down with a sinus infection. His medical condition actually turned out to be his savior, although only his wife thought so at the time. Alone in the barracks, while waiting to join the next company of recruits, he was assigned to wash windows for six weeks. His commanding officer claimed never to have seen anyone wash windows so thoroughly and with such enthusiasm. Employing typical Army logic, he recommended Horn for officer's training at Fort Benning. From there, he went to Camp Ritchie in Maryland, where he met Felix Rosenthal, who joined him in England and then in Germany. Horn's chance encounter with Mason Hammond in London and then his interrogation of Private Hüber had now brought him to Nürnberg.

It was only natural for the two men, together after so many years, to ponder how different things might have been if Horn had stayed in Germany. As Troche remarked, he would have been a prime candidate for a leadership position in the Third Reich. The Nazis would have rolled out a red carpet for a javelin thrower, German history scholar, and fifth-generation German national.

Troche was probably right. Athletics aside, with his degrees from the University of Heidelberg and pan-Germanic studies in Berlin, Munich, and Hamburg, Horn might have risen quickly up the Nazi ranks. But he couldn't have lived with himself.

Troche didn't volunteer many specifics of his own journey after they had last seen each other in Berlin, but he described enough for Horn to know that he profoundly regretted refusing Panofsky's advice.

He justified not leaving the country by telling himself that in Berlin, he could do something to effect his lover's release from Dachau. But that didn't happen. He was too frightened to join Jan's friends publicly speaking out against Nazi tyranny. Those who protested found themselves wearing the inverted pink triangle sewn on the uniforms of Dachau inmates, in what had become by this time a concentration camp. It wasn't long afterward that the crematorium was installed.

The Nazis took hundreds, perhaps thousands, of homosexuals to the camps. Troche's friends who weren't picked up refused to acknowledge him in the streets. He, too, lay low. He continued working in the archives at the National Museum and did his best to stay out of the military. In a strange way, difficult for him to describe, he had begun to believe the picture that Hitler had created of the "new world order," even though there wasn't a place in it for him. He was in disguise—pretending heterosexuality as he pretended disdain for Jews, when in fact he was homosexual and a lover of Jews.

To keep his job in Berlin, he had to join the Nazi Party, and once he joined the party, he had to fall into line. Children joined the Hitler Youth. Men capable and willing volunteered for the army, navy, or air force. Museum curators and scholars joined the ranks of the Deutsches Ahnenerbe, an elite Nazi research institute that Himmler and some of his associates had founded.

Horn hadn't heard the name of the Ahnenerbe organization before and had seen nothing about it in the foreign press and only a reference or two in the G-2 intelligence reports, but he suspected, based on things his brother Rudolf and brother-in-law Erich had said before the war, that this was the same corps of Nazi intellectuals who oversaw curricula at the universities and sponsored academic-related research expeditions abroad.

Troche told Horn that it was this and much more.

The Deutsches Ahnenerbe, or German Ancestral Heritage Research and Teaching Society, Troche explained, was a Nazi think tank founded by Himmler and dedicated to rediscovering the accomplishments of Germany's supposed Aryan ancestors and conveying these findings to the public by educating the youth; publishing magazines, articles, and books; sponsoring museum exhibitions; and conducting scientific research. It was especially attractive to scholars and intellectuals seeking to avoid active military service, as its work was considered "war essential." Ranking members had their own specially created SS uniforms, complete with distinctive signet rings and ceremonial daggers.

Troche became involved in Ahnenerbe activities while he was with the Berlin Museum. At first, he helped gather research data, but gradually, as he became more involved, he attended lectures at the Ahnenerbe headquarters in a grand mansion in Dahlem, one of Berlin's wealthiest neighborhoods. The lecture that most impressed Troche was delivered by Dr. Otto Rahn, Berlin's noted medievalist. He was also, according to Troche, once a well-known fixture in the city's homosexual underground, an example of what perhaps was possible for Troche himself if he followed in Rahn's footsteps.

Horn remembered Rahn's dissertation on Guyot de Provence, a nobleman, knight, and poet whose writing on the lost Holy Grail was said to have inspired Wolfram von Eschenbach to write *Parzival*, the epic poem featuring the "bleeding lance." Rahn had a fanciful notion that his research would lead him to the secret hiding place of the fabled Temple of Solomon treasures, which included the Grail Chalice and the Ark of the Covenant.

When Troche attended Rahn's lecture, he had no idea that Rahn had already become a leading Nazi with a distinguished rank in the SS. Nor did he know that the Ahnenerbe's sprawling headquarters, with its tall hedges and wrought-iron gates, had been purchased at a "bargain" price from a Jewish family forced to flee the country.

Troche was merely impressed by its extensive library, fully outfitted laboratories, and research archives and was pleased to discover that it was supportive of Rahn and his quest to find the Holy Grail. "No dream is too big or unattainable under the Nazis," Rahn had told his audience.

Troche was won over. At that time—just before the invasion of Poland—the Ahnenerbe had more than a hundred scholars and scientists on its payroll and nearly twice as many filmmakers, photographers, artists, laboratory technicians, accountants, and secretaries. Many thousands more people were part of the expansion into the schools. Professors unwilling to take direction from the Ahnenerbe were gradually replaced. If a professor wanted a chair in the university, he had to join the Ahnenerbe's ranks or at least pay the organization lip service. It was only later that Troche would learn the darker, more ruthless side of the Ahnenerbe and its connection to the Nazi high command.

Rahn too belatedly learned the truth. Having failed to find the Holy Grail and embarrassed by the scholar's homosexual lifestyle, Himmler had Rahn arrested for sexual misconduct, after which—according to the Reich press—he committed suicide. Following Rahn's demise, any member of the SS found guilty of homosexual offenses faced a mandatory death sentence.

Troche hadn't known what was to befall the man who had inspired him to join the Ahnenerbe. Like Rahn, he rose quickly and was promoted up the ranks from an archivist to the director of an art museum in Breslau, the capital of the predominantly German province of Silesia, in Poland. He might well have risen higher in the Ahnenerbe's ranks but was reluctant to join Himmler's SS, a prerequisite for all senior staff. Doing so would have meant undergoing a mandatory six-month "boot camp" at Dachau or one of the other concentration camps and then graduate training at Himmler's private castle in Wewelsburg, in the district of Büren, northeast of Nürnberg. But it didn't take a tour of Dachau or a visit to the Ahnenerbe castle for Troche to experience personally the horrors of the Nazi regime. A tour of duty in Breslau was enough.

Horn knew what had happened from G-2 reports. The first order of business in Breslau was to clear Jews, ethnic Poles, and Slavs from the city. To advance Hitler's projected repopulation of

the Aryan race and culture to its colonies, Himmler set about reset-
tling hundreds and thousands of Germans across the border into
the newly vacant homes of the displaced. No expense was spared in
opening universities, museums, and other cultural institutions that
were to extend the Fatherland. Breslau was to be the showcase for
the Führer's Eastern Empire.

Thus, Troche was brought to the city to help turn Breslau into
a model community that showcased German spirit and culture. The
museum was not only to display ancient and traditional German art
but also to export an Aryan vision of the future rooted in the past.

To this end, Troche had helped to oversee building a model
farm, where visitors could view an idyllic version of traditional German homesteads and learn about time-honored German agricul-
tural practices. There was also to be a separate Jewish wing of the
museum, where German schoolchildren could learn of vanquished
"inferior" cultures. Near the museum, the Ahnenerbe scientists established an Aryan breeding center, a kind of baby factory to help
repopulate Poland with genetically superior Germans.

Like so many of Hitler's grand schemes, the model city of
Breslau, the Ahnenerbe utopia, ended in a tragedy beyond compre-
hension for the German people. After the battle for Stalingrad, the
Red Army began retaking Poland. Breslau became an armed camp
to hold back the Communist hordes. The German civilian population, most of whom had willingly given up the homeland to resettle
Breslau and who still held dreams of the ideal community they had
sought to create, were boxed in by two armies. Hitler had left them
to be massacred by the Soviets.

The story of Breslau's ill-fated airport, the German population's
only avenue of escape, exemplified how the Nazis had shown their
true colors to their own people. A thousand or more German homes
had been demolished, and ten thousand German and Polish civilians
killed, to build an airstrip that saw but a single plane land and take
off. That plane was not occupied by any of the settlers. It rescued
the city's SS officers.

Troche didn't have to endure the final destruction in Breslau. He
had been transferred to the Germanic Museum in Nürnberg to work
as an assistant curator. He wasn't privy to the decisions being made by
Reich leadership, but he observed enough activity at the museum to

realize that the highest-ranking Ahnenerbe official, Heinrich Himmler, had grandiose plans for Nürnberg. Among the shipments of treasures that Troche's Ahnenerbe colleagues brought back with them to Nürnberg from Poland was the Viet Stoss altar, removed from Cracow, which was to join the Crown Jewels, previously removed from Austria. "It was part of the master plan," Troche said.

Horn was not unfamiliar with the phrase *master plan*. Intelligence officers referred to it when discussing Hitler's strategy to crush Poland and invade France and England and his ambition to exterminate the Jewish race. Horn hadn't heard it used before in reference to the treasures of the Holy Roman Empire.

To hear Troche describe it, the treasures of the Holy Roman Empire and the ancient pan-Germanic traditions, rituals, and arcane religious beliefs of the soldier-kings who once possessed them represented substantively more than mere loot for the supposed master race. In the hands of Adolf Hitler and his chief henchman, Heinrich Himmler, the Holy Lance and the Crown Jewels were a seductively potent weapon that the Nazis had used to legitimate the Führer's "Thousand-Year Reich." Hitler had used these treasures to transform Nürnberg and all of Germany.

Horn's three-hour hotel lecture on cult veneration notwithstanding, what Troche had to say shocked and unsettled the lieutenant. He might well have dismissed what the curator had to say next, had Troche not brought along documentary evidence.

In addition to several books and files on the Crown Jewels that he had retrieved from the museum archive, Troche had a map, which he unrolled on the cloister's paved-tile floor. Unlike the World War I–era map that Thompson had been issued, this one, prepared by the Nazis, showed the prison camp and parade grounds. In addition, it detailed improvements and renovations in various stages of completion throughout the city. As Horn could easily see, Nazi architect and city planner Albert Speer—Hitler's favorite—had been busily planning for the future.

Troche took a curator's grease pencil and outlined the Nazi improvements as they appeared on the parade grounds. The image created was unmistakable. The outline was in the shape of a spear or, more precisely, the Holy Lance. And its tip pointed directly to the old inner city, to Blacksmith's Alley.

CHAPTER 9

THE ARYAN JESUS

July 22, 1945

Like the planchette on a Ouija board, the spear tip outlined in grease pencil unmistakably pointed to Blacksmith's Alley. But it wasn't to the renovated beer cellar that Troche directed Horn's attention. Nazi cartographers hadn't incorporated the hidden bunker and its vault on the map at all. The important compass point could be located among the buildings in the castle complex positioned directly above the bunker. The outline of the spear pointed to a small square structure perched on the sandstone bluff overlooking Blacksmith's Alley, to the west of the Knights Hall, where the medieval Teutonic Knights had once met, and east of Heathen's Tower, named for the pagan images that covered its walls.

"The King's Chapel," Horn said, putting his index finger on what might well be the most historically important structure in the entire castle complex.

Horn had guessed correctly. In this chapel, Troche explained, the Holy Roman Emperors attended services, and in the fifteenth century, the Teutonic Knights kept the Crown Jewels safe from invaders. Although the Heilig Geist Spital, or Hospital Church of the Holy Ghost, was where the Crown Jewels were traditionally kept, it was in the King's Chapel, the spiritual capital of the city, where the emperor could more easily keep an eye on them. Hitler, Troche went on to say, knew and studied the legends of the ancient city. That was why he ordered Nürnberg's ancient spiritual capital aligned with the new holy ground where the party rallies were held.

Troche said that it was a mistake for Horn to think of the Nazi Party as merely a political movement; no, it was a cult, which grew from the twisted imagination of its creator. Hitler, assisted by Himmler and others, did not want so much to erase the past as systematically to reinvent it as justification for world conquest. This was what Troche meant by the master-plan, and it was as relevant to understanding the creation of the Dachau concentration camp as it was to the Blacksmith's Alley bunker. Horn, Troche said, would not discover who took the Crown Jewels, and why, until he understood how Hitler had intended to use them.

Horn had spent the previous night at the hotel lecturing occupation officers on the significance of the Crown Jewels to the Holy Roman Emperors. It was now Troche, in the confines of the museum cloister, who lectured Horn on what they meant to the Nazis.

Troche began by covering familiar territory. The Hitler cult was founded on a core belief: the superiority of Aryan man. Military conquest and the extermination of the Jews was not the Nazis' stated or overt intention. Rather, they viewed it as the natural result of Aryan man's evolution on the world stage. This was the message put forth in *Mein Kampf* and the substance of the Führer's mad diatribes at the party rallies.

Horn couldn't argue with what Troche was saying. Everyone who lived in the shadow of the Third Reich understood Hitler's racist agenda. Troche, however, was trying to steer Horn into a deeper understanding of Hitler's thought processes and what it was about the Aryan man, in Hitler's mind, that made him superior.

To Troche, Hitler's cult was little more than an amalgam of arcane beliefs popular throughout Europe at the turn of the century. One was the caste system of races, which placed Aryans, the supposed white race of tall flaxen-haired men and women from northern Europe, at the apex of the genetic-superiority pyramid. Aryan man's alphabet, known as runes, was found inscribed on stone monoliths and vellum scrolls in locations throughout the world, most notably in northern Germany and other Teutonic or Nordic nations. Aryan man's ancient origins, according to this esoteric mysticism, rested in the Himalayas and, before that, in some undefined polar region known as Thule.

Hitler, and Himmler, too, believed that God himself had created Aryans to be physically and spiritually a perfect race. They possessed the spark of genius needed to create civilization and were endowed with superhuman abilities such as telepathy. They could see into the past and preview the future. Before Aryan man's demise—the direct result of interbreeding with genetically inferior races—they had brought into the world all that was truly great and lasting. By studying Aryan man's accomplishments and cosmic truths, by embracing the ancient Aryan community spirit, what the Nazis called *Volk*, modern-day Germans, their direct descendants, could once again manifest such abilities and take their rightful place on the world stage.

"Hitler didn't just recycle the old Teutonic folklore, myths, and mysticism to lend credibility to his racist agenda," Troche said. "He and his inner circle actually believed them."

Most significant, Troche pointed out, was the role that Himmler's scholars, the Ahnenerbe, had played in furthering Hitler's agenda. They were the ones, Troche said, who studied the ancient practices, arcane lore, and cosmic truths of Aryan man as a way to reawaken the ancient *Volk* spirit in modern man. Doing so meant locating Aryan settlements and holy places, deciphering the runes they found there, and identifying the iconic or spiritually charged images Aryan man had created. Ahnenerbe archaeologists, Troche claimed, mined historic sites for evidence of Aryan culture, linguists studied ancient place names to create maps tracing Aryan migrations, and geomancers, studying electromagnetic fields, divined sacred Aryan sites that were conducive to future Nazi settlements. They studied ancient buildings, from prehistoric megaliths to the Parthenon in Athens and the Colosseum in Rome, as these structures were believed to be tangible relics, created by artisans and architects whose blood coursed with Aryan purity. These structures were measured to reveal sacred geometry—the reason, Ahnenerbe scholars maintained, that these monuments had withstood the test of time. All of this learning, Troche said, was to be inscribed into Nürnberg's urban landscape.

Everyone attending the party rallies understood Hitler's message of racial superiority, Troche said. But only the Nazi elite were overtly aware of the arcane doctrines and practices that informed Hitler's beliefs or of how these beliefs were being made an integral part of life in the Reich.

Troche described how the massed Nazi Party pilgrims marched in lockstep at the Nürnberg rallies, ignorant of how and why Hitler had chosen the particular cadence to which they marched. Millions of party members marveled at the majesty of the massive golden eagle atop the Nazi grandstand, yet few were aware that Hitler had envisioned this particular image in a mystical dream. Nor did they realize that the parade route was a carefully constructed and measured roadway designed and built in accordance with an arcane formula. They knew that the Holy Lance and the Crown Jewels—important symbols of German monarchy—were returned to the city that had long coveted them, but they didn't know how they contributed to the Nazis' engine of destruction.

Horn was aware of much that Troche was telling him. His former classmate, however, was taking him in a new and unexpected direction. In Hitler's vision of significant world events, Troche said, it was no coincidence that his favorite opera celebrated Parsifal's discovery of the "bleeding lance" that revitalized the mythic German kingdom. It was also no coincidence that March 15, the day Saint Longinus is honored in the Catholic Church, was the same date Hitler had the Holy Lance and the Crown Jewels removed from their glass cases in Vienna's Hofburg. Based on the things Troche had seen and heard from colleagues at the Germanic Museum, Hitler may well have timed the invasion of Austria for that very reason. The Holy Roman Empire treasure contained the very first and most important artworks the Nazis looted and the last, Troche said, they would give up to the Allies.

Horn was stunned by what he heard. He knew that the Nazis had used Nürnberg as a stage on which to create and project an image of historical greatness, political legitimacy, and the promise of future grandeur. He also intellectually understood that the Holy Lance and the Crown Jewels were politically charged props, which Hitler and his regime could use to win the hearts and minds of Germans. But what Troche claimed was altogether more frightening:

that Hitler and his inner circle believed the artifacts themselves were invested with mystical significance. Fantastic as this might be, the spear-shaped image on the Nazi map Troche showed him, the seeming congruity of the hidden vault directly under the castle chapel, and the timing of the Anschluss were evidence that this might actually be the case. And although Horn hadn't consulted the MFAA records, Troche could be correct that the Crown Jewels were the first artifacts that the Nazis removed to Germany.

Hitler's interest in the Reich treasures, as Horn himself had conjectured and Troche now confirmed, dated back to 1909, when the twenty-year-old was living hand-to-mouth as a struggling artist in Vienna. He had failed twice to gain entrance to the Vienna Academy of Arts, and Hitler's life to that moment had been one of frustration and disappointment, made more painful by the tragic and excruciating death of his mother from breast cancer and his estrangement from the rest of the family. Hitler sometimes slept on park benches and took his meals in charity kitchens. He had no future. Life seemed meaningless. His escape may well have been in fantasy.

Rosenthal, the Third Army's Hitler scholar, would certainly have concurred with Troche's assessment. The young Hitler, a lover of Germanic art and architecture, had wandered Vienna's massive public parks and open spaces, watching how pedestrians moved about the city. He would sit for hours contemplating the subliminal effects that certain monuments and particular configurations of buildings had on the population. He filled notebooks with sketches of futuristic improvements that could be made on existing city spaces and reimagined public transportation, laying down designs for motorways, bus systems, and the vehicles that would use them. The young Hitler's love of art and architecture also took him to the Hofburg, to the Kunsthistorisches Museum, in what had previously been the imperial palace, where he first saw the Holy Lance and the Crown Jewels.

Upon entering room 11 of the Kunsthistorisches Museum, he would have learned from the catalogue description that the treasures on display were the sacred objects of the German kings, passed down by divine right. Despite the fact that the lance had none of the jeweled opulence of the crown, scepter, orb, and royal swords, this object reportedly fired his imagination: a simple iron spear point, blackened with age, wrapped with gold and silver bands, with a nail in the center of the blade, resting on a red velvet dais.

Troche had no way of knowing if Hitler actually took any more than a casual interest in the old relic or if, indeed, as people who knew the young Hitler claimed, it was a revelatory moment in his early life. But Troche supposed that Hitler indeed had had some kind of epiphany. To the impressionable young man—a former Catholic choirboy and aspirant to the priesthood, whose known reading habits ranged from treatises on ancient Rome to the dynastic succession of Frankish kings and pan-Germanic mysticism—the treasures were surely more than mementos of a bygone age. They had the power to shape the destiny of mankind.

Exactly what Hitler experienced when viewing the Holy Lance and other Crown Jewels would remain a mystery. Troche, however, saw it as no coincidence that the future Führer, around the time he first viewed the Crown Jewels, associated with members of secret occult societies. Among Hitler's reputed intimates were two Austrians, Guido von List and Lanz von Liebenfels, proponents of Ariosophy, whose belief in mystical Christianity, *Volk* nationalism, and anti-Semitism may have become Hitler's own. Harking back to traditions and practices rooted in medieval Germanic cult practices—in which Christ's blood and wounds were the principal objects and symbols of veneration—List and Liebenfels espoused general persecution of the Jews and a return to blood as the central theme that connected Christian mystics with their pagan ancestors.

Better documented but no less significant was Hitler's association with Dietrich Eckart and members of the Thule Society, a study group that combined an Aryan racial philosophy with virulent militarism. Taking their group's name from the legendary homeland of the Aryans, Thulists studied the ancient rune alphabet to draw from it secrets of man's origins. Around the time of the Führer's rise to power, an entire book was written on Hitler's connections with the Thule Society, but the book and any public discussion of the subject were subsequently suppressed by the Nazis, who feared a backlash from the Lutheran and Catholic churches.

As Horn knew, Hitler was well aware of his need for support from Germany's mainstream Christian community. It was also no secret that he adopted Ariosophy's swastika banner and that Himmler, another wayward Catholic and longtime friend of the Thulists, would choose runes for symbols for the Waffen-SS, which acted as his private army. Horn, his brother Rudolf, and his brother-in-law Erich had discussed these things.

How much or how little Hitler actually believed the myths, magic, and pseudoscience was all a matter of speculation and, as Rosenthal knew, difficult to prove. Beyond Hitler's decision to dedicate the second volume of *Mein Kampf* to Dietrich Eckart and several references he made in speeches, Hitler never overtly referred to his associations with Ariosophy, the Thule Society, or their founders. All that could be said for certain of Hitler's first visit to the Hofburg was that he remembered the Holy Lance and other Reich treasures and would, twenty-six years later, make it his duty, some would say his divine obligation, to return them to the Fatherland.

Himmler, who was steeped in much the same mystical traditions, was Hitler's willing accomplice. He took what may have been Hitler's passing interest or infatuation with arcane beliefs several steps further, creating his own research bureau and engaging scholars to study a wide range of mystical beliefs and practices. Under his tenure, the amalgam of cult beliefs and practices became the "new church" of the Nazis, known to many members of the Ahnenerbe and prominent theologians as the German Christian movement.

Neither Hitler nor Himmler publicly stated or defined the new religion. Nor did they ever develop a coherent religious system that could be practiced. Like Emperor Constantine, Hitler was content to point the way, letting his Christian supporters believe what they would. All Hitler and his inner circle would publicly state was that their faith was distinctly Nordic or Germanic, uncorrupted by the institution of Roman Catholicism and the foreign influence of non-Aryan Jews and Marxists.

Within their own ranks, it was this and much more, Troche claimed. Hitler and Himmler were laying the groundwork to make Germanic Christianity the new national religion of Germany. A group of influential Protestant theologians, he said, had gone so far as to create a version of the New Testament in which scripture was cleverly manipulated to suggest that Jesus was making a holy war against the Jews and that Jesus' inner circle of followers were not Jews but Gentiles. The Holy Lance and the Crown Jewels, like the

Nazis' "updated" gospels, were to figure prominently in the conversion of the German people.

The role that the Holy Roman Empire artifacts were to play in the Nazi agenda, according to Troche, was evident very early in the creation of the Third Reich. No sooner did Hitler rise to power than Himmler ordered Wolfram Sievers, a former antiquarian and the Ahnenerbe's future executive secretary, to research the history of the Reich treasures in Austria. The stories were collected, and the seductively potent medieval legends of the spear's power were presented in Germany as fact. And just as the lance legends were cleverly corrupted and enhanced, so were centuries of Christian doctrine. Not only was Longinus an Aryan, but Jesus was, too.

To support these racist theories, Nazi scholars cited contradictions in Jesus' infancy narratives, inconsistencies related to Jesus' genealogy, and a revisionist picture of the racial demographics of Galilee. They pointed out that Aryan tribes, known to have been present in Galilee, were never expelled from Israelite settlements and that, according to Nazi scholars, after the Assyrian conquest, Galilee was devoid of Jews. Jesus' parents, descendants of King Herod's Aryan cavalrymen, were Jews by "confession," not racial identity. The Nazi scholars maintained that Jesus was actually born not in Bethlehem in Judea but in another Bethlehem near Nazareth in Galilee. A wide range of other arguments was put forth seeking to show that Jesus, from the inception of his ministry, stood in direct opposition to Jewish thought and practices and that he preached a "kingdom of God" in the human heart, a concept foreign to Judaism.

More than this, in lectures and from the German pulpits, Nazi scholars and theologians suggested that the ancient soldier-kings of the Holy Roman Empire were aware of the hidden knowledge of Jesus' Aryan pedigree and that the Catholic Church sought to suppress it. This had been one of the supposed reasons King Frederick I, in a power struggle with Pope Alexander III in Vatican City, conspired to install antipope Victor IV as the Holy Roman Empire's new Vicar of Christ.

Troche could understand how Horn, gone from Germany since just before the war began, might find all of this far-fetched, yet these were the theories that Himmler's Ahnenerbe think tank and proponents of the German Christian movement produced. It was also why Himmler sent teams of scholar-soldiers to Jerusalem, Tibet, and elsewhere around the world to collect artifacts deemed valuable to the Reich.

Himmler, according to Troche, went about laying the groundwork for the return of the Crown Jewels at the same time as his Ahnenerbe scholars were feverishly revising world history to accommodate the new theology of Aryan superiority. Attorney Walter Buch, father-in-law to Martin Bormann, was ordered to find legal means to effect the recovery of Holy Roman Empire treasures from Austria. The original documents promising the Crown Jewels to Nürnberg, signed by Holy Roman Emperor Sigismund, were laid out and studied.

Extraordinary as the rest of what Troche was telling him seemed, it was more remarkable that the Nazis, who wantonly plundered what they considered theirs and used their own creative license to reinterpret the legends and myths of the past, should expend the effort to study the legal issues and find ways to legitimate their actions regarding the Crown Jewels.

Troche pointed out another paradox. The very people endeavoring to liberate distinctly Christian artifacts were also involved in destroying the secret societies that gave rise to Hitler's beliefs and compiling dossiers that they would use to undermine those leading figures in German churches unwilling to endorse Nazi doctrine. The cult of the Nazis was to have no competitors.

Backed by Hitler's authority, Buch made several attempts to arrange for an art exchange so that the royal regalia could be displayed in Germany. There was to be no trade of art. Kunsthistorisches Museum officials in Vienna justifiably believed that they would never see the treasures again should they loan them to a German museum.

This did not stop Hitler from continuing his effort by publicizing the historic importance of the Crown Jewels. His first step was to build a replica of the wooden shrine that housed the treasures in medieval times. At the first of Nürnberg's Nazi Party rallies, held in 1933, the reproduction shrine was duly installed in the market square, just as the real artifact would have appeared centuries earlier during the weeklong festival celebrating the Holy Roman Empire treasure. This shrine, though, was left empty, a not so subtle means of conveying the greater message that Nürnberg had been robbed of its cultural and spiritual inheritance.

Hitler's efforts to raise his nation's consciousness of the treasure were welcomed by Nürnberg's new mayor. Willy Liebel was as preoccupied with the Crown Jewels as Hitler himself, and in addition to publishing books and articles celebrating their venerated history, he publicly demanded their return to Nürnberg.

Liebel's interest, however, was not in any arcane or mystical properties attributed to the artifacts. He barely touched on this in his many speeches or in the meetings he convened with his city council. His obsession was in having the emblems of world monarchy returned to Germany's "imperial city." Just as Berlin had the Brandenburg Gate, surmounted by its chariot symbolizing Germanic solidarity, Nürnberg would have the Crown Jewels. The imperial crown, Troche said, was always more important to Liebel than the Holy Lance.

In preparation for Nürnberg's 1935 party rally, Liebel had an expensive reproduction of the ceremonial sword made. During his traditional opening speech welcoming Hitler, he presented the sword as a "symbol of unity, stature, power, and strength of the German nation." Liebel referred to the research of Walter Buch, now a major in Himmler's Waffen-SS, which gave Nürnberg legal claim to the regalia. And for the first time, Hitler spoke directly of the regalia as a "symbol of German imperial power" and a reminder of the significance of the National Socialist revolution.

After his speech, Hitler promised Liebel that the actual artifacts would be returned to Nürnberg after Germany successfully annexed Austria. This was especially important, Troche pointed out, because Hitler was alleged to have said this a full three years before storm troopers crossed the German border into Austria. In other words, plans for the invasion were already under way while Hitler was publicly pledging to preserve the peace.

Principal among the players in the "recovery" of the authentic artifacts was Himmler, assisted by Kaltenbrunner, then leader of the Austrian SS underground, and Major Buch, who had become chief of the Nazi Party's secret police. Mayor Liebel and his city council handled other administrative and public relations work related to the "repatriation" of the artifacts back to Nürnberg.

As the story was told in Nazi circles, the operation got under way in early March 1938. Buch, traveling incognito ahead of the invading German forces, checked into a small hotel near the Hofburg. Inside the major's innocent-looking suitcase was his SS uniform, a Luger pistol, and secret orders to kill anyone who might attempt to hide or remove the Holy Lance and the Crown Jewels from the Kunsthistorisches Museum before storm troopers could take the city. On March 12, the night of the Anschluss, as Panzer divisions crossed the border into Austria, Buch donned his uniform and secured the treasure.

There followed a glittering reception in the Royal Palace in Vienna three days later, when Buch presented a selection of items from the collection for Hitler to view. Buch was reported to have raised his arm in a Nazi salute and announced, "Die Heilige Lanze, mein Führer."

Hitler didn't just take the lance and other treasures back with him to Berlin. Everything was to appear perfectly legal. It was only after Austria was formally incorporated into the Reich and the Austrian ambassador to Germany presented the treasures to the city of Nürnberg that the Crown Jewels were returned to their ancestral home.

Mayor Liebel himself and members of the city council arrived in Vienna to escort them to Nürnberg on a heavily guarded special eight-car train. The treasures arrived at the Nürnberg station on August 30, 1938, and, amid a phalanx of SS guards, were brought for display to Saint Catherine's Church. Troche, one of the Germanic Museum's new curators, saw them for the first time there.

"Everything the Nazis did was by design," Troche told Horn, repeating his earlier assessment. Having said this, he removed his smock, rolled up the map, collected his books and files, and indicated that it was time for them to leave the museum cloister. Hitler had had big plans for the city, the Reich, and his holy treasures, and he wanted Horn to see these things for himself.

CHAPTER 10

HITLER'S FAIRY-TALE KINGDOM

July 22, 1945

Troche led Horn out of the herb-scented sanctuary of the museum cloister into the exhaust-filled street. Trucks still idled in the warehouse bay, and now the morning traffic brought a steady stream of jeeps ferrying dignitaries from the Nürnberg-Fürth Airport, troop transports carrying laborers detailed to hotel repair, and dispatch riders on motorcycles shuttling between the Palace of Justice and the U.S. military government offices. All of the transport in the city, it seemed, was devoted to preparing Nürnberg for the upcoming war-crimes tribunals.

The two men moved easily through the traffic, making their way east on a wide boulevard along the old city wall. Their ultimate destination was the King's Chapel in the castle complex, but along the way, Troche wanted to stop at Laufer Tor, one of five medieval stone towers that once guarded the gates of old Nürnberg. From its parapet, they would have the best view of the old inner city to the north and the Nazi Party parade grounds to the south.

Fire had gutted the interiors and burned the roofs on the rows of buildings on either side of Laufer Tor. The ancient tower, however, built from massive blocks of quarried stone, still stood at the entrance to the old inner city, as it had five hundred years earlier, when knights in chain mail rained all manner of flaming debris upon would-be conquerors assaulting Nürnberg.

How the tower's low-pitched wooden roof escaped serious damage in the bombing raids and during the last offensive was a mystery. Captain Peterson's E Company, on its drive to Blacksmith's Alley, had exchanged a few rounds with sharpshooters perched on its parapets, but it was not E Company that fought a pitched battle for the eighty-foot tower. That honor went to an antitank platoon that had shelled Laufer Tor for twenty minutes before its one hundred twenty-five defenders surrendered.

An all-female German labor brigade was clearing the debris from around the entrance when Troche and Horn arrived. As everywhere else in the city, the women wore head scarves, and their faces were covered with kerchiefs for protection from the clouds of dusty grit and the odious stench of what they inevitably uncovered in the course of their labors. As Horn would note on subsequent trips throughout the city, he couldn't help wondering how often the work crews came upon bodies still buried under the rubble and if, after months of such backbreaking labor, they had become immune to the cloying fetor of rot. Horn certainly hadn't. He nearly gagged as he maneuvered between the women and followed Troche inside the tower and up a spiral stone staircase.

The large, circular lookout room at the top contained bedrolls, a kerosene cooking stove, and an assortment of old dressers and other furniture. Like virtually everywhere else in the city, anything with a roof over it was considered suitable lodging. The tower was prime real estate, as it provided adequate shelter, and its hinged door could be locked from within, offering a modicum of protection from the former camp laborers, youth gangs, and packs of stray dogs roaming the city at night.

The tower's occupants weren't home. Perhaps they were out foraging for food and supplies or among the women at the foot of the tower removing rubble from the street. Troche, more accustomed to the deprivations of life in Nürnberg, strode into the room without concern. His interest was in the panoramic vista.

It was to be a virtual straight line, Troche said, through the parade grounds to the King's Chapel. This was not by accident, as he had previously noted. The Nazis had moved buildings and drained a small lake so that the roadway connecting the inner city to the parade grounds would someday be arrow-straight and the view to the castle unobstructed. Hitler himself, accompanied by Himmler, had walked the proposed route.

Just as the Nazis had transformed a park and pastureland on the outskirts of the city with their monumental architecture, massive public spaces, and their main thoroughfare, they had revitalized and restored the historic inner city. Their plan for old Nürnberg, Troche understood, was to reflect the storybook romanticism of the Middle Ages and to project an unsullied image of past greatness. The Third Reich's "Via Appia" was to connect the old inner city, the nation's past glories, to the parade grounds, the nation's future. They were complementary elements of the regime's program to create a sense of Nürnberg as a sacred place, an environment where the cult of Germanic Christianity and the *Volk* would reawaken in visitors and residents alike a truly German national culture.

From their position atop the tower, Troche pointed out the salient aspects of the Nazis' handiwork on the parade grounds. That which had already been completed was impressive by anyone's reckoning, but what Hitler had envisioned, outlined on the Reich map and which Troche now described, was like a Nazi amusement park, where the fantasy was to become the reality.

The grandest building in the entire rally complex was the horseshoe-shaped arena, the Deutsches Stadion, a truly colossal affair, which was ultimately intended to seat nearly half a million, making it the largest arena in the world. Hitler's avowed aim was that it would one day be the permanent home of the Olympic Games. The massive pylons, portals, and galleries, all built on an epic scale, were designed to diminish those who passed beneath them and tower, cathedral-like, over the spaces they enclosed. Nürnberg was not to be like other modern public spaces but to emulate ancient Greece and Rome, where visitors and participants in spectacle looked to one another, and upward. Those who attended weren't to watch the action but to be the action.

The pageantry planned for the arena elaborated on this fundamental theme. Massed torchlit processions, with trumpet fanfares and thundering drumrolls, epitomized the conceit. The heads of the various contingents—Hitler Youth, storm troopers, members of the Labor League—would lead the way in legionnaire costumes, carrying Roman standards.

Mysticism accompanied the majesty, grandeur, and spectacle, Troche explained, in the "sacred" formulas that determined a building's proportion and placement. The Ahnenerbe were alleged to have arrived at the correct formulas by studying ancient texts and the masterworks of previous civilizations. The grandstand from which Hitler delivered his message at the rallies, what the Nazis called the Tribune, copied the Hellenistic Pergamon Altar on the Turkish coast, while the accompanying Deutsches Stadion emulated the one built by Herodes Atticus in Athens. These buildings, Hitler was convinced, had lasted for a reason: they were spiritually charged designs following universal laws.

The position and height of the Tribune's podium were determined by dowsers, and the original building site itself was relocated several hundred feet to the west to take advantage of what the dowsers claimed were significant electromagnetic "lay lines," underground streams and magnetic currents that would enhance the activities taking place above them. The repositioning of the Tribune was no small undertaking, Troche said, as it required draining a lake and rerouting a railroad.

Many other examples of arcane beliefs and "sacred geometry" influenced the construction and design of the buildings. Twelve, for example, was the "magic number," as there were twelve signs of the zodiac and twelve apostles. Sets of twelve columns, twelve pillars, and twelve avenues were to open onto the main thoroughfare leading from the old city into the new. This was not surprising, as Horn would later note, as there were twelve divisions or bureaus in Himmler's SS.

Troche went on to describe how parade-ground architects found many other opportunities to incorporate the number twelve into their designs. The most elaborate swastika designs featured a wheel with twelve arms, referred to as the Black Sun, which the Ahnenerbe and Thulists believed to be Nordic or Teutonic man's most ancient and potent representation of the Aryan God.

Polarity figured into their thinking as well. Like the main road leading from the parade grounds to the chapel, virtually all designs, when feasible, were said to be directed north to the legendary land of Thule. To hear Troche describe it, the hundreds of thousands of people who came to the rallies didn't begin to know the full truth of the urban planning or the more subtle subliminal messages being imparted.

The location, placement, and design of the structures weren't all that was determined by mystical or arcane considerations. The ornamentation and symbols attached to the buildings, like the Black Sun, were equally significant.

Troche claimed that the enormous eagle with outstretched wings, placed above the stadium, was designed in the shape of a rune from the ancient Aryan alphabet. The particular rune—chosen by the Ahnenerbe's official runologist, Karl Marie Wiligut—was that of the Tyr or "spear rune," symbolizing the legendary female eagle consort of Zeus, the god of war, giver of victory and protector from harm. This rune was also significant because it was the symbol Aryan warriors were said to have cut into their own flesh in order to enter Valhalla.

After discussing the construction in the parade grounds, Troche walked across Laufer Tor's parapet and directed Horn's attention to the old inner city, where Hitler had devoted similar attention and Reich funds.

The inner city, he said, was not intended as a mere footnote to the rallies. It was to legitimize the activities taking place to the south. The changes, as such, were not promoted as new building projects but as renovation and preservation of existing structures. They were to reinforce the concept of the greatness of Germany, to herald the new and glorious age under Nazi leadership, and to promote the Führer as the true keeper, guardian, and heroic reformer of the imperial city of the ancient Holy Roman Empire.

The Nazis' first step was restoration of the city's historical structures to "cleanse and beautify" its image. Anything that might blur the message or detract from the symbolic connection with the city's medieval greatness was removed. Billboards and signs came down, sloping tiled roofs replaced modern flat ones, and stone work and half-timbered construction emerged from centuries of facing. Dilapidated or unimportant buildings were replaced altogether with replicas of structures designed to harmonize with their surroundings.

The Nazis employed craftsmen from all over Germany and Europe. Artisans cast statuary, memorial busts, and placards commemorating the glories of the city's ancient past and the genius of the musicians, painters, and sculptors who lived and worked within its walls.

Early in the process, any evidence of Jewish or Slavic influences vanished, a campaign Troche said was guided by Julius Streicher, Nürnberg's first defense minister and Gauleiter, who championed the passage of the notorious anti-Jewish "Nürnberg Laws." That Jewish businessmen and artisans had contributed significantly to the building of the authentic medieval city and its institutions was conveniently ignored.

Removing the Jewish presence from the city, Horn knew, was not a new idea, as the market square—renamed Adolf Hitler Plaza during the Nazi regime—had been the site of a Jewish synagogue before a wave of medieval anti-Semitism swept the city and the Church of Our Lady was built over its ruins. The Nazis merely picked up where city fathers had left off centuries before.

The largest of the Nazi renovation projects was the old city telegraph building on the market square, which Troche said was singled out as an "unbearable foreign body" that disturbed the city's medieval charm. In a major facelift, the building's simplified façade and pitched roof aimed to complement neighboring structures for a more orderly aesthetic, and new anti-Semitic murals, made to look old, were added to the façade.

Other renovation projects were undertaken to restore the city's town hall, the Holy Ghost Hospital, and Saint Lorenz Church, which was to become, on Hitler's orders and with the support of the German Christian movement, the Third Reich's national cathedral. Equally important was Saint Catherine's, the former Dominican convent where the Crown Jewels were lodged after their arrival from Austria. That the Mastersingers performed here and in later years Nürnberg's opera company celebrated Parsifal's discovery of the "bleeding lance" here put it high on the Nazi priority list.

The centerpiece of the renovation projects was Nürnberg Castle, which was to be cleansed of its nineteenth-century adulterations, the better to present the structure as a potent symbol of medieval Germany's greatness. The Nazis' magisterial desire to re-create a symbol of Reich greatness, however, conflicted with historical reality. The problem, as Germanic Museum curators well knew, was that there had never existed a single castle representing a golden era of German supremacy. The castle was an amalgam of past constructions representing its cyclical rise and decline and defied any attempt to date discrete elements or envision it as it had been centuries ago.

Rather than attempt historical accuracy, the Nazis chose to create a storybook castle. Anything that didn't look grand or romantically appealing was removed. In several notable cases, spires and arched entryways were added, and the martial aspects of the structure, as represented by its battlements and drawbridges, were enhanced. The Nazis' message was obvious: the castle was a fortress, the *feste Burg* of the empire.

Just as the rally grounds were designed to promote the grandeur of the Nazi message, the castle's main buildings, which included the Knight's Hall and imperial residence, were redesigned for use by the Nazi hierarchy. The stables were transformed into a Hitler Youth hostel, and the King's Chapel, which had for decades been the sleeping quarters for the castle caretaker, was rededicated to the Holy Roman Emperors and Teutonic Knights who had worshipped there.

Here and throughout the old city, the Nazis wished to impress upon visitors that the ancient kingdom of the Reich was a magnificent and grand place, where enlightened soldier-kings presided over prosperous tradesmen, artisans, and musicians living in relative splendor in neatly kept, idyllic homes. Never mind that in medieval days, the city streets were a sea of mud and raw sewage, that disease-carrying rats ran rampant, pigsties fronted nearly every home, and the city walls existed for a purpose beyond protection of the empire from foreign invasion. It simply wasn't safe outside the walls. All manner of thieves and brigands, and in one notable case the disgruntled members of an emperor's own family, preyed on those who ventured into the supposed idyllic forests and glens of medieval Germany.

Into the fairy-tale kingdom that Hitler and his inner circle had created in Nürnberg, he brought the Holy Lance and the Crown Jewels. As Troche described what happened, it was as if the Knights of the Round Table had returned to Avalon, and King Arthur, or his evil twin, accompanied by Merlin—which was how Himmler must have viewed himself—strode into Camelot bearing Excalibur.

Erwin Panofsky, Horn's and Troche's mentor, would no doubt have bridled at the comparison between Arthurian chivalry and the murderous Third Reich. Yet he surely would have delighted in Troche's explanation of art and architecture's prominence in the culture the Nazi regime created in Nürnberg, not because of the more arcane details of the story that Troche presented but for his approach: that the landscape or environment informed and gave significance to an artwork. Ancient treasures shouldn't be studied in museums but in the context of their original usage and display. In the case of the Holy Lance and the Crown Jewels, how they were displayed, venerated, and protected in medieval times directly related to how the Nazis sought to display, venerate, and use the treasures in modern times.

In the world of Nazi cosmology, past and present merged beyond what Horn had previously imagined. Horn was fascinated, as this was his academic specialty: how art and architecture informed the cultural life of a city and its residents. The important difference was that Horn had previously confined himself to studying ancient cultures long swept away. Never before had he seen or examined in such detail how the same principles and modes of inquiry related so directly to modern times.

Still, there was the matter of the Crown Jewels. If Horn understood the thrust of what Troche was saying, the Nazis accorded the Crown Jewels an exalted and mystical status and thus required them to be suitably housed and protected. It also stood to reason that they would hide them during the invasion, as had occurred when Napoleon's troops arrived on Nürnberg's doorstep. Yet the entire collection was not removed as the Nazis' fantasy kingdom burned. Only five items were taken from the bunker, and the item that Troche said might have been the most important to Hitler—the Holy Lance—was not among them. If Troche was correct, surely the Nazis, as they secreted away the other treasures, would have taken Hitler's Excalibur.

Impatient as the lieutenant was for his former classmate to address the subject of the Crown Jewels, he couldn't hurry Troche. There were things that Horn must first know and understand; otherwise, he wouldn't believe what Troche had to show and tell him next.

CHAPTER 11

TEUTONIC KNIGHTS

July 22, 1945

Troche described the drama that played out in Nürnberg as if it were the opening act of a Wagnerian opera, but the players and backdrop were real. He half imagined Hitler, as Parsifal, appearing at center stage to confer with Himmler, the evil magician. What new twists and turns in the story did Troche have to share?

Horn, still feeling unnerved and shaken by his colleague's revelations, silently followed Troche out of the tower, up the cobbled thoroughfare into the old inner city, across the market square, and then through a series of winding alleyways to Saint Catherine's, the thirteenth-century convent church that had been transformed into a showroom for the Crown Jewels. Another crew of laborers, wearing the same head scarves, worked here, but they were not clearing debris to rehabilitate the old chapel and Mastersingers' choir room. It was beyond saving, except perhaps as an example of Allied airborne destructive power.

Horn stepped through the jagged hole where an Allied bomb had exploded the arched hallway. Here, in this stone corridor, five hundred years earlier, Dominican nuns with black veils and white tunics had entered the chapel and been met with an astonishingly rich candlelit display of art and architecture: omega-shaped arches over a magnificent choir and transept, stained-glass windows, and a delicately carved and much-loved statue of their patron saint, the martyred Catherine of Alexandria. Now there was nothing but bare, fire-scorched stone walls, Gothic window holes, piles of burned wood, and heaps of slate where the roof had collapsed into the sanctuary. Troche helped him to imagine how it had looked when the Nazis used the building to display the Holy Lance and the Crown Jewels.

He described how an enormous crimson carpet led from the church's nave to the ambulatory. Red and black floor-to-ceiling drapes were hung to cover the walls, and the windows were shaded to heighten the effect of spotlights focused on the display cases. The crown, orb, scepter, lance, and swords—polished and radiant—were arrayed on a delicately carved medieval stone box in the chancel.

The opening-day exhibition ceremonies on September 6, 1938, when the treasures were officially handed over to the city, were officiated by Arthur Seyss-Inquart, the Nazi governor of Austria, who, echoing the declaration by Emperor Sigismund, presented the treasures to Nürnberg "for all eternity." A week later, at Nürnberg's sixth party rally, the Führer saw the Crown Jewels for himself. A phalanx of SS guards, dressed in formal black uniforms, stood at attention in the aisles. On the balcony stood trumpeters dressed in heraldic medieval costumes. As the Führer stepped into the sanctuary, Nürnberg's choral society sang the "Awake" chorus from Wagner's *Die Meistersinger.*

Hitler, standing on a rostrum where the pulpit had once been, was most eloquent that day. Troche quoted the Führer from a commemorative album published by Mayor Liebel: "In no other German city is there as strong a connection between the past and present . . . as in Nürnberg, the old and new imperial city. This city, which the old German Reich deemed fit to defend the regalia behind its walls, has regained ownership of these symbols which testifies to the power and strength of the old Reich . . . and is a manifestation of German power and greatness in a New German Reich."

Touching the crown, Hitler said, "The German people have declared themselves the bearers of the thousand-year crown."

Troche pointedly noted that Hitler did not refer to the crown as the "imperial crown" or "crown of the Holy Roman Empire." He called it his thousand-year crown.

Troche and an estimated two hundred thousand people saw the Holy Lance and other Crown Jewels that first day. In the coming months, several million more had the same privilege.

No doubt, Hitler had every reason to believe in the protective power of the Holy Lance, Troche said.

Horn concurred. The Führer's powers of invincibility must have seemed real, as one European nation after another fell before the blitzkrieg of the German army and air force.

It wasn't long, however, before the climate began to shift. Hitler and his armies were still unstoppable in the summer of 1940, but the RAF had begun bombing German cities. Not long after the first Nürnberg raids, the Saint Catherine's exhibition was quietly closed. Without fanfare but accompanied by the same phalanx of SS officers, the Crown Jewels were moved for safekeeping to the vault of the Kohn Bank, on the corner of König and Brunnengasse, a facility whose Jewish owners had been conveniently removed from Nürnberg.

There were unsubstantiated rumors that Hitler borrowed the lance for days or months at a time. Troche didn't know. All he had heard about the collection from fellow curators and museum staff was that Himmler and the Ahnenerbe were making a movie that would tell the story of the Crown Jewels and Nürnberg's emergence as the Mecca of the Third Reich. Troche and other curators were assigned to scout filming locations and provide suitable props from the museum collection. The movie, however, was never completed, for by this time, the bombing raids had destroyed entire sections of the restored city.

Perhaps, too, Troche said, the invincibility of the Nazi regime was being seriously questioned. The mystical formulas that were to ensure the longevity of the thousand-year Reich were no protection against bomber streams. The party rallies were suspended, and the city renovations were halted. By the early 1940s, money and supplies that had been earmarked for the projects were now directed to the war effort. But not all construction projects in the old inner city ceased, Troche said. The Nazis were building the bunker under Nürnberg Castle.

The actual construction of the Blacksmith's Alley facility, Troche explained, was not a secret. Many bomb shelters were being built throughout Nürnberg, and this one was seemingly no different. But few people outside Mayor Liebel's inner circle were aware of the special improvements under way.

Horn, of course, had seen those improvements firsthand. But Troche wanted Horn to understand why Himmler and the Ahnenerbe had selected this particular site to store the treasures, when many equally suitable underground chambers existed in Nürnberg.

With this in mind, they left the ruins of Saint Catherine's and trudged slowly uphill through the maze of rubble-strewn streets to the castle. In many respects, they were walking backward in time to the very spot where, centuries before, the city had been founded. No trucks hauled men and equipment; no couriers on motorcycles passed by. The old city was eerily deserted in the shadows of its toppled buildings and columns, hauntingly and mysteriously beautiful.

Horn and Troche climbed a winding series of stone steps, worn smooth from centuries of use, and entered the complex through the "Heaven's Gate" portal, its naming lost to history. A likely explanation, however, was that the gate led to an open courtyard where, in medieval times, criminals were granted asylum if they could sneak past or overcome the gatekeepers.

The sentries now on guard, two MPs lounging on the battlements, barely gave Horn and Troche a second glance, for obvious reasons: the bombing raids had destroyed virtually everything but the castle walls, and waves of looters had already carried off anything of value. Here, as elsewhere, the MPs' duty was to keep German nationals and freed camp laborers from congregating.

Horn and Troche lingered for a few minutes to survey the imperial courtyard. Nearly every guidebook to the old city mentioned a "sacred tree," alleged to have been planted by the consort of Holy Roman Emperor Heinrich II in the early eleventh century. According to superstition, as long as the tree flourished, the castle and its accompanying "burg" would thrive.

No records were kept of how many times, and under what circumstances, the tree had been replanted. According to Troche, the Nazi one, reportedly blessed by the Führer himself, had withered long before the Allied invasion. All that remained was a charred stump.

They hadn't come to see the tree. Troche led Horn down a narrow stairwell between the Knight's Hall and the Heathen's

Tower, which opened into the lower portion of the King's Chapel, which consisted of two separate Romanesque galleries, one atop the other. Except for pigeons fluttering about inside, the two men were alone.

The square opening connecting the upper and lower galleries had survived the bombing. Sections of the upper gallery's vaulted ceiling and portions of four massive white marble columns supporting it had not fared as well. Massive chunks of masonry had smashed down and filled the lower gallery with debris. As the chapel, like the rest of the castle, was neither relevant to the war-crimes tribunals nor linked to any of the city's vital services, no work crew had been dispatched to clean up the mess.

Troche directed Horn's attention to a spot in the middle of the rubble-filled lower gallery. This area, resembling a crypt, had never been used for burials. It was where the Teutonic Knights guarded the portable shrine containing the Holy Lance and the Crown Jewels. The emperor, from his gallery above, could look down to see that it was being properly tended.

Peering down between the fallen chunks of dusty masonry, Horn wondered if there was anything yet to discover under the debris. Did clues exist, after centuries of renovations, to how the knightly order protected the treasures? More important, was the Teutonic Knights' manner of protecting the treasures in medieval times connected to the Nazis' method of securing them for future generations?

Horn couldn't overlook the apparent coincidence that Himmler had chosen to rehabilitate a beer cellar directly under the chapel any more than he could ignore the spear-shaped image on what might have been a Nazi treasure map. Perhaps the bunker's secret exit shaft, hidden in its auxiliary exhaust ventilation unit, led directly to the chapel's lower gallery. If so, it would take more than Private Dollar to excavate the passage.

Troche anticipated what was on Horn's mind. He didn't know for certain that this was where the hidden shaft led, but it was not an unreasonable supposition. The medieval Teutonic Knights, he said, figured prominently in Himmler's mystical worldview.

Yet again, Troche referred to the master plan and the Hitler cult, but now he wanted to emphasize that understanding what the Nazis did in Nürnberg required connecting it to the ancient past.

Troche reminded Horn that in addition to the role the Teutonic Knights played in protecting the Crown Jewels, significant differences separated this ancient religious brotherhood from its counterparts, the Knights Templar and the Knights Hospitaller. All three knightly orders originated in the Holy Land during the Crusades, and all three for a time flourished in medieval Europe. However, the Teutonic Knights viewed the recovery of Palestine and protection of travelers on pilgrimage as only one of their primary tasks or religious callings. Additionally, the German brotherhood of soldier-priests aided the Holy Roman Emperors in their conquest of greater Europe and led the invasions into Poland, Hungary, and Russia, just as Himmler's SS assisted the Third Reich. And, unlike the Teutonic Knights, the Templars and Hospitallers were multinational. The Teutonic Knights had to prove their Germanic descent back three or more generations, just as pure Aryans were the only soldiers permitted to join the SS.

As Horn knew from his own scholarship, the Teutonic Knights, for a time, were a major force within the Holy Roman Empire. It was not until the Protestant Reformation and the subsequent war between Protestants and Catholics that their numbers greatly decreased. The order was finally abolished by Napoleon, whose failed quest to become Holy Roman Emperor had brought an end to the once vast agglomeration of European territories. Around this time, the Crown Jewels, no longer under the protection of the Teutonic Knights, were taken to Vienna and were not seen again in Germany until the Nazis marched into Austria and reclaimed them.

As Rosenthal had once discussed with him and Troche now drew to Horn's attention, Himmler had a deep and abiding interest in the Teutonic Knights. The highest honor an SS officer could receive was the "Blood Order," or *Deutscher Orden*, a Nazi version of the decoration conferred upon the Teutonic Knights. The black and white colors of the brotherhood also became the official colors of the SS. The first SS uniform, after the Nazis did away with the brown shirts worn by Hitler's street thugs, was the Teutonic Knights' black tunic and peaked cap. Himmler modeled not only these outward symbols but also the hierarchic structure of SS leadership itself after the pattern of the orders blessed by the Holy Roman Emperors. "Never forget," Himmler had told his officers, "we are a knightly order."

A recruiting poster, in wide circulation throughout Germany, had gone so far as to show the Führer dressed as a medieval Teutonic knight.

Horn followed what Troche had to say with growing interest, but he didn't anticipate what came next. Based on things his fellow curators had told him and what he gleaned from references in Mayor Liebel's writings, he had reason to believe that Himmler did more than borrow the symbols of the Teutonic Knights. He might have reinstated the actual order, which had continued to exist in Germany as a charitable and ceremonial body. Despite Hitler's sweeping edict calling for the dissolution of the Teutonic Knights, along with the Freemasons, Rosicrucians, Anthroposophists, and myriad other arcane societies and fraternities, Himmler might have revitalized the brotherhood of soldier-priests.

According to Troche, the new order of knights might have met at Himmler's Wewelsburg castle, a triangular medieval fortress overlooking the Alme Valley, north of Nürnberg. There was one tower for Hitler's exclusive use, another for Himmler, and a third tower, facing north, where all manner of arcane ceremonies were conducted. Troche admitted that he hadn't been to the castle; few besides the Reichsführer's inner circle had. But he had certainly heard it discussed among museum staff in Berlin. The castle and nearby Externsteine, an excavation site a few miles away, were where Horn could take the full measure of the Nazis' cult fascination with Germanic history, mysticism, and the Teutonic Knights.

Troche was convinced that Mayor Liebel and possibly other prominent residents of Nürnberg were members of the supposed Teutonic brotherhood and that their specific task was to oversee the protection of the Holy Lance and the Crown Jewels. Troche couldn't be sure, however, because membership in the alleged order and everything else about it was secret. He was, as he had said several times before, an outsider. Yet he saw it as no coincidence that in ancient times, three Nürnberg residents, members of the Teutonic Knights in the imperial city, were charged with overseeing the protection of the treasures and that in modern times, under the Nazis, Mayor Liebel entrusted three members of the Nürnberg city council to hold the keys and the lock combination to the Blacksmith's Alley vault.

For the second time that day, Horn's mind reeled with the import of the museum curator's words. In effect, Troche was telling him that Himmler hadn't just marshaled the army of men under his command to research and retrieve the treasures of the Holy Roman Empire but that he might have gone farther and re-created a medieval brotherhood, and the specific task of the resurrected order, Troche presumed, was to guard the treasures.

Troche's theory, however, didn't answer the more pertinent question about who might have removed the Crown Jewels from the bunker. But it went a long way toward explaining the preponderance of coincidences involving the Nazis' recovery and handling of the Crown Jewels, the decision to secure the treasures in a vault under the King's Chapel, and the confluence of architectural improvements in Nürnberg that pointed spearlike from the Nazi Party rally grounds to the ancient seat of the Holy Roman Emperors.

If indeed what Troche said was true and not a figment of the curator's imagination, it suggested that those deemed worthy to possess the keys to the vault had been derelict in their duties. Either that, or they were the very ones who had removed what they determined were the five most valuable treasures. And if the modern-day Teutonic Knights had removed the treasures, this presented an additional dilemma, one that had troubled Horn since he had lectured Thompson and his fellow officers at the hotel and Troche had shown him the Reich map of the city. If indeed the Holy Lance was as significant to Hitler as he supposed, why hadn't this relic also been removed from the greater collection of artifacts stored in the Nazi bunker? If there actually was a modern equivalent of the Teutonic Knights, had they failed in their endeavor to safeguard all of the important treasures, or was this, too, somehow part of the master plan?

Troche had no definitive answer. He did, however, posit an explanation. As the bombers appeared over Nürnberg and the rest of Germany, as Allied troops crossed the Rhine River into the Fatherland, the Holy Lance lost its luster. It was plain for everyone to see that the relic provided no supernatural protection from the infidels.

The Führer, Troche said, turned his back on the holy talisman as he did on the German Christian movement. Plans to expand the Nazi Party rally grounds, renovate the city, and make the Saint

Lorenz Church the national cathedral abruptly came to an end. Attention shifted to establishing antiaircraft guns on the city's perimeter and also to protecting the imperial emblems of the German monarchy, those that Mayor Liebel had most coveted.

Four of the treasures that were removed from the Blacksmith's Alley bunker—the crown, the orb, the scepter, and the imperial sword—were the objects necessary for coronation. The fifth item, the ceremonial sword, was in a different category. This was what the king, in later times, used to bestow knighthood on aspiring soldier-priests.

To Troche's way of thinking, it was no surprise that Liebel, before the actual Crown Jewels were returned to Nürnberg, had presented a reproduction of the ceremonial sword to the Führer on the occasion of the opening ceremonies of the 1935 party rally. Liebel didn't present a facsimile of the imperial sword, crown, or Holy Lance. He gave Hitler a copy of the sword with which a German king knighted his Teutonic warriors.

Horn followed Troche's reasoning. The master plan had gone astray. Hitler's avowed intention to resurrect Nürnberg as the imperial city of the Germanic Empire was no longer feasible as Allied bombers rained destruction down upon the city. The mystical protection provided by the Holy Lance hadn't proven effective. It was the crown and other artifacts of the monarchy that were to be preserved for future generations. The ceremonial sword was important in ways that the Holy Lance wasn't. It was the means by which future generations could be brought into the knighthood.

As true as this might be—and Horn wasn't convinced of Troche's theory—this still didn't identify who had removed the five missing treasures from the Blacksmith's Alley bunker.

Troche had an answer for this, too. Mayor Liebel was dead, but his supposed Teutonic Knights, or their underlings, were still in the city. "They won't be too difficult to find," Troche assured him. "Two of them are on the U.S. occupation payroll."

CHAPTER 12

THE ENEMY
AT THE GATES

July 23–25, 1945

If what Troche described was true, Hitler had used the Holy Roman Empire treasure to legitimize his rule. He had installed the cherished symbols of Reich authority in his nation's ancestral capital, which he had transformed into an elaborate pilgrimage site. And like the soldier-kings who came before him, Hitler had a brotherhood of Teutonic Knights dedicated to protecting and preserving his kingdom's holy treasure from invading armies. As it had been in ancient times, so it was in the Third Reich.

Horn didn't doubt the substance of what his former classmate had told him. Hitler might indeed have believed himself to be part of a long line of ordained rulers. Possession of the Crown Jewels might have actually been, in his mind, a means to justify his quest to conquer the Western world. This could also explain, Horn reasoned, why Hitler believed he had the authority to commit the atrocities for which his henchmen were soon to stand trial. There could be no greater distortion of power than one man believing that his authority came from God. But Horn, at this point in his investigation, didn't pause to consider the implications. He had a mystery to solve. And although every answer led to new questions, forcing him to assess the role that Himmler's corps of scholar-soldiers had played in the emergence of a would-be world dictator, at the very least, Horn now had a theory about the treasure thieves' identity. The next step was to find the members of this "Teutonic brotherhood" or, barring that, their willing foot soldiers.

Two of the three people topping Troche's list of suspected conspirators were names that Horn already had noted. Heinz Schmeissner and Dr. Konrad Fries, city councilmen in the Liebel administration, currently served in the same capacity for the occupation government and were on Captain Thompson's MFAA Historical Committee. The third suspect on Troche's list, former city councilman Julius Lincke, promised to be more difficult to track down. He had vanished immediately before the invasion of the city and hadn't been seen since. He could be in hiding, locked in one of the labor camps, or, as Dreykorn and Thompson believed, among the anonymous Nürnberg dead.

It was not these men, however, whom Horn chose to interrogate first. Even if he could find Lincke, obtaining truthful answers from him or the others might be difficult. They wouldn't likely acknowledge complicity in a theft that could land them in jail but could be counted on to cleverly conceal their role in the conspiracy. Far better, Horn thought, to interview them, along with Albert Dreykorn, Mayor Liebel's former secretary, after he knew the right questions to ask. He first needed to familiarize himself with details of the bunker's construction and daily operation and to create a chronology of events that could help pinpoint the date that the Crown Jewels had been removed from the vault.

Interviewing Private Hüber, whom he hadn't seen since Camp Namur, was not feasible, given the difficulty of locating him among the hundreds of thousands of prisoners in work camps throughout Belgium, France, and England. Finding his family, if they hadn't been crushed to death in the collapse of the medieval buildings on Blacksmith's Alley, would be as difficult as tracking down Julius Lincke. However, with Troche's help, Horn could obtain significant information from the more important museum personnel, civil engineers, masons, secretaries, and assorted laborers who toiled to build and fill the bunker's storage chambers.

Horn wouldn't have to raid his footlocker of black-market goods to elicit their cooperation. He had a much more powerful tool at his disposal: the ability to make recommendations to the military occupation employment review board. He had, in effect, both carrot and stick. All adult German citizens were required to file a *Fragenbogen,* designed by U.S. Customs, which listed their previous Nazi affiliations. Since virtually every adult in Nürnberg was a party member or had some other objectionable Nazi affiliation and hence was technically unemployable, the only way an individual could legally obtain work was to appeal the case to the review board, which could weigh mitigating factors regarding a candidate's employment. Intercession from a ranking occupation officer, such as Captain Thompson, could make the difference between employment and starvation.

Lining up potential informants would not be a challenge. Troche needed only to put the word out among museum staff and their friends that anyone willing to speak with investigators would receive favorable employment consideration. The hurdle, Horn imagined, would be persuading Thompson to support his plan.

In the brief discussion with Thompson that followed, Horn didn't inform the captain that the interviews he wished to conduct were a prelude to his interrogation of Dreykorn, Fries, and Schmeissner. Nor did he raise the subject of a supposed Teutonic brotherhood of covert neo-Nazis who might be operating within the ranks of the city's civilian administration. Rather, he impressed upon Thompson his desire to confirm, as the captain himself had said, that the Nazis themselves had removed the treasures before the U.S. Army invaded the city. In all likelihood, Horn suggested, he would tie up a few loose ends and be on his way back to Frankfurt with a report substantiating the rumors the captain had first brought to Major Hammond's attention.

Thompson yielded to Horn's requests without much wrangling. Perhaps the lecture Horn had delivered at the hotel had tempered the captain's previous hostility toward him, or Thompson was merely eager to have the lieutenant out of his way. Horn didn't know. The captain, without conditions, simply agreed to let the lieutenant spend a few days interviewing low-level bunker personnel, consented to intercede with the employment review board on behalf of informants who helped the investigation, and offered Horn the use of his office at occupation headquarters.

Horn, with Troche's help, got started right away. On July 25, the fifth day of his investigation, twenty-one people discussed what they knew about the bunker. They ranged in age from late teens to early fifties and included two former building contractors, a civil engineer, a structural and electrical inspector, an air-raid warden, and a clerk for the city planning department. They were invariably dressed in soiled and torn clothing and had experienced nothing but misery since the invasion. More than anything else, they wanted work in their areas of expertise.

Most informants appeared in person at occupation headquarters, but there were several others, desiring not to be seen speaking directly to investigators, who made arrangements to meet privately with Horn at the Grand Hotel. Private Dollar, seated with Troche at a desk in front of the MFAA offices, conducted the initial screenings. The informants were then brought singly into Thompson's office for interviews, which lasted anywhere from a few minutes to an hour.

No one Horn spoke to on his first day of interviews claimed any knowledge of the disappearance of the Crown Jewels from the bunker. However, the time Horn invested was not wasted; nearly everyone he spoke to confirmed Troche's identification of Mayor Liebel's choices to run the Blacksmith's Alley facility. Julius Lincke's name appeared on blueprints provided to contractors, Heinz Schmeissner's office did the legal work, Konrad Fries wrote money orders and signed off on requisitions, and Albert Dreykorn handled routine business-related matters.

The name Horn expected to hear—Heinrich Himmler—did not initially arise in connection with the building or operation of the bunker. Either the bunker was not technically under his supervision, as both Private Hüber and Troche claimed, or the informants Horn interviewed that first day were not privy to high-level discussions. Also disappointing to Horn, these workers appeared to know nothing about any secret order of modern-day knights. The workers viewed the bunker as a city-owned and city-run facility, albeit secret, under the direct supervision of Mayor Liebel.

Similarly, no one Horn spoke to on that first day of interviews suggested that there was any mystical or arcane reason for Blacksmith's Alley to be selected as the site for the bunker. If there had been debate over any particular location, that discussion took place behind closed doors in Liebel's office at town hall or in Himmler's Berlin offices or more secluded Wewelsburg castle. Informants said only that the former beer cellar was property that had long been owned by the city and, before its renovation into a high-security facility to house city art treasures, had been one of several locations where equipment, lighting fixtures, and props were stored for the annual Nazi Party rallies. Hitler's favorite podium, in fact, was said to have been stored there.

Renovation of the former beer cellar took place in great secrecy over a six-month period beginning in September 1939, just days after the outbreak of the war on Poland. This date was confirmed by informant Paul Müller, a contractor who delivered concrete and steel to the site, and by Friedrich Lammerman, who had requisitioned building materials from supplies earmarked for the Nazi Party rally grounds. Besides the air-conditioning, heating, and ventilation units, the largest single expense was the bank vault, manufactured in Nürnberg by the Carl Hermann Company, the same firm that had also supplied locks and shock-resistant steel doors for the storage rooms.

The destruction of the Carl Hermann Company, as a shipping agent reported, would make it difficult to track down details of how its bills were paid or, more precisely, who footed the bills. Most noteworthy, however, was the presumed timing of payments. As more than one informant explained, the Carl Hermann Company was delivering high-end goods and services to the Blacksmith's Alley facility long before any city funds were allocated for bomb shelters or other installations related to city defenses.

Clerks Luis Hirsch and Grete Weigel didn't know the financial relationship between the Carl Hermann Company and Mayor Liebel, but they were certain that the funds that passed through their hands came directly from resources given to Liebel for the parade-grounds facilities. These funds, they said, were provided by Bureau II of the RSHA, the Reich Security Main Office, but controlled by Mayor Liebel and his city council. Although Ernst Kaltenbrunner, Himmler's second in command, technically provided the funding, Hirsch and Weigel were unaware that the Reichsführer himself took any personal or professional interest in how the funds were spent. Everything was handled through Liebel's office.

A third detail concerning the bunker's construction was also worth noting. According to Harold Claub, a draftsman, and Wilhelm Schwemmer, a custodian, the original bunker design had called for only three storage rooms—two ten-by-twelve-foot units and the vault—in addition to the utility, ventilation, and guards' quarters. This suggested that the facility was not initially intended to store the vast collection of city valuables that was ultimately placed inside. Rather, the bunker had been enlarged over a two-year period to become a seven-chamber multifunction facility.

This knowledge might not matter to Horn's investigation into the disappearance of the five missing treasures, but it did suggest that the bunker might originally have been designed to house only the vault for the Crown Jewels and the Cracow altar and that later, perhaps as a result of the bombing, it was enlarged. No one could say for certain who made the decision, but credit was invariably given to Mayor Liebel and Germanic Museum directors Heinrich Kohlhaussen and Eberhard Lutze.

The transfer of the Holy Roman Empire treasures from the Kohn Bank to the bunker took place on February 23, 1940, a year and a half after their arrival in Germany. Museum porters were dispatched to move twenty crates from the bank to the newly constructed Blacksmith's Alley shelter, under the cover of darkness. According to a museum porter, Mayor Liebel and a company of SS guards were present—the only new evidence Horn had yet elicited from his interviews that Himmler's men had a hand in both the facility's creation and its later security.

The shipments of Germanic Museum artifacts into the bunker and expansion of the storage area to accommodate them were ongoing. The dates given by staff workers tallied with the card-catalogue records and could, as Horn learned, be positively correlated to the bombing raids that had become a daily fact of life in Nürnberg. Like the events of Pearl Harbor to Americans, the dates and consequences of the raids were deeply embedded in the consciousness of everyone he interviewed.

Mention of the raids invariably elicited a strong reaction. RAF Air Marshal Arthur Harris, known to residents as Butcher Harris, was the most loathed Allied commander of the war because of his decision to bomb the civilian population as a means of crushing

German resistance. This, of course, didn't come as a surprise, as almost everyone Horn spoke to had lost a family member, a home, and livelihood as a consequence of the Harris missions and those later conducted by the Americans. A metropolis of nearly half a million people shrank by almost two-thirds before the actual invasion of the city took place.

As a direct consequence of one particular air raid, on October 13, 1944, Himmler's name would finally appear in connection with the bunker. Eight major bombing raids had already targeted Nürnberg, and construction had been completed on fourteen above-ground air-raid shelters and eight underground facilities. Also in place around the city was the ring of antiaircraft guns, which would eventually be repositioned to fire on the U.S. invasion force.

Residents, by this time, had become dispirited and hardened to the destruction caused by the bomber streams. Horn's informants described how they were no longer proud to wear their party badges. The massive party rallies, which ended five years before, were a distant memory. The greeting "Heil, Hitler" was seldom heard. Not only were people in the street, civilians and soldiers alike, not saluting the Nazi flag, but local party officers sometimes failed to reprimand those who breached standard Nazi etiquette.

The October 13 bombing raid was neither as severe as previous raids nor would it result in a firestorm such as the one that obliterated Dresden four months later. But it did blast apart the camouflaged Blacksmith's Alley tunnel entrance, exposing its existence to hundreds of residents, perhaps more. According to several informants, Mayor Liebel hurried to the old town the next morning, where his worst fears were confirmed. The tunnel's innocent-looking outer portals, disguised as garage doors to the antiques shop, had been blown wide open.

Liebel at once ordered workmen to repair the damage, and more than twenty people labored in the reconstruction. Among them was Anton Kiesel, a low-level labor-crew administrator. Most of the work was concentrated outside the bunker by the loading dock, but several alterations were made to the facility's interior. Twenty or more large beams were installed as additional supports in the corridor leading from the end of the tunnel into the vault area. A few days into the new construction, around October 16, Himmler and a contingent of SS officers arrived in Nürnberg in the Reichsführer's personal train and, with Mayor Liebel, inspected the construction work and inventoried the contents of the vault.

Himmler's presence provided an important new clue in establishing the time line that Horn was creating. Although the lieutenant could not be absolutely certain, it seemed logical that the Crown Jewels were still in the bunker, as Himmler—at this point one of the most powerful men in Germany—would not otherwise have made a personal inspection. As minister of the interior, he had far more important things to be concerned about than a minor construction project. The only reasonable explanation was that he was worried for the safety of the collection. This may have been when he and Liebel decided to remove what they considered the most valuable and easily transported of the treasures.

But the contents of the bunker interested Horn's informants not at all. They wanted to talk about the air raids that followed. Loath as Horn was to veer from discussion of the bunker, he let them express the suffering they had experienced as conditions in the city steadily deteriorated. Each had a personal story, and they all wanted an American officer to listen to their plight, to let the army of occupation know that hardships and suffering debilitated both sides.

Three months before the Allied invasion, Nürnberg suffered its heaviest bombing raids, which brought the city's administration and economy to a standstill. On January 2, 1945, most of the old city center and many outlying areas were destroyed, nearly two thousand people were killed, and one hundred thousand were made homeless.

Nürnberg did not recover. On February 20 and 21, raids killed another thousand or more people and left another seventy thousand without shelter. As more than one witness described it, bombs were already falling on ruins, and the listing of destroyed properties was abandoned. The registry that once was used to inventory damaged structures now indexed only those still standing.

Virtually all of the people Horn interviewed were actually looking forward to the Allied invasion by this time. Food was difficult to find. There was no fuel, potable water, or electricity, and most of the streets were blocked by collapsed ruins. As there was no wood for coffins, the dead were wrapped in paper for burial, and the gravediggers were paid in bottles of schnapps. The arrival of the enemy, most residents believed, would be a release from the suffering. Better to have an end with horror than to have horror without an end, was the prevailing wisdom.

Horn was sympathetic to their plight. At the same time, however, he couldn't ignore the failure of residents to own up to the truth of their situation. The residents presumed that the Allied nations were unjustified in bombing their city. Perhaps this was true. As he knew from G-2 intelligence reports, more bombs were dropped on Nürnberg on January 2, 1945, than in all of the raids the Germans had unleashed on England during the entire war. But as Horn also knew, Nürnberg's citizens—who claimed to be unaware of the consequences of their supporting the Nazi regime and were simultaneously incapable of doing anything about it—had done significantly more than supply men, armaments, and food to the Nazi war machine. They provided the venue, propaganda, and pageantry that Hitler used to mesmerize the nation.

The lieutenant didn't voice his ambivalence. This wasn't the time or place to fix blame. He simply returned to the point of the interview sessions, probing for specific details about the Nazis' operation of the bunker and their administration of the city.

Julius Streicher, by this point in the war, had dropped out of the picture altogether. Although he was still the city's defense minister, his status was nominal. In a scandal that eventually left many prominent Nürnberg citizens pointing their fingers at one another, Liebel accused Streicher of stealing confiscated Jewish property and using the funds he received for personal gain. By the time of the presumed removal of the Crown Jewels from the bunker, Streicher had stopped appearing at the government headquarters at all and was living on a small farm on the outskirts of the city.

The de facto defense minister in Nürnberg was now Karl Holz, who resorted to the kinds of extreme Nazi tactics that the Germans had previously exercised only outside Germany. At his side was Gestapo chief Benno Martin, who was reputed to be friends with Himmler. But according to informants, and very interesting to Horn, Martin and Holz did not get along. Informants claimed that the two men argued over several important matters, especially the need to defend Nürnberg, which to Martin's mind had no militarily strategic importance.

Holz overruled Martin as he eventually did Liebel. He issued orders that anyone fleeing the city would be shot and that laborers failing to appear for work at the factories would be arrested. Further, anyone hanging a white flag or waving one would be executed for treason. "Who does not want to live with honor must die in shame," Holz had broadcast from the city's loudspeakers.

This was no empty threat. As one witness after another testified, four residents were publicly executed for "disgrace and shame" in the week before the invasion, and another thirty-five "criminals" were sent to Dachau. And if the testimony of several informants was to be believed, as the U.S. Army arrived in Fürth, on the outskirts of the city, Holz laid plans to destroy entire sections of Nürnberg. Demolition teams were assigned to each of the government buildings and all of the remaining factories and bridges. Of special note to Horn, among the locations allegedly slated to be destroyed was the Blacksmith's Alley bunker.

No one Horn spoke to knew who had been assigned the demolition duty or who had prevented them from carrying out Holz's orders. In the confusion of the invasion, as U.S. artillery pounded the city and Peterson's E Company liberated the Nazi prison camp adjacent to the parade grounds, Nürnberg residents didn't give the Blacksmith's Alley vault much thought. The lucky few had already fled into the warren of bomb shelters to escape the enemy at the gates.

1

Nürnberg, which Hitler called "the soul of the Nazi Party," paid dearly for its participation in World War II. Allied air squadrons in eleven bombing missions dropped 14,000 tons of high explosives into an area no larger than a London suburb. This view of the devastation, photographed in April 1945, shortly after the American invasion, looks across the Pegnitz River toward the Church of Our Lady, in the upper right corner.

The Crown Jewels, coveted by Hitler, illustrated in early-eighteenth-century manuscripts. These millennium-old relics, which had resided in Nürnberg for 450 years, were removed to Austria after the collapse of the Holy Roman Empire in 1806.

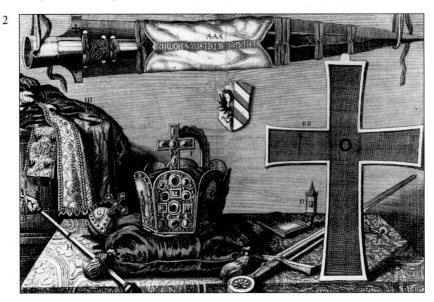

Top: (III) imperial robes, (H) scepter, (AAA) Holy Lance, (G) orb of worldwide Christian rulership, (F) crown, (E) sword, (D) ecclesiastical reliquary, (BB) cross said to have been made from the wood of the crucifixion cross.

Adolf Hitler leaving the Church of St. Mary in Bremershaven in 1932, the year before he became Führer. Members of the Nazi Party would soon champion their own heavily revised "Aryan" edition of the New Testament.

The triumphant Hitler swore that one day Germany would rule the world. Here he stands in Nürnberg's market square in front of the Church of Our Lady clock tower, at the 1934 Nazi Party rally.

Left: (1) pilgrims medallion of Holy Roman Emperor Sigismund; (2) medallion of the ecclesiastical treasures, featuring the Holy Lance; (3) Holy Roman Empire crown; (4) Austrian imperial crown; (5) scepter; (6) slippers; (7) orb; (8) imperial sword; (9) dagger; (10) the shrine box where the Crown Jewels were traditionally kept; (11) pilgrims medallion for the Feast of the Holy Lance; (12) the ceremonial sword; (13) Holy Roman Emperor Sigismund in full coronation regalia.

6

Left to right: Heinrich Himmler, Adolf Hitler, and Victor Lutze (head of the Nazi Party "storm trooper" division) leave Nürnberg stadium in 1934.

7

Hitler proudly struts down the stadium steps at the 1935 Nazi Party rally.

Top: Nürnberg mayor Willy Liebel at the 1934 Nazi Party rally, demanding that the Crown Jewels be returned to Germany from Austria. Pictured behind Liebel is the "symbolically" empty Holy Roman Empire relic shrine. Lower Left: the September 6, 1938, ceremony at St. Catherine's Church, when Nazi officials "repatriated" the looted Crown Jewels to Nürnberg. The advent of war, a year later, resulted in the treasures' being hidden in a fortified Nazi bunker under Nürnberg Castle. Lower right: The Holy Lance or Spear of Destiny, alleged to have been the lance that pierced Christ at the crucifixion, long venerated by the Holy Roman Emperors and believed by the Nazis to possess mystical power.

11

12

13

Top: Hitler viewing the Crown
Jewels at St. Catherine's Church
on September 12, 1938. Middle:
the gold and bejeweled orb of
worldwide Christian rulership; the
imperial crown, consisting of eight
gold plates studded with precious
stones and a cross. Bottom: the
embroidered coronation slippers.

14

Left: Nazi poster warning residents to dim their lights to make it more difficult for Allied pilots to locate ground targets at night. Bottom: Before the war, Nürnberg had approximately 130,000 homes and buildings. After the invasion, 67,000 were totally destroyed, 16,000 were partly destroyed, and 30,000 were seriously damaged. Out of a prewar population of 450,000, only 160,000 residents were still residing in Nürnberg when hostilities ceased, and 20,000 residents were living in makeshift hovels and bomb shelters.

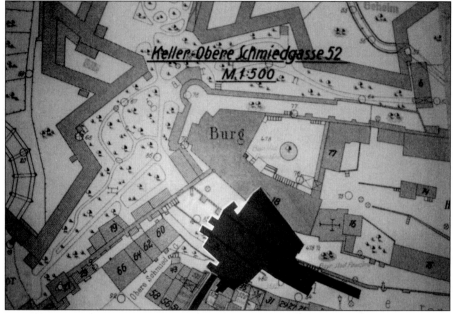

17

Top: Map of Nürnberg Castle with the Nazi bunker at 52 Blacksmith's
Alley highlighted. The entrance tunnel is on the lower left portion of
the highlighted area, the vault room is on the far right. The Imperial
Chapel in Nürnberg Castle is designated with a cross. Bottom: View in
1935 from Albrecht Dürer's house looking across Tiergärtner Plaza with
Nürnberg Castle looming overhead. Blacksmith's Alley (to the right,
arrow), with the disguised garage entrance to the Nazi bunker (to the far
right) where the Crown Jewels were kept hidden.

18

Inside the Blacksmith's Alley bunker. Top left: Tunnel entrance leading from street level into the bunker. Top Right: entrance to the vault, with its foot-thick steel outer door, where the Crown Jewels were kept. Left: SS guards room. Bottom: Carved figurines in the storage room containing the famed Viet Stoss altar, plundered by the Nazis from the Basilica of the Virgin Mary in Cracow, Poland.

Thirty-seven-year-old Walter Horn, U.S. Third Army interrogator and G-2 intelligence officer, whom Generals Dwight D. Eisenhower and George S. Patton ordered to Nürnberg to recover the Crown Jewels. Horn, the German-born son of a Lutheran minister, received his doctoral degree in art history under the mentorship of the renowned Erwin Panofsky at the University of Hamburg in 1933, before emigrating to the United States and then volunteering to serve in the U.S. Army in 1943.

Top: Horn family in
Heidelberg—left to right:
Walter, brother Rudolf (on
archway), father Karl, mother
Mathilde, brother-in-law
Erich Maschke, and sister
Elsbeth, circa 1917. Bottom:
Mrs. Anne Binkley Horn,
Walter's American-born first
wife, circa 1943.

Twenty-eight-year-old Master Sergeant and G-2 investigator Felix Rosenthal. A German-born engineer and bibliophile before emigrating to the United States, Rosenthal became Horn's colleague and best friend. He is pictured here in 1945, around the time he helped Horn to solve the mystery of the missing Crown Jewels.

26

On July 19, 1945, Horn was put in charge of a special investigative unit of the Monuments, Fine Arts and Archives division of the U.S. Army, charged with recovering the missing Crown Jewels. Left: MFAA Chief Major Mason Hammond, a Harvard classics professor before and after the war, and (right) MFAA field officer Lieutenant James Rorimer, a museum curator and the future Director of the Metropolitan Museum of Art in New York.

28

Nürnberg city councilmen suspected of being complicit in the removal of the Crown Jewels from the Nazi bunker: counterclockwise, Heinz Schmeissner, Julius Lincke, and Konrad Fries.

29

30

Top: Horn's former classmate and friend, Nürnberg museum curator Günter Troche (center), who would play a key role in locating the missing Crown Jewels, is pictured here showing Nazi visitors a display at the Germanic Museum, circa 1938. Bottom: Deutsches Ahnenerbe (German Ancestral Society) headquarters in Dahlem, outside of Berlin, where Himmler's corps of Nazi scholars oversaw curricula in German universities and organized international research expeditions for the purpose of scientifically proving the superiority of Aryan man and collecting Germanic art and antiquities for display and veneration in the fatherland.

Top: Ahnenerbe presentation to SS staff, circa 1943. Note the Spear or Tyr rune to the left of the eagle, and the upside-down Ansuz rune, suggesting secrecy, to the right. Bottom: An outdoors Ahnenerbe education program for young Nazi officers.

The Externsteine rock formation in the Teutoburg Forest in northwestern Germany was a sacred site used by pagans before Christian worshipers claimed it as their own in the 12th century. Himmler funded archaeological excavations here, believing that this was where the German people's Aryan ancestors conducted religious ceremonies. Top: note the chapel entrance in the foreground with the Crucifixion and the pagan Irminsul relief. Bottom: Heinrich Himmler and his staff pay homage to the sacred site.

35

CHAPTER 13

CHAIN OF COMMAND

July 26, 1945

Albert Dreykorn topped the list of people Horn interviewed the next day. The threat of losing his position on Thompson's historic-renovation committee was all the encouragement necessary to bring him, hat in hand, into Thompson's office. Motivating him to share specifics of what he knew was the greater challenge. An articulate and crafty bureaucrat, he chose his words with care.

"Mayor Liebel was a good and honorable man," Dreykorn declared. "A more kind and dedicated civil servant didn't exist in Nürnberg or anywhere else in Germany."

Horn, taking notes of what was said for later review, had fully expected to hear Dreykorn defend his former employer, but he had hardly anticipated that the mild-mannered secretary would champion Liebel in such a fervent and unbridled manner. Liebel was indeed a dedicated civil servant and by all accounts an effective administrator, but it was with Liebel's acquiescence that Julius Streicher published the virulent anti-Semitic schoolbooks and newspapers that fomented widespread support for the Nürnberg Laws, introduced at the 1935 party rally, which ultimately led to the creation of death camps.

A time would come for Horn to confront Dreykorn with the unpleasant reality of Liebel's administration. For now, the lieutenant focused his attention on the mayor's role in the construction and maintenance of the bunker. Rather than deny Liebel's involvement, Dreykorn gave full credit to the mayor as the man who foresaw the calamities to befall the city and took steps to protect its population, historic monuments, and treasures.

"The bunker was entirely Dr. Liebel's idea," Dreykorn said. "The city's treasures had to be protected, whatever the cost, whatever the sacrifice. He ordered the facility built despite the risk of infuriating the Nazi high command in Berlin."

The danger, Dreykorn said, was disregarding Nazi policy on resource allocation. Instead of putting all funds into the war effort, Liebel secretly siphoned Reich dollars from city coffers for the Blacksmith's Alley bunker and, later, to construct other shelters and facilities in the city. According to him, the Nazi high command specifically forbade the building of shelters because it believed it sent the wrong message to the people. Nürnberg residents were not to think that the Fatherland could ever be invaded.

Dreykorn went on to explain that with the help of Julius Lincke, who directed the city planning office, Liebel had skirted the letter of the law by declaring the Blacksmith's Alley facility to be a city-operated storage site, not a bunker or a bomb shelter, which under law couldn't be built. Thanks to Liebel and Schmeissner's adroit interpretation of the legal provisions, Nürnberg had more shelters for its residents than any other city in Germany.

"Do you mean to tell me that Heinrich Himmler was unaware that Liebel had built the Blacksmith's Alley facility to house the Crown Jewels?"

Dreykorn didn't answer Horn's question directly. He would say only that the treasures of the Holy Roman Empire belonged to the city of Nürnberg, not to the Nazi government. As city property, the mayor was entirely within his legal right to move them from one city-owned facility to another, as he eventually did Nürnberg's collections of museum treasures. The only concession that Liebel made was to extend to Himmler the same courtesies he offered other ranking Nazi visitors. This included, but was not limited to, showing the Reichsführer the city's home guard defenses and emergency evacuation plans. Liebel and Himmler, he said, shared the same appreciation for the city's historical significance and worked amicably together.

Horn briefly steered the conversation away from Himmler and back to the bunker. Dreykorn confirmed that Lincke, Schmeissner, and Fries were the principal players in the bunker's construction and maintenance. Liebel had trusted them implicitly, which was why he had given them the keys to the vault. Dreykorn alleged that after the invasion, the councilmen didn't come forward with the keys to the facility because they feared retribution from Nazi hard-liners who they believed were still operating in the city. Liebel's confidence in Schmeissner and Fries, he further stated, was well founded in that they carried on the "sacred trust" by working with occupation authorities to rebuild the city.

"As Teutonic Knights?" Horn asked.

If the supposedly reinstated medieval brotherhood meant anything to Dreykorn, he didn't acknowledge it. He merely repeated much of what he had said before, adding only that bunker documents had been burned before the Allies arrived. These records were stored, Dreykorn said, in a locked cupboard in Liebel's town hall office. That office and much of the rest of the building were destroyed in the devastating bombing raids the previous January. Dreykorn alleged that they contained all of the important papers related to the bunker and its contents, specifically the Crown Jewels.

Upon further questioning, Dreykorn acknowledged, as Horn suspected, that there had been other files. The mayor kept a secret cupboard at Gestapo headquarters, which contained restricted correspondence between city officials and the Reich high command. Dreykorn claimed that this correspondence had been burned by Nürnberg defense minister Holz, who Dreykorn said was the real criminal.

To hear Dreykorn tell the story, Holz was Hitler's man. He fully intended to carry out the Führer's plan to leave nothing behind for the invaders. "Everything was to be destroyed. Buildings, bridges, the airport, and the train station. All of it."

Liebel and Holz, according to Dreykorn, had a long-simmering rivalry on matters ranging from the treatment of Reich laborers to the deportation of Jews. Holz, who answered directly to the Führer, always prevailed. But Liebel, according to Dreykorn, found ways around Holz to help the Jews. He and Benno Martin, Liebel's personal friend and confidant and second in command of the city's defenses, couldn't stop the deportations, but they did manage to tip Jewish authorities off when roundups were about to take place. Liebel and Martin, Dreykorn declared, conspired to rid the city of Julius Streicher.

The story, as Dreykorn presented it, was that Liebel and Gestapo chief Martin had assembled considerable evidence of Streicher's personally profiteering on the forced sale of Jewish assets. But ridding the city of Streicher was not enough, because that, in effect, gave Holz total military authority over the city, which served only to compound an already difficult situation after the Allies crossed the Rhine River. Benno Martin had considerable clout with Himmler, as did Liebel, but not enough, according to Dreykorn, to remove Holz from office.

Dreykorn alleged that the most serious confrontations between Liebel and Holz occurred shortly before the invasion, when it was evident to everyone that Nürnberg would be overrun. According to Dreykorn, Liebel was determined to surrender the city, regardless of the orders Hitler was issuing from his bunker in Berlin. When Liebel found out that Holz intended to fight to the last man and blow up the municipal gas, electric, and water buildings, as well as the city's bridges—as Hitler had instructed—Liebel was livid, accusing Holz of hurting not the enemy but their own people. As Horn had previously learned, and Dreykorn now confirmed, the Blacksmith's Alley bunker was on the list of installations to be destroyed. Liebel's secretary described the facility as the mayor's pride and joy, his single comfort in the horror that had befallen his city.

"It contained all that Dr. Liebel believed most sacred to Nürnberg," Dreykorn said. "He sooner would have died than seen these treasures go up in flames."

The situation between Liebel and Holz reached a crisis when Benno Martin, who was charged with the various demolition projects, fled the city, leaving Holz in charge two days before Allied artillery began their assault.

"Dr. Liebel had made plans to surrender," Dreykorn said. "He spoke by telephone with U.S. General Alexander Patch."

Horn had heard nothing about such a conversation, although he didn't doubt it could have taken place. Thompson had said the enemy was given every opportunity to surrender. Thousands of leaflets had been air-dropped over Nürnberg.

"Liebel had only to raise a white flag and there wouldn't have been an invasion," Horn said. "Did he give in to Holz's authority?"

Dreykorn said that Liebel, from his office in the bunker under Gestapo headquarters, had gone ahead and issued the order for a citywide surrender. Holz discovered what Liebel had done and paid the mayor a final visit. "The defense minister was the last person to see Dr. Liebel alive," Dreykorn declared.

Horn questioned Dreykorn further on the subject. As Dreykorn explained the confrontation, Holz had stormed into the office demanding that Liebel rescind the order to surrender. Dreykorn, sitting in the outer office, saw Holz arrive, steaming mad. Holz then marched into Liebel's inner office and slammed the door behind him. A few minutes later, Dreykorn heard a gunshot. Holz then exited the office and announced that the mayor had committed suicide.

"Dr. Liebel didn't shoot himself," Dreykorn told Horn. "He was murdered."

If Dreykorn, the faithful acolyte, believed that his words would elicit the lieutenant's sympathy or somehow expiate the mayor's guilt, he was sorely mistaken. Liebel had sealed his own ghoulish fate long before Holz put a pistol to his head.

"What happened next?" Horn asked.

"Holz went ahead with his plans to destroy bridges, utilities, and public buildings."

"Did this include the Blacksmith's Alley facility?"

Dreykorn repeated what he had said earlier. The bunker had been on the list of buildings and monuments to be destroyed. But Benno Martin and Dr. Liebel, anticipating trouble from Holz, had already issued orders to evacuate the personnel and seal the bunker. Without access to the locked and shock-resistant storage cells, the only thing Holz's demolition experts had time to do was destroy the tunnel entrance.

"It was a tribute to Dr. Liebel's legacy that the treasures inside have survived," Dreykorn said.

Horn considered what he had been told. If Dreykorn was to be believed, Mayor Liebel, with or without Himmler's help and knowledge, had built the facility in secret, not only to protect the Crown Jewels but because Nazi policy forbade construction of defensive facilities. Only later, after the bunker was fully operational, did the Reich policy makers finally allow Nürnberg to install defenses, and the Germanic Museum and other city treasures were moved into the facility. Further, and perhaps more significant, Liebel and Holz were enemies. Suspecting that the defense minister would countermand his orders to surrender the city, Liebel had apparently gone ahead, in a last desperate and ultimately fatal decision, to keep the Blacksmith's Alley bunker safe. This was why Captain Peterson and E Company had found the facility evacuated. Karl Holz's demolition team, not U.S. artillery, might have been responsible for blowing up the tunnel entrance.

Had Liebel, with Benno Martin's help, done more than just this? Had the mayor issued orders that the five most important treasures be removed from the facility altogether? It was the logical conclusion, and Dreykorn, as Liebel's personal secretary, was clearly in a position to know.

Horn looked Dreykorn squarely in the eyes, willing him to reveal the truth. "Did Heinrich Himmler order Liebel to remove the missing Crown Jewels?"

Dreykorn chose his words carefully. Initially, he said only that Dr. Liebel, a patriot, had given his life to protect Germany's greatest treasure. After much more questioning, Dreykorn finally admitted to knowing more. Liebel had received an important telephone call concerning the Crown Jewels.

"About a month or so before the invasion, in February or early March, Dr. Liebel received a call from Berlin," Dreykorn said.

"From Himmler?"

Dreykorn confirmed that the call had indeed come from the Reichsführer. Just as Horn had suspected and as Dreykorn now also confirmed, contradicting what he had told Horn earlier, Himmler had ordered the creation of the facility. But the reason was not entirely what the lieutenant had supposed. The construction was to be kept secret, according to Dreykorn, because Himmler and the Führer feared that not only the invading Allies but also elements within the Reich would try to steal the imperial treasure. "No one could be trusted," Dreykorn said.

Horn jumped ahead to the logical conclusion. The facility was no longer a secret after the January bombing raids. The hidden entrance to the tunnel had been blown off its hinges and had to be repaired. Something had to be done to keep the collection safe. But the entire collection could not be removed, because there was no safe place to put it.

Dreykorn confirmed this and more. Himmler had ordered the most valuable items removed for safekeeping. Liebel hadn't shared with Dreykorn any details, only that this was the subject of the telephone conversation between the mayor and Reichsführer Himmler.

"To whom would be entrusted the responsibility of removing the Crown Jewels?"

"The city council," Dreykorn said flatly. "Heinz Schmeissner, Julius Lincke, and Dr. Konrad Fries. This was what I told Captain Thompson."

CHAPTER 14

HIMMLER'S COURIER

July 26, 1945

Horn wasn't entirely convinced of the veracity of Dreykorn's story, but he had to admit that, except for the mayor's alleged "kindness" to Jews, the story fit the basic facts that Horn believed to be true. The most troublesome aspect of the interrogation was Dreykorn's revelation that he had previously discussed his suspicions with Captain Thompson. The captain had mentioned hearing rumors but had not revealed their origin.

If Thompson had actually desired to investigate the case in a timely manner, he surely would have followed up by interviewing Schmeissner and Fries. These men, along with Dreykorn, sat on the occupation team's historical committee. Had Thompson purposely failed to call this to Horn's attention? Was the captain somehow complicit in covering up how the missing Crown Jewels had been removed from the bunker?

Eager to move his investigation forward and feeling prepared to confront Schmeissner and Fries, Horn thanked Dreykorn for coming to see him. "This will be all for now," he said. "Your help is most appreciated."

After Dreykorn left, Horn discussed what he had learned with

Troche and declared his intention to confront Schmeissner and Fries. Finding two of the three councilmen was no problem, Troche assured Horn. Schmeissner and Fries had offices in Nürnberg's Palace of Justice. Troche, however, encouraged the lieutenant to talk to one other potential informant—his immediate superior at the Germanic Museum, Dr. Eberhard Lutze—before he approached the two city councilmen.

Horn knew Lutze only by reputation, as the world's leading Viet Stoss scholar, a man Panofsky turned to for help and advice on the famous city artist. According to Troche, he had been intimately involved with the transfer of the Stoss altar from Cracow and had overseen the shipment of the various Germanic Museum collections to the Blacksmith's Alley bunker.

Most significant for Horn's investigation, Troche said, was a conversation Lutze reportedly had with Liebel before the invasion, just after Himmler's tour of the city's underground facilities, when Allied bombers had blown the doors off the tunnel entrance. It had been the subject of much discussion among the Germanic Museum staff, and he urged Horn to query Lutze about it.

Rather than talk with Lutze at occupation headquarters, Troche arranged for them to meet at the Grand Hotel, where they could speak more privately. Like others Horn had interviewed, Lutze desired the lieutenant's help in putting in a good word with the military government, whose influence on the review board would help clarify certain unspecified problems he had stemming from his previous associations with the Nazi hierarchy, most notably his participation in the removal of the Stoss altar from Poland. But at the same time, Lutze didn't wish to be seen entering or leaving occupation headquarters. Why was not at first clear but would soon become evident.

The middle-aged and overweight Lutze didn't make small talk or detail what suffering he had experienced in the city before the invasion. Like Troche and the rest of the museum staff, he had sat out the final four days before the occupation in a bomb shelter under Nürnberg's Pannier Plaza elementary school.

Lutze got right to the point. He had first learned about the bunker's creation from Mayor Liebel during the beginning stages of the facility's renovation. Lutze believed, as had Dreykorn, that the bunker's original and sole purpose had been to store the Holy Roman Empire treasures and the Stoss altar then held at the Kohn Bank, a facility judged unsuitable for art storage. The bank vault was designed for cash, bonds, and gold, not for priceless fabrics, delicate woodwork, and bulky crates containing holy artifacts, so Liebel, presumably with Himmler's knowledge and approval, set about finding a more suitable space.

Lutze's involvement with the artifacts, however, predated the creation of the bunker. Because of his expertise and oversight of the Stoss collection at the Germanic Museum, Liebel had invited Lutze to participate in the removal of the Stoss altar from Cracow's venerated Basilica of the Virgin Mary. Lutze admitted without apology that he and Heinz Schmeissner arrived in Cracow by train and, with help from twenty or so members of a special SS Ahnenerbe unit and under the direction of Dr. Peter Paulson from the University of Berlin, dismantled the altar piece by piece for shipment to Germany, where, as Lutze said, it could be better protected. As his presence in the basilica was only in an advisory capacity and the real hands-on work of removing the altar was undertaken by Himmler's government-sanctioned troops, Lutze considered his participation in the altar's removal to be marginal at best.

Listening to Lutze, as with Dreykorn before him, it was difficult for Horn to maintain his composure. The theft of the Stoss altar did not take place in the heat of battle but was part of a systematic and ideologically driven program to steal the artistic and cultural patrimony of another nation. Lutze, the consummate museum professional, surely comprehended the nature of his acts. Yet to hear Lutze describe it, he was doing Poland a favor. The altar had to be removed from war-torn Cracow for its own safety. The only difficulty, he said, was bringing the altar to Nürnberg, as various ranking Nazis desired that the Stoss masterpiece be safeguarded elsewhere.

Despite Liebel's protests, the altar was sidetracked to Berlin, where Nazi architect Albert Speer thought it ought to be displayed. Other high-ranking Nazis, too, had ideas about where the altar should go. Foremost among them was Hermann Göring, who thought it would be a wonderful new addition to his palatial mansion, Karinhall. Conversely, propaganda minister Josef Göbbels thought it ought to be made part of a traveling exhibition of German artwork.

The altar's arrival in Nürnberg, Lutze claimed, came only after intervention from Himmler and with help from Julius Streicher. With a conceit that bordered on arrogance, Lutze further admitted that he had personally contributed to the presentation that had won Hitler over to Mayor Liebel's claim on the trophy. The altar, installed in Nürnberg, was to be the centerpiece for a proposed 1947 celebration of the artist's five-hundredth birthday. And after the war, it was to be installed at the Saint Lorenz Church, which was slated to become Germany's national cathedral. No mention was made of the altar's ever being returned to Poland.

Plans for the Stoss birthday celebration, like the plans to inaugurate Saint Lorenz as Germany's national cathedral, were put on hold as the war continued and bomber streams darkened the skies over the city. The result was the creation of the Blacksmith's Alley bunker and the decision by Mayor Liebel and Germanic Museum director Heinrich Kohlhaussen to expand the existing structure to house more artwork.

"Did Himmler know about the expansion of the bunker?" Horn asked.

"He must have known," Lutze said, "though he couldn't have been happy about it."

Exactly what had transpired between Liebel and the Reichsführer, and if, as Troche had said, the modern-day Teutonic Knights were involved, Lutze didn't know or wouldn't say. He had no direct contact with Himmler, and what he knew was limited to comments that Mayor Liebel had made. Lutze's responsibility was to see that the altar and the Germanic Museum art stored in the bunker were properly tended. Even then, he had only limited access to the facility. Whenever he needed to check on the altar and other artwork in the storage units, Liebel had Schmeissner, Fries, or Lincke meet him at the entrance. Lutze always had to sign in and sign out, and there were always SS guards present. He hadn't even been in the vault room where the Crown Jewels were kept, only the various separate storage units. The guards themselves, he claimed, didn't go inside the vault unless Liebel, Fries, Schmeissner, or Lincke was there.

Just as there had been a tug-of-war over whether Nürnberg would get the altar, various high-ranking Nazi officials had their own ideas about where the Crown Jewels were to go. Lutze had no direct knowledge of what behind-the-scenes negotiations had taken place, but he was aware that Göring fancied having some or all of the treasures for himself. At the 1935 Nazi Party rally, where Liebel had presented the Führer with the jewel-encrusted reproduction of the ceremonial sword, Lutze and others were standing near Hitler when Göring commented that he wanted the real sword for his own collection. According to rumors circulated among Germanic Museum curators, this had incensed Hitler. Göring obviously hadn't known how badly the Führer coveted the treasure.

Beyond this, however, Lutze was unaware of any rivalries among the Nazi elite that may have necessitated Himmler's guarding the treasure in the Blacksmith's Alley bunker. Liebel, he said, was concerned only that the artifacts would be damaged by the bombing raids or that when the invasion inevitably came, thieves would take advantage of the confusion, break into the vault, and steal the treasure.

"Was Liebel worried about Karl Holz?" Horn asked.

Lutze was of the same opinion as Dreykorn. The mayor and the defense minister were at odds with each other. But Liebel had other enemies as well. Holz had the support of Brigadeführer Erich Naumann, a Holz underling who sought to replace Gestapo chief Benno Martin. Naumann, Lutze said, might have been the officer charged with destroying the city's bridges, utilities, and other public facilities just before the invasion of the city. Lutze, however, couldn't say this for certain, as he had little or no contact with the Nazi hard-liners in the city. His sole responsibility was caring for the Stoss altar.

Horn mentally added Naumann to his list of suspects. As he knew from G-2 reports, Brigadeführer Naumann, of Himmler's RSHA, operated the mobile SS killing squads that had slaughtered tens of thousands of men, women, and children in Russia. The manhunt for Naumann, as for Martin Bormann and Gestapo chief Heinrich Müller, was still going on. According to Lutze, Naumann had been transferred to Nürnberg in the last days of the war and shared offices with Holz.

Lutze went on to confirm details discussed in Horn's previous interrogations of bunker personnel. He impressed on the lieutenant the tight security and his sincere doubt that anything could have been removed from the facility without direct orders from Liebel and Himmler. Although he didn't know anything about the bunker being evacuated or Holz's alleged order to blow it up, he admitted that this might indeed have been the case.

"Then who took the Crown Jewels?" Horn asked.

Lutze didn't know, but he suspected what may have happened. "There's a rumor," he said. "I spoke to your Captain Thompson about it and filed a report. Check, you'll see."

Horn bristled at learning, once again, that clues significant to his investigation had been withheld by Thompson from him. But rather than address this subject with the museum director, he focused on the more critical question of what Lutze knew. "Please go ahead and tell me what you told the captain."

"There's a man, Herr Baum," Lutze said. "I sometimes work with him at the museum. Likely he's still around if he didn't die or flee the city in the last days before the invasion."

According to Lutze, Baum was a noted metalworker whom museum curators routinely hired to manufacture specialty display cases.

"Dr. Liebel wanted some containers built," Lutze said. "He asked me for a recommendation, and I gave him Baum's name."

Lutze, ignorant of the specifics of Liebel's arrangement with Baum, knew only that the mayor had asked the metalsmith to make four large, airtight, reinforced copper containers, two short and two long.

"How were they to be used?"

Lutze said that the two short containers would easily have accommodated the crown, orb, and scepter. The two long ones would have been suitable for the swords.

"What did Baum do with them?"

"He delivered them to Councilman Lincke to give to Dr. Liebel."

The rest of what Lutze knew came from remarks the mayor made during a final inspection tour of the facility a month before the invasion. The mayor, Lutze said, told him that a team of SS officers had visited the bunker just after Baum delivered the containers. They had come, Lutze said, on special assignment from Reichsführer Himmler.

CHAPTER 15

KEYS TO THE VAULT

July 27, 1945

Thompson didn't deny having read Lutze's report. He merely dismissed it as "rumors and speculation."

How many other reports and potential leads Thompson had deemed to be unimportant Horn didn't know, and the captain wouldn't tell him. The evidence, however, was stacking up against him. They were sitting across from each other at the same table in the officers' club where, exactly one week earlier, Thompson had erroneously assured Horn that everyone of importance to his investigation either had fled the city, had been sent to labor camps, or was buried under the rubble.

"I can understand your not talking to Julius Lincke," Horn said. "He fled the city. But you could have questioned the two other councilmen Mayor Liebel put in charge of the bunker. They're the ones who had the keys to the vault."

To Horn's mounting frustration, Thompson repeated the same litany of justifications he had used in their earlier meeting. There was no point in investigating further because the city's Nazi past was a debris-strewn trail of toppled buildings. Nürnberg was one large morgue, and the only corpse that mattered was Liebel, who had engineered the removal of the missing Crown Jewels before the invasion.

"You're wrong," Horn countered. "The two city councilmen, Schmeissner and Fries, are witnesses to the crime, and Dr. Lutze and perhaps Liebel's secretary, Dreykorn, are accessories."

Thompson was unwilling to concede that a crime had actually been committed, as the removal of the missing Crown Jewels from the bunker had taken place before the U.S. Army had taken over from the Third Reich. Nor did Thompson admit that Horn had made any genuine progress in his investigation. Dr. Eberhard Lutze wasn't a trustworthy witness to the events, because he had been among the members of the raiding party that had plundered Cracow's Basilica of the Virgin Mary. He would be willing, Thompson suggested, to tell Horn what he wanted to hear to avoid being held accountable to the war-crimes tribunals. Dreykorn might be cleverly shifting the blame away from Liebel, whom he clearly venerated. And Troche was obviously looking to protect his curatorial position at the Germanic Museum and might have his own personal motives for pointing his finger at former colleagues.

Horn acknowledged that what the captain said might be true. However, he was convinced, based on what he had learned, that he could pressure Schmeissner and Fries into revealing what they knew. Further, he wasn't going to leave the city until he had interrogated them.

The captain's response was brief and to the point. Under no circumstances was Horn to contact Schmeissner and Fries. The occupation review committee had vouched for their character, and they had proven their loyalty by the help they had given Thompson's historical-renovation committee. These men—civilians—couldn't be held accountable for clerical and other services they may or may not have provided to the city's former Nazi administration. If Horn wanted to pursue the matter, he should draft a letter with the questions that the lieutenant wished to ask them, and the captain would take the matter up with the new military governor, Colonel Andrews, who was expected to arrive in Nürnberg shortly.

Horn wasn't about to let Thompson tie him up with bureaucratic red tape. If a telephone call from Mason Hammond was required, or a telex from Eisenhower himself, the lieutenant was fully prepared to take the matter to the next level. Either that, or he would go ahead and interrogate them on Hammond's authority alone. He already knew, from Troche, where to find them. They had offices at the Palace of Justice.

Thompson responded to Horn's insistence on pursuing his investigation with a tirade of threats to shut it down, according to Horn. Lacking any corroboration from Thompson or any other military documents, it is possible the captain might not actually have lost his temper to the degree the lieutenant claimed, or conversely, Thompson might have been entirely justified in castigating a lesser-ranking officer for insubordination.

In the heated exchange that followed, Thompson told Horn that he wouldn't be permitted within a hundred yards of the palace unless he was led there in handcuffs. Further, if the lieutenant defied the commands from his immediate superior officer and talked his way inside, the two councilmen wouldn't speak to anyone of lesser rank than a full colonel. They would be on the phone to Frankfurt and have the lieutenant's stripes before the end of the day.

"I'm here to do my job," Horn responded. "And I intend to do it whether you like it or not."

Thompson declared that he, too, had a job to do and wouldn't stand by while Horn harassed members of the city's civilian administration. Nor would governor-designate Andrews, who, Thompson pointed out, had been appointed by President Truman and had the full support of USFET. They would have the lieutenant court-martialed.

Horn, as stubborn as Thompson was hot-headed, turned and left the room.

To the lieutenant's relief, the captain didn't call for an MP. He reached for his coat and tie and pursued Horn into the hotel lobby, where their conversation was less combative. Thompson wasn't acceding to the interrogation, he informed Horn. He wished only to advise the lieutenant that it wasn't just Horn's career that was in jeopardy. More important U.S. interests were at stake.

Thompson then revealed what Troche had only hinted at. The two former city councilmen weren't merely on the occupation payroll. They stood at the very top of the administration's civilian chain of command. Heinz Schmeissner was in charge of renovating the

Palace of Justice courtrooms and prison. Konrad Fries headed the civil affairs division. There would be hell to pay if their work was interrupted or, worse still, if they were implicated in a Nazi conspiracy to steal the Crown Jewels.

Horn was still playing catch-up, but the larger picture had finally emerged. If renovations on the Palace of Justice were not finished in time for the tribunals, the occupation team would take the blame. If food distribution was interrupted, they might well have a riot on their hands. Either scenario would be a disaster for U.S. interests. The tribunals might well have to be moved to the Soviet zone in Berlin, the British zone in Hamburg, or the French zone in Baden-Baden.

Still, Horn wasn't to be intimidated or dissuaded from following the only real lead he had. "You are with me on this, or you're not."

Thompson, it turned out, had decided to join him. His job, too, the captain said, was on the line.

Horn didn't know whether to compliment Thompson on his decision finally to do the right thing or chastise him for failing to act more promptly. He decided that praise was in order. Even if Thompson's only motivation was to try to keep himself out of trouble, the captain was on board. That was enough for now.

Private Dollar, parked outside, drove Horn and Thompson the short distance to the Palace of Justice. Advice from the captain was forthcoming at every stop along the way. Thompson counseled the lieutenant to adopt a civil tone when speaking to the councilmen. This was not to be an interrogation but a friendly meeting between members of the historical committee to tie up some loose ends that would help the MFAA to find and return the city treasures.

"But they're not city treasures," Horn protested. "The Nazis removed them at gunpoint from Vienna."

Thompson reminded Horn that everything in the bunker was technically still Nürnberg city property and would remain that way until the Allied military government declared otherwise. This was not a decision that was up to him or the captain. Horn was to refer to the missing items only as "Reich treasure." The captain would handle the rest.

Horn wasn't about to let Thompson take charge of the interrogation. The lieutenant did, however, see the value in having the captain along for the ride as they passed through one military checkpoint after the next. Although the trials were not scheduled to begin until November, the huge palace complex was already on alert, and no one was granted access without clearance from one of ten ranking occupation officers. The reason, as Hammond had previously told Horn, was that no one knew what the Germans would do when the nation saw its former leaders on trial. If there was a Nazi-led resistance movement waiting to show itself, it would be here.

In anticipation of trouble, an entire garrison of men was stationed behind the barbed-wire palace entrance gates, and bomb-sniffing dogs patrolled the perimeter. The irony, not lost on Horn, was that the courtrooms and jail they guarded had been used as courtrooms and a jail under the Nazi regime. In all likelihood, the Allies were now using Nazi-trained dogs. The jail's inmates and gatekeepers had changed sides—although even this was not a certainty, given who was in charge of the renovations.

The scene inside the massive building promised to be quite a circus when the tribunals began, as Horn knew from G-2 reports. Truman and Stalin might make an appearance, along with the army of reporters that traveled with them. However, the majority of those most responsible for the trial being held wouldn't be attending.

Hitler, Himmler, Göbbels, and several hundred other Nazis had chosen to end their lives rather than be put on public display. Still, there would be something for the reporters to write about. Göring was sure to stand trial, as would architect Albert Speer and former deputy Party chief Rudolf Hess. Horn and Rosenthal themselves had helped to prepare the evidence on Julius Streicher and Ernst Kaltenbrunner and might very well be called by the prosecution to testify at their trials.

The prospect of a return visit to Nürnberg troubled Horn much less than the fact that the two men they were about to interview, now on the U.S. payroll, might well have been as complicit in promoting the Nazi platform as their more notorious colleagues. They merely lacked uniforms or high profiles.

Horn and Thompson were shown into a large suite of offices in the east wing. Just as in the rest of the city, Allied bombs had done their work here. But the palace renovation teams had more to work with, as only the roof suffered major damage. The rest was cosmetic.

The room that the two officers were eventually shown into was already outfitted with a full complement of amenities. There were plush carpets on the floor, furniture, telephones, and filing cabinets. A large table occupied the center, covered with blueprints and schematics of the building complex. Schmeissner and Fries were waiting just inside the door.

Finding the two men together, Horn later noted, might have been a coincidence. However, the lieutenant couldn't help but remember the serendipitous arrival of Mayor Liebel's secretary at the bunker just as Thompson was about to blow open the vault. As Horn would note and the detailed military records of the subsequent interrogation session would document, there existed an underground network of informants working for both civilian and military governments. Horn couldn't say with certainty whose side anyone was truly on.

Schmeissner, forty years old, was the taller of the two men. Nearly bald, clean-shaven, with narrow lips, he had the grim countenance of a prison warden. Fries, six years older, frailer, balding, and slightly stooped, resembled a monk. Neither man looked as though he had been out in the sun in months.

Thompson made the introductions. He apologized in advance for the inconvenience and said that there was a matter concerning the bunker that he hoped the councilmen might clear up.

As Horn later reported in his unpublished notes on the meeting, he balked at letting Thompson have the first word. The interview was too important to be left to an occupation toady.

"It's about the missing Crown Jewels," Horn cut in. "I want to know what you did with them."

Schmeissner, speaking in perfect English, said that the lieutenant must be referring to the art bunker. He considered it a masterpiece of construction.

"Yes," Horn responded. "Himmler's bunker. The one you and Julius Lincke built and outfitted."

Directing his attention to Fries, Horn continued the interrogation. "And the one you administered on behalf of the Nazis."

The two men looked to Thompson, as if waiting for an explanation.

The captain pointed out that the occupation government had

not technically established that the bunker was a Nazi facility. It was used to store city art treasures.

Schmeissner and Fries acknowledged the captain's remarks for what they were: a conciliatory statement intended to chastise the lieutenant.

Horn wasn't about to let Thompson or the councilmen relax. "I believe that you and Dr. Fries were present on the day that Himmler's couriers removed five treasures from the collection of Crown Jewels stored in the vault."

Thompson interrupted once again, no doubt trying to defuse Horn's remark with an explanation of his own. The brash young lieutenant, he suggested, wanted to know about the rumors that former Mayor Liebel had turned five pieces of the Crown Jewels over to the SS before occupation forces arrived in the city.

"I mean exactly what I said," Horn interjected. "The two of you took possession of four reinforced copper containers in which you placed the missing Crown Jewels. You then delivered them to Himmler's men."

Schmeissner denied ever handling the items in the vault. Dr. Liebel would never have permitted it.

"Mayor Liebel asked you to open the vault, you took the treasures, and you turned them over to the SS."

Schmeissner's face, as Horn would later describe it, was cold and hard. Fries, too, had become tense. He was no longer a weary monk accustomed to bending over a wooden scriptorium. He was a naughty child caught with his hands in the cookie jar.

"Are you accusing us of stealing from the vault?" Schmeissner retorted.

Thompson once again intervened, saying that no one had yet made any accusations. The lieutenant merely wanted to know what had happened in the vault. He had reason to believe that five items belonging to the collection of Crown Jewels of the Holy Roman Empire were put into copper containers and taken from the bunker.

Horn refused to be silenced or to have Thompson rephrase his questions. "I want to know who took the Crown Jewels and why you and your colleague, Dr. Fries, didn't come forward and report what you knew when the vault was first opened for inspection."

Thompson, perhaps knowing that Horn wouldn't back off and

that there was no retreat from what had been said, finally let Horn take charge. The exchange that followed, based on Horn's recollections, was like that of a prosecutor cross-examining witnesses, except that there wasn't a judge in the room to restrain the lieutenant.

"Tell me what you know, or you'll answer to a military court," Horn swore.

After an awkward silence, Schmeissner adopted a less defensive tone, stepped back, and invited him and Thompson to take seats at the table.

He told Horn that he and Dr. Fries had nothing to hide and that no one, before now, had asked them what their contributions were to building and operating the art bunker. They wanted nothing more than to see the Crown Jewels, or whatever Horn said was stolen from the vault, returned to their rightful owners.

Schmeissner then continued distantly, almost reflectively. He apparently didn't like to think about the unpleasant days of the war and how the city's infrastructure—the sum of his life's work—was destroyed. Horn didn't point out the obvious. Nürnberg had indeed been reduced to rubble by Allied bombers. But in a very real way, it had been destroyed more than a decade earlier when the city council unanimously voted to turn the parade grounds over to Hitler and his henchmen.

"You were in the bunker on the day the Crown Jewels were removed?" Horn asked, less as a question than as a statement of fact.

Schmeissner confirmed it. He and Fries had both been there. They also admitted that they should have come forward earlier. The truth, according to Schmeissner, was that he and Fries were ashamed of many things that Dr. Liebel was forced to do during his tenure as mayor.

Fries, speaking for the first time, came directly to the point. He said that he and Schmeissner had been called to the bunker just before the invasion of the city.

"After the garage doors camouflaging the tunnel entrance were repaired?" Horn asked.

"Yes. After repairs were made," Schmeissner confirmed.

"The date?"

Schmeissner and Fries looked at each other. "Late March or early April," Schmeissner said.

Fries was also uncertain. He, however, seemed to be making a sincere effort to remember the exact date. "I know it was before Easter Sunday."

Fries told Horn that Dr. Liebel had called him and Schmeissner to the bunker very early in the morning.

"Was he waiting at the tunnel entrance, or was he already in the bunker?" Horn asked.

Fries confirmed that they had met Liebel at the entrance.

"Was he alone?"

Schmeissner shook his head. The mayor, he said, was accompanied by an SS officer and two privates—a driver and an armed escort. Their car was parked in front of the loading dock.

Fries nodded in agreement. As Schmeissner went on to explain, it was unusual for Dr. Liebel to call them to the vault so early in the morning. "But these were unusual times," he said. "Everyone knew that the Americans would be arriving soon. They had already crossed the Rhine. Neither of us knew what would happen next as we stood in front of the bunker."

"And what did happen?"

Dr. Liebel, they said, had them open the vault.

"That was all?"

"No," Schmeissner admitted. He let his colleague describe what had happened. Fries said that Liebel and the SS officer, carrying the heavy containers, went into the bunker. He and Schmeissner were told to unlock the vault. The mayor and the SS officer then went inside. A few minutes later, they exited with the metal boxes.

"How many were there?"

Fries didn't at first admit to knowing, until Horn pressed him.

"Surely you must know. You were there."

Schmeissner warily confirmed what Fries could not. There were four, two short and two long.

"What happened next?"

"The two privates stepped forward and took the metal boxes. Heinz and I closed and locked the vault door. The Nazis went to their automobile and loaded the boxes into the backseat. After that, we were dismissed."

Fries nodded in confirmation.

"You must have known what was in the boxes."

"No, not for certain," Schmeissner said. "Konrad and I didn't go into the vault with Dr. Liebel and the officer. We never actually saw the artifacts put into the containers."

"But you suspected they were for the Crown Jewels."

Schmeissner nodded. "The five missing items: the crown, the orb, the scepter, the imperial sword, and the ceremonial sword."

Horn hadn't specified which items were removed from the bunker but supposed that if the two councilmen hadn't actually helped to pack the items in the containers for Liebel, Dreykorn had shared the details of Horn's investigation with them. Still, Horn wanted the councilmen to acknowledge that they knew exactly what had taken place in the vault that day and, further, that they were, as Troche had indicated, two of the three people Liebel had charged with protecting the treasures.

"You knew what was in the boxes because it was your responsibility, with Councilman Lincke, to safeguard the Crown Jewels," Horn said. "You had also visited the vault many times before. You showed curators inside for inspections. And you had previously been there with Himmler."

Horn had gone out on a limb by referring to the Reichsführer. He had only guessed that Liebel had called Schmeissner and Fries to open the vault on the day of Himmler's inspection.

Schmeissner was apparently unruffled at the mention of Himmler. He admitted that he, Fries, and Lincke were the only people permitted to open the vault door or go inside.

"Except, of course, Dr. Liebel," Fries added. "He was always the one to show important dignitaries into the facility."

"Was the SS officer who took the metal containers an important dignitary?"

Schmeissner answered for Fries. "He must have been. Otherwise, the mayor wouldn't have been there."

"How long were the mayor and the SS officer inside the vault?"

According to Schmeissner, the transfer had taken five minutes, perhaps less. They were in a hurry, and as the councilman intimated, he didn't think Liebel wanted anything removed from the vault but had had no choice in the matter. Liebel was alleged to be upset. He wanted the entire matter over and done with. After all, Schmeissner said, these were treasures that the mayor had gone to great lengths to obtain for the city, and he had risked his career by building the vault in the first place.

"But he acted with Himmler's blessing. What risk was there in that?"

Schmeissner was silent. After a long pause, Fries answered for him. Everything concerning the bunker was done with great secrecy. But when the bombs came night and day, the city's treasures had to be protected.

"As they had in medieval times, by the Teutonic Knights?"

Like Lutze before them, neither man reacted discernibly at the mention of the brotherhood of knights. All the two men would say was that Himmler authorized the construction of the bunker.

"And the Reichsführer ordered the Crown Jewels to be removed? He sent an officer to retrieve what could be easily transported?"

"Yes, this is how it happened," Schmeissner said.

"You will testify to that? You are willing to put this into writing?"

Both city councilmen said they would put this into writing.

Thompson, who had remained silent while Horn conducted the interview, was noticeably relieved. The interrogation session hadn't been the painful ordeal he had dreaded.

Horn, however, wasn't finished. "Who took the boxes from Dr. Liebel? What is the officer's name?"

"His name?" Fries seemed surprised that Horn should ask. "How should I know?"

"You mean to say you don't know the name of the man to whom you delivered the Crown Jewels of the Holy Roman Empire?"

"Liebel knew him," Schmeissner said quickly. "Else we wouldn't have done it."

"Surely there was paperwork? You signed a release."

"Yes," he admitted. "There must have been paperwork. But Dr. Liebel handled everything. Konrad and I were never introduced to the officer or his men."

"It wasn't for us to sign a release," Fries added. "I couldn't even swear that the Crown Jewels were inside the containers."

Horn's heart sank. Had they told him all they knew? He needed more—something he could use to take his investigation to the next step.

"What was the officer's rank?" Horn asked.

Schmeissner looked to Fries. "A major, perhaps. I don't think it was a lieutenant colonel or a colonel."

"No, certainly not a colonel," Fries agreed. "Must have been a major."

"What branch of service?"

Beyond the officer's general designation as belonging to the SS, the councilmen didn't seem to know.

Horn tried a different tack. "What color were his shoulder straps and the piping on his hat? How many stripes were on his cuffs? Did he have a Death's Head ring on his finger? Think about it. You must remember."

Try as the councilmen appeared to be doing, they couldn't remember or hadn't noticed.

"What was the make and model of the car?" Horn asked. "Did it have a bumper flag?"

They were certain that it was a black, four-door Mercedes sedan, without a flag or other distinguishing insignia.

"What was the license number?"

"I didn't think to look," Schmeissner said.

"It was dark," Fries pointed out. "Very early in the morning."

"The driver and the guard put the boxes into the backseat," Schmeissner said. "The officer sat in the front with the driver, and the guard in the back. They left immediately."

"So you don't know who took delivery of the Crown Jewels, and you don't know the license number," Horn said, now exasperated. "Where were they going?"

Schmeissner said that he assumed they were leaving Nürnberg. Fries suggested the Nürnberg-Fürth Airport. He said that planes were still landing and taking off, right until the end.

"Didn't Liebel say anything to you about it?"

The two councilmen admitted that Liebel was upset but that he also suggested that it was a relief.

"What makes you say that?" Horn asked.

According to Schmeissner, Liebel didn't enter the vault again after that. He and Fries were never called back to the bunker until after the invasion, when the mayor's secretary came and told them that the Allied occupation troops were about to blow the vault door open.

Fries concurred with his colleague's narrative. It was a relief, as the Crown Jewels, he suggested, brought Nürnberg nothing but trouble. Horn, in retrospect, wished Fries had expanded on what he meant by his last remark, but Thompson concluded the interrogation before Horn could press the councilmen for more details.

Thompson thanked the two men for sharing what they knew. Unless they had something to add, he and the lieutenant would let them get back to work.

Horn resisted the impulse to continue the interrogation, saying only that he would write a statement for the councilmen to sign. "Just to be certain that I've got the story straight."

That wouldn't be necessary, Thompson told the councilmen, as they would not be going anywhere soon. There was plenty of work to be done before the tribunals started.

Horn said he would write up a statement just the same. And with that, he and Thompson left the office.

The captain was noticeably relieved that the interview had come off as well as it did. Rather than rattling his saber and harping about Horn's wasting his time rooting around in the toppled debris of Hitler's Nürnberg or harassing civilian administrators, the captain was actually contrite and complimented the lieutenant on doing a good job. He promised Horn that next time, he would give him the help he needed.

Horn doubted there would be a next time. If the two city councilmen were to be believed, only the first two acts of Hitler's demonic opera were set in old Nürnberg. Himmler, the evil magician, had secreted the treasures out of the city.

CHAPTER 16

HITLER'S HOLY REICH

July 27–28, 1945

Later that night, Horn vented his frustration about what he had seen and heard in Nürnberg over a game of chess and a bottle of wine with Rosenthal in the library of their Camp Freising home. The Nazis who had helped to bring the Crown Jewels from Vienna to Nürnberg were the same as those who had conspired to remove them from the Blacksmith's Alley vault. And to the shame of the American military, several of the key Nazi conspirators held the same or similar positions in the U.S.-appointed occupation government as they did during the Third Reich. Besides these revelations, all Horn had to show for his first week of investigation was what Rosenthal had said from the start. Himmler had ordered the five missing pieces of the Crown Jewels removed from the vault before the Allied invasion. It was still too great a leap, however, to suppose, as Rosenthal did, that Himmler's courier had subsequently sunk them in a lake in Austria.

"No Teutonic Knight would do such a thing," Horn said.

Rosenthal felt doubtful about Troche's theory of a brotherhood of modern-day knights whose resistance mission was to protect the Crown Jewels. He couldn't, however, dismiss the possibility that such a covert organization existed in the Third Reich or that there were links between the vault treasures and Himmler's army of Aryan scholars. Nazis with textbooks, he readily admitted, could be just as dangerous as commandos with guns.

Like Horn, Rosenthal had heard stories and seen things that would have seemed far-fetched before the invasion. The medical experiments conducted at Dachau and Auschwitz were prime examples. Never in their wildest nightmare would they have believed that fellow Germans could be capable, for instance, of murdering inmates for the sole purpose of measuring unusually small or large body parts. But this was what G-2 intelligence had just reported.

Investigators had found what they identified as a "Jewish skull collection" in a German-operated French research lab. Along with the specimen collection were Jewish cadavers in various stages of decomposition and a special custom-made elevator that moved corpses from one floor to the next, where physicians using large tanks filled with chemicals removed hair, nails, tendons, cartilage, and other soft tissue to transform bodies into pristine skeletons. The program was dwarfed by the death camps and armament factories, but it couldn't be dismissed as insignificant. It, too, had Reich funding and support from a hierarchy of bureaucrats that oversaw its functioning. And as Rosenthal informed Horn that evening, this program was sponsored by the Deutsches Ahnenerbe, the same team of Aryan scholars and scientists Troche had referred to. This alone was reason not to dismiss the museum curator's theories of a Teutonic brotherhood, however fantastical they appeared.

"Nothing is off the table where the Nazis are involved," Rosenthal said as he arranged the chess pieces. "The sooner we accept this and get down to the real business of studying Hitler and his henchmen, the better off we'll all be."

Rosenthal and Troche were on more common ground in their belief that the basis for both the Ahnenerbe's medical and its scholarly programs was the Führer's pathological hatred of the Jews and twisted notions of Aryan supremacy. The challenge for intelligence officers was to connect the dots. One could either declare Hitler and his inner circle certifiably insane and be done with the matter, as many in the Allied command did, or one could, with difficulty, trace the evolution of the monstrous Nazi scheme point by point, from the rantings of a political dissident in a Munich beer hall to a skull collection in France.

Rosenthal and Horn believed that the Holocaust could not be understood without connecting the dots. Although it was doubtful that the upcoming war-crimes tribunals would seek to trace Nazi doctrine to the years before Hitler's appearance in the Munich beer hall, Rosenthal concurred with Troche that the place to begin probing the roots of Hitler's psychosis was not in Germany but in Vienna, when he was an itinerant art student, hating Jews and romanticizing his personal destiny. Rosenthal, the Allied Army's Hitler scholar, had as much to say on this subject as Troche. "Everyone now knows how the Third Reich ended," he said. "No one knows how it began."

Hitler's prewar membership in various arcane spiritual societies was likely only speculation, but his associations with members of those societies, their virulent anti-Semitism, and the books he studied were a matter of record. The operative word, Rosenthal said, was *study*. Hitler read incessantly, whence came his deep and abiding appreciation for the Holy Roman Emperors and their ancient traditions. That these soldier-kings believed their divine calling was to remove pagans from their empire was reflected in Hitler's own pathological desire to eradicate the "Jewish conspiracy." The greatness of Germany's supposed Aryan ancestors was for Hitler the template for a more exalted Reich future.

In addition to his fascination with all things German, Hitler was deeply superstitious. Before the war, as later, he consulted astrologers. Despite his denial of any faith or belief system rooted in Roman Catholicism, he had, as Troche correctly stated, once aspired to become a priest. Years later, Hitler would choose a Catholic priest to edit *Mein Kampf.* Not that the Führer was a Catholic or even a Christian; rather, one could not dismiss the myriad influences that had created the half-baked mysticism he brought to Munich, which would, in succeeding years, fuel his inexorable rise to power and, according to Troche, influence his decision to renovate Nürnberg. He surely was a madman. But he was more than just a raving lunatic, pounding his fists on the floor, bullying and cowing those around him. He was a shrewd and calculating politician who read a book a day, kept one foot rooted in the past, and charted the course of future events decades in advance. "It was all right there in *Mein Kampf*, only no one took the time to read it," Rosenthal said. "The German people believed what they wanted about him."

Then there was Himmler. Although Allied intelligence officers enjoyed the comic-book image of the Reichsführer as a failed chicken farmer turned psychotic killer, he was a bright, studious, well-read, and well-educated son of a prominent Bavarian educator, who had turned to animal husbandry to help create an agriculturally sustainable future for his nation. In addition to conducting experiments to raise genetically superior livestock, his Munich-based company sold enhanced fertilizers and promoted state-of-the-art farming techniques. The racist Himmler, besides believing in the ultimate ascendancy of Aryan man, was enamored of the rites and traditions of the Holy Roman Emperors. He had studied archaeology, anthropology, and medieval history, as he had chemistry, physics, and botany. At some point, caught up in the wave of patriotism, hero worship, and economic depression that swept Hitler into office, he became convinced that something more than deportation and prison camps was required to protect the Aryan bloodline from the perils of racial mixing.

Himmler took on the task with a single-minded fanaticism and meticulous attention to detail. Connecting these dots was not as difficult as understanding just how sick and demented the architect of the "Final Solution" became after giving up his chicken farm. As Reichsführer, Himmler not only created the SS machinery and death industry but also romanticized the cruelty as a historical necessity to purify the Aryan race.

Knowing this, it was easier to believe that the Reichsführer, with Hitler's blessing, had actually reconstituted the Teutonic Knights, whose historic mission was to protect Germany's sovereignty and to preserve its culture for future generations. Although reluctant to speculate further on the existence of the brotherhood and other arcane matters of which Troche had spoken, Rosenthal reminded Horn of two critical things Rosenthal had learned in his years of studying Hitler and the Third Reich.

First, and most important, Hitler's regime did not operate as efficiently as Allied command reported to the press. The Nazi high command was highly organized but not monolithic. Rivalries abounded, with each camp spying on and at times undermining the other's effectiveness. Intelligence officers puzzled over this, seeking a reason. Many in the G-2 believed that the rivalries among the Nazi high command resulted from Hitler's sloppy management style; others believed them to be the result of an intentional strategy to incite factionalism within the ranks, thereby increasing the Führer's own power and prestige. Whatever the reason, Nazi leaders such as Himmler, Göring, and Göbbels independently constructed personal bases of power by hoarding whatever resources in manpower, funds, and property they managed to acquire from the common pool.

The second point Rosenthal made was directly related to the first. Because the Third Reich was not a unified totalitarian state but a patch-work of bureaucratic principalities, Reich leaders were free to create their own mini-empires, or fiefdoms. This was as true for Admiral Karl Dönitz and his U-boat crews as it was for Air Marshal Göring and his Messerschmitt pilots. Dönitz's naval officers had their own private re-sorts, complete with brothels, to service fighters who had been at sea for months at a time. Göring's pilots were pampered in similar luxury, and the officers who distinguished themselves were entertained at the air marshal's Karinhall palace, where their host sometimes met them at the door dressed in an eccentric medieval hunting costume. As long as the Reich leaders were successful in their individual responsibilities, Hitler stayed out of their way. He didn't interfere with their lifestyles the way Eisenhower kept a tight rein over his generals.

The significance of Rosenthal's words was not lost on Horn. He chose to interpret them, however, from the point of view of a scholar steeped in Germanic history. The Third Reich, Rosenthal was saying, operated similarly to the ancient Holy Roman Empire. Just like the medieval lords and other electors of the empire, each Nazi leader vied for control of individual fiefdoms within the greater kingdom. This feudal discord increased the emperor's hold over his individual vassals. Transfer of the crown from one emperor to the next, or *translatio imperii,* depended on deal making on an epic scale. Candidates for the crown had to make concessions to warlords, the clergy, and secular princes alike. The more adept the would-be emperor was in pitting one party against another, the more likely he was to maintain the precarious balance he needed to assume the throne.

In Hitler's Holy Reich, Himmler was left to create his own very specialized SS subculture, as long as his death camps operated smoothly, as long as SS infantry distinguished themselves on the battlefield. Just because Göring and Dönitz were not known to have a convert brotherhood of Teutonic Knights operating under their command or a small army of Aryan pseudo-scholars installed in their own castles didn't mean that the same was true for Himmler, guardian of the Crown Jewels.

Hitler's Nürnberg was indeed the perfect place to display a treasure fit for an emperor. And this was precisely what Horn—after considering the implications of all he had learned over the past week—found deeply disturbing. He wasn't so much investigating the disappearance of five holy relics missing from the Third Reich's treasure room as he was unraveling a Nazi plot to keep the symbols of world monarchy from falling into the hands of the Allies. Had General Patton known or suspected that this might be the case?

Rosenthal had something to say on this point as well. While Horn was interviewing former bunker personnel in Nürnberg, Rosenthal had made discreet inquiries to fellow G-2 officers and Patton's general staff to try to find out exactly what Patton's interest in the Crown Jewels was.

Himmler and Hitler, according to Rosenthal, were not the only commanding officers obsessed with ancient history, Catholic mysticism, and the conquests of medieval Holy Roman Emperors. Patton was as obsessed with these subjects as his enemies were. This came as no great revelation to Horn, as everyone serving in Third Army intelligence knew that Patton was unique among the Allied commanders in the variety of assignments he gave his officers. He commissioned entire studies on the morale of German soldiers in the field, how many attended church services, and the number of cases of venereal disease. Of more interest to Horn's investigation were the reports the general had demanded on where and how battles had been fought centuries earlier on terrain his Third Army intended soon to invade. Horn himself had contributed to one study itemizing the preparations Roman legionnaires had taken before crossing the Alps.

According to officers Rosenthal had spoken to, General Patton had written on the subject of Longinus, a poem speculating on what the Roman centurion had thought when he plunged his lance into Christ's side and how the single act of a fellow soldier had changed the course of world history. And although Patton was an Episcopalian and a dedicated Bible reader, there had been much talk at headquarters about the general's belief in arcane ideas such as reincarnation. At one staff meeting, Patton surprised commanders with references to having fought on the same battlefields centuries ago. "Imagine, if you will, the conversation Patton might have had with Himmler on the subject," Rosenthal suggested ruefully.

Rosenthal had not raised the subject to make light of a man for whom both he and Horn had supreme respect. He wanted to call attention to Patton's knowledge and appreciation of the more mystical aspects and attributes of the collection of Holy Roman Empire treasure. This was perhaps why, according to what a fellow officer from command headquarters had told Rosenthal, Patton had flown into Nürnberg a few days after the invasion. He paid his respects at a cemetery where the Allied dead were being buried, then left for the old inner city to view the Holy Roman Empire collection. Governor Fuller, however, wouldn't let him inside the bunker. The vault was still locked, and no one knew how to open it without risking damage to the artifacts. This had prompted Patton to call Mason Hammond, who in turn contacted Horn. But although Patton had been the one to light the fire under Hammond to launch an investigation, the general's purpose in securing the treasures and dealing with them differed from that of Eisenhower, who desired that the treasure be returned to Austria, where Hitler had stolen them. Patton believed the Crown Jewels ought to be the property of the U.S. Army.

"Just remember who you are working for," Rosenthal counseled Horn. Patton might have brought him into the investigation, but Eisenhower's signature was on his travel vouchers and MFAA credentials. Rosenthal wanted his colleague to make certain of his conclusions before going off on a wild tangent about a covert brotherhood of neo-Nazi knights and a treasure fit for an emperor. This was just the kind of incendiary ammunition, Rosenthal said, that Patton could use to remove the Crown Jewels from Europe altogether, something no self-respecting art historian would stand for.

Horn couldn't know for certain how Patton's interests in the

Holy Roman Empire collection might figure into his investigation of the Crown Jewels, but at least now he better understood why his report from Camp Namur had climbed the chain of command so quickly. Like Hitler and Napoleon before him, Patton wanted the treasures for himself.

"What will you do next?" Rosenthal asked after claiming yet another victory in their ongoing chess rivalry.

Horn had already begun to formulate his plan of action. He had two logical avenues of pursuit to find the missing treasure. He could delve deeper into Himmler's secret operations at his castle fortress in Wewelsburg and at the same time mine the wealth of intelligence that the Allies had collected on Himmler's subordinates. Foremost among them were the very men Rosenthal had referred to in his first conversation with Horn about the missing artifacts. The Counter Intelligence Corps had captured several highly placed RSHA officers and were using them with great success to track the movements of Nazi gold and other treasure. From what Rosenthal had found out from fellow interrogators, these captured officers were the source of the rumors that the Crown Jewels had been sunk in Lake Zell.

Rosenthal supposed, in advance, that the records they would be searching related to Ernst Kaltenbrunner, who had navigated among the Nazi high command with unusual ease. He probably knew more about what Himmler was up to than Hitler himself. The CIC had upward of twenty file cabinets of depositions, dossiers, and interrogation reports devoted to the former RSHA commander, and one, Rosenthal surmised, must contain references to the Crown Jewels.

Obtaining access to the CIC's inner sanctum, however, would not be easy. A highly secretive investigative arm of Army intelligence, the CIC rarely permitted officers from outside its ranks access to its records. Even Mason Hammond, at headquarters in Frankfurt, might not have the clout to open doors of the spy agency wide enough for Horn, a mere MFAA officer, to peruse its files. The matter would have to be approached unofficially, from one intelligence officer to another. Rosenthal had done plenty of favors for the CIC, mostly translating documents, and he would ask for a favor in return.

"Do whatever it takes," Horn told him.

Rosenthal agreed to use everything at his disposal, including giving his CIC contact a case of liquor from the cache of supplies in their locked closet. He would try to make arrangements for Horn, accompanied by Rosenthal, to meet at CIC headquarters two days hence, where they could review the files together. In the meantime, Horn, on Troche's recommendation, would leave with Private Dollar for Wewelsburg to see what could be found at Himmler's castle.

Horn communicated this to Mason Hammond when he called Frankfurt the next day to report on his progress in Nürnberg. If Hammond was surprised by Horn's decision to visit the castle, he kept it to himself. Himmler's fortress, the major said, was not known to have contained a trove of looted artifacts as had Göring's Karinhall. Hammond, however, had received a report that the Reichsführer had kept replicas of one or all of the Crown Jewels there. He promised to call ahead and alert the MFAA officer in charge of the site, Major Sydney Markham of the British Army, stationed in nearby Büren, to expect Horn's visit. Markham had written a report, Hammond said, that the major had found as intriguing to read as Horn's own report from Namur. Markham would surely provide him with a copy of the report and discuss it with the lieutenant.

There remained still the disposition of Schmeissner and Fries. The two councilmen were not blameless. They hadn't stepped forward with everything they knew when the bunker was first opened, and despite Governor Fuller's vote of confidence in their allegiance, they had been and perhaps still were dedicated Nazis. Surely there were others like them among those working for the Nürnberg occupation team.

"Shall I have them arrested?" Horn asked. "At the very least, they ought to be held for further questioning and relieved of their posts."

Hammond agreed to do what Horn thought best but counseled the lieutenant to move cautiously. Beyond the political fallout that was sure to result, arresting the councilmen would certainly end any future cooperation the two men might offer the investigation. They might still know more than they had revealed. As Horn himself always liked to say, "Better to catch the big fish before hauling in the small fry."

After checking in with Hammond, Horn was ready to set off on the next leg of his investigation. He had only to collect his mail while Dollar fueled up the jeep and plotted the route through the Teutoburg Forest to Büren.

To the lieutenant's disappointment, there was still no word from his brother and sister in Heidelberg or his mother and half-sister in Soviet-occupied Jena. Family news came instead in the form of a thick envelope from his wife, postmarked Chicago. Unbelievable as it seemed, while he was still receiving months-old postcards forwarded to him from Belgium and France, his divorce papers had found him in less than a week.

The document was short and contained no surprises. The good news was that his Lake Forest beauty queen had fulfilled her promise to give him possession of their Point Richmond house. He would not be returning to her when he had had enough of trying to help solve his birth nation's problems, but he would have a home to return to. She would remain in Chicago. Horn saw this as positive; it would be all the easier for each of them to make a fresh start.

Horn read through the document twice, affixed his signature, and left it in a return envelope for Rosenthal to post. Doing so brought him an unexpected sense of relief. Beyond his desire someday to return to Berkeley, he no longer had any pressing obligations in America and could remain in Germany for as long as he chose. He might actually teach a class or two at Heidelberg University and help Felix open his antiquarian bookstore in Munich.

Also on a positive note, he was now free to explore other relationships without guilt or recrimination. As Rosenthal frequently reminded him, and Dollar noted whenever they passed an attractive unescorted female in the street, there were twenty or more women for each eligible man in occupied Germany. Every male in uniform, regardless of rank, was viewed as a potential mate, and officers were considered the most desirable. Horn had the stripes on his uniform, and for the time being, a jeep and a driver. Most important, he spoke German, which put him miles ahead of the competition. The more vexing question was whether, after revisiting the crushed cities and unfulfilled dreams of his youth, he could open his heart as easily as he could unbuckle his pants.

CHAPTER 17

EXTERNSTEINE

July 29, 1945

Horn and Dollar reached the hilly uplands of the Teutoburg Forest by mid-morning. Driving on the narrow two-lane road between thick groves of pines and firs, their arching green limbs intertwining overhead, brought back many pleasant memories of family hiking and camping trips in these same dark woods. Thoughts of his family, specifically of the scholarship of his older brother Rudolf, stirred Horn to change their plans. Before driving to Büren to meet Major Markham, they would make a half-hour detour to visit Externsteine, the archaeological site Troche had mentioned.

The lieutenant knew the route. It was along a winding moss-covered trail just off the main roadway. Even if they missed the turnoff, there was no mistaking their destination. Externsteine was visible from nearly half a mile away: five enormous limestone pillars that jutted straight up out of the forest canopy. The tallest pillar towered 123 feet high and with the four others formed a wall nearly a thousand feet wide.

Horn started in right away lecturing Dollar on what made Externsteine special. Beyond the unusual geology, the site had been a place of habitation and pagan worship since Neolithic times. Many such sites existed in the area, but this one was unique because it had also been occupied by Germany's first Christians, who had built a chapel in one of the formation's many grottos and lived in caves carved into the rock wall. The site had fascinated historians and archaeologists for centuries. Because of its myriad of religious links, it had also captured his father's attention and eventually his brother's. Rudolf had written a paper on the site while studying for his doctoral degree under the mentorship of the eminent Dr. Eugen Fehrle at the University of Heidelberg.

Horn assumed, given the recent war, that archaeological activity at the site had stopped. The paving on a formerly dirt trail, adjacent excavation pits, and several large equipment shelters at the foot of the main towers suggested otherwise. Although no one was at work that day—he and Dollar had the monument and grounds entirely to themselves—archeological research had continued under the Nazi regime. A large tourist map and guide to the site, displayed at the entrance, told the story. In bold letters at the bottom, the Society for the Protection and Maintenance of German Cultural Monuments gratefully acknowledged its patron, Heinrich Himmler.

After parking, they followed a footpath between the trees to the chapel carved into the base of the main tower. Archaeologists and scholars debated about the activities that had taken place elsewhere on the site, but there was no question that the grotto had been used by the early Christians. Carved into the rock wall was an ancient mural depicting Christ being lowered from the cross. After having listened to Horn's lengthy discussion in Nürnberg about Saint Longinus and the piercing of Christ, Dollar expected to find an image of the spearman alongside Joseph of Arimathea and Nicodemus standing beneath the cross. But no; this depiction of the Crucifixion was significant to Germanic Christianity for a different reason. It predated the popular Passion narratives and Longinus legends that had given rise to the blood cults and relic worship of the Middle Ages. The message here was Christ's conquering of the pagans.

Dollar listened intently as Horn pointed to the salient feature. Christ was portrayed being lowered onto an image of a tree or pillar with two spread limbs, a holy symbol known variously by pagans as the Irminsul, the "Pillar of Heaven," and the "Tree of Life." Exactly what the Irminsul actually was and how it figured into pagan cosmology were hotly debated among scholars when Horn and his brother had studied Germanic prehistory. Many believed the Irminsul to be a tree, or a large tree trunk, around which ceremonies took place. Just the same, it could have been a depiction of one of the Externsteine monoliths. No one could say. The runes that told the story could be interpreted in different ways. That was the mystery.

Horn knew only that the various caves and grottos carved into the rocks were constructed according to astronomical orientations, much like Stonehenge in Britain. A round windowlike opening in the base of one of the rooms had been demonstrated to have significant celestial alignments, including a view of the moon at its northern extreme and the sun at sunrise on the summer solstice.

The early Christians who came to Externsteine must have been aware of its significance to the pagans, and perhaps this was why they had combined the scene of the Crucifixion with that of the Irminsul. The most obvious interpretation was Christ's ascendancy over the heathens. But another interpretation had also become fashionable. Christianity, as it spread through what became Germany, was informed by more ancient pagan beliefs and practices. In the century before Charlemagne abolished the old ways of the Germanic tribes and metaphorically and perhaps literally cut down the Irminsul tree, pagans and Christians had coexisted. At least, this was one of the theories his brother had been researching when he took his doctoral degree.

Horn and Dollar peeked into the caves before climbing to the top of the central spire where the pagans were said to have had their temple. That this had not been destroyed, as had many other pagan sites presumed by medieval Christians to be places of devil worship, was further evidence, from his brother's perspective, that paganism and Christianity, or a hybrid of the two, had coexisted in ancient German history. There was nothing now to see except a reinforced concrete platform of recent construction and the incredible panorama of the lush forest below.

From the summit, Horn pointed out sites he had visited as a youth. Foremost among them, hidden by the canopy of trees, was a park and statue dedicated to Arminius, the legendary Germanic tribal leader who had annihilated the Roman legions of Varus, forever establishing the border between the Roman Empire and Germania. Although Arminius ultimately failed to unify the Germanic tribes, his upset victory—the worst defeat in Roman history—had a far-reaching effect on the Aryan tribes, the Roman Empire, and, ultimately, the map of Europe. The surrounding area was similarly rich in historical significance. A nearby forest was widely believed to have been the site of the legendary battles where ancient Germanic tribes had held off the Huns.

Perhaps, Horn mused, the region's storied history was why Himmler had chosen to establish a base of operations for his Aryan scholars in a nearby castle and why the Nazis had continued the excavations at Externsteine. Troche would certainly have drawn such a conclusion. Externsteine and the lands surrounding it were a symbol of German unity, Christian and pagan alike, and a demonstration that a united Germany could defeat powerful enemies. The attraction of taking over a castle amid such legendary battlefields must have been irresistible.

Horn considered this as he and Dollar returned to their jeep for the drive through the countryside to Büren, to meet MFAA officer Markham. However, as Horn would later note, a new and equally unsettling thought distracted him as they passed the excavation pits. Had his own brother contributed his scholarship to Himmler's army of academics and scientists? And what of his brother-in-law, Erich Maschke, dean of prehistory and archaeology at the University of Leipzig, who had risen to the very top of his profession under the Nazi regime? Troche, who knew both Rudolf and Erich and had been a member of the Ahnenerbe, hadn't said, and Horn hadn't asked.

Horn and Dollar shortly left the green tunnel of forest and wound between moss-covered glens and pastures, passing occasional small dairy farms and old stone houses. Finding their way to the British Army's occupation headquarters was not difficult. An entire company of soldiers was camped in neat rows of tents in a rolling pasture just outside Büren's town center. A British flag flying over city hall identified the administration offices.

Dollar stayed out front with the parked jeep while Horn presented his credentials to the guards at the door and was shown into Markham's office.

Like his American MFAA counterparts, the major wore the uniform of a soldier; there was little else about him to suggest he had ever carried a weapon in combat. Tall and spindly, Markham had the retiring demeanor and thick spectacles of an academic, which in fact he had been in his previous career as scholar in residence at the British Museum. He warmly welcomed the lieutenant into his office, prepared a pot of tea over a portable stove, and offered whatever assistance his colleague required.

Horn greatly appreciated Markham's gracious manner, especially after the reception he had received in Nürnberg. Perhaps the officer recognized a kindred spirit in Horn, or, as Hammond had intimated, he was merely grateful for Horn's attention. There had been only one visitor to the castle before him, a CIC officer who hadn't known before his arrival that no less a figure than Himmler had held court in its spacious Knights' Hall.

Markham served the tea from a shell-white porcelain service decorated with Germanic runes, the ancient alphabet of Aryan man. Horn couldn't resist commenting.

The major was delighted that the lieutenant recognized the symbols. Himmler had had the tea service specially made, and the British occupation force had borrowed it from the castle kitchens. These same ancient images, as Troche had told Horn, had been used by Hitler in the reconstruction of Nürnberg and the designs for the Party rally grounds. Himmler's taking over the castle and inscribing runes on his tea service were clearly more evidence of his recycling the past to celebrate the future.

"I'm looking forward to touring the castle and reviewing the Reichsführer's papers," Horn said. "I've been led to believe he turned the old fortress into a study and research center."

Markham, with scholarly enthusiasm, said that it had indeed been a research center. He was, however, disappointed to report that the Nazis had removed most of the documents before the U.S. Army arrived on the scene. A fire, he said, had destroyed practically everything else.

Horn's heart sank. Neither Troche nor Hammond had said anything about a fire.

The fire, Markham went on to explain, had been set by the Nazis themselves. Himmler had ordered his personal demolition team to do the dirty work.

Markham pointed on a wall map to Himmler's castle in the village of Wewelsburg and, nearby, the U.S. Third Army's former encampment position. Using a pointer to identify key locations, he explained that the Nazi garrison had abandoned the castle just before Easter 1945, leaving in a fleet of trucks a few days before the U.S. Army reached the outskirts of the village. Himmler had then dispatched a crack team of commandos to destroy the castle. The Reichsführer hadn't wanted it to fall into enemy hands, no matter what the risk, and apparently didn't trust his castle staff to do a proper job. The major knew the details, because everyone in the village, as well as prison-camp laborers Himmler had imported to refurbish and enlarge the structure, saw what had happened.

Horn sat back, sipping his tea, as the major recounted what he had learned.

Himmler's ten-member team, led by SS captain Heinz Macher, arrived in nearby Paderborn on the Saturday before Easter, but since the United States had control of the nearby roads and the village was surrounded on all three sides, his team needed help gaining access to the castle. After an initial attempt to slip past the American forces failed, the unit recruited a local guide to show them a route between enemy lines.

The Nazi commandos arrived in three jeeps at around 10:00 A.M. that Sunday. Most of those in the village were in church, directly across the street from the castle. They didn't see the commandos until they heard an explosion and rushed outside. As the castle staff and Himmler's officers had left the site several days before, the villagers thought that the Americans were firing on the castle. In their confusion as they helped put out the flames, they were met by Macher and his gun-toting crew.

The actual demolition did not come off as Macher envisioned. He hadn't visited the castle before and grossly underestimated the amount of explosives necessary to complete the task. Although the castle was comparatively small—no larger than a London city block—it had been built on a foundation of bedrock with massive slabs of quarried stone. After setting off the initial rounds of ordnance, to no serious effect on the old castle walls or battlements, Macher resorted to placing tank mines in key locations. Even this wasn't enough. His team eventually went from room to room with torches. The next day, when U.S. tanks began rolling up the street in front of the church, the fires were still burning.

Not everything was consumed by the inferno, however. Markham said that there were a few rooms in the east wing, near where the Führer had his personal quarters, and in the west wing, where Himmler stayed, that survived destruction. The only area that was relatively unscathed was the north tower, the very area of the castle that Himmler desired leveled.

"Why was this?" Horn asked.

Markham couldn't say for certain, but from what he had been told by former camp laborers, Himmler thought it was the center of the universe, his Axis Mundi.

Horn had guessed correctly back at Externsteine. The Teuto-burg Forest and neighboring Paderborn were clearly why Himmler chose an otherwise remote castle to house his Aryan scholars and provide intellectual and spiritual training to his SS officers.

Markham said that it was indeed a very special place. But that feeling wasn't shared by everyone. The townspeople in Wewelsburg thought it was cursed.

The major explained that the fears of the villagers were not rooted only in the evil of the more recent occupants of the castle, though this certainly contributed to their reluctance to venture inside. Their fear arose as well from lurid stories of townspeople being tortured and murdered by a Teutonic Knight who had first built his stronghold atop the site and, later, by the bishop-electors of Paderborn, who constructed the more recent fortress on top of and around it.

There was plenty of other history, Markham noted, to attract Himmler. Archaeologists had discovered a Stone Age burial pit containing human remains when the castle foundations were first excavated. Nearby digs had uncovered Neanderthal skulls, as well as items of Bronze Age jewelry and other signs of early human habitation.

Markham's connecting the site with ancient Aryan man and a well-known Teutonic Knight and its later use as a home to electors of the Holy Roman Empire—the lords who jointly chose the emperor—fit squarely with the things that Troche had said.

The major had much more to share. According to the local historian, who had helped Markham prepare his MFAA report, the stronghold, or keep, the oldest part of the castle, had held off invasions as far back as Attila the Hun. Like Nürnberg Castle, it developed an aura of Germanic power and mysticism. The important difference between this structure and the far larger Nürnberg Castle, however, was that Himmler had this one completely to himself, nestled away in a forest far from Munich and Berlin. He was free to do with it whatever he wanted. He didn't have to share it like the Führer, who turned Nürnberg Castle and its accompanying parade grounds over to Mayor Liebel and the Nazi Party. This was his own fief.

In addition to the Himmler connection, as Markham had said, the locals' fears had been fueled by lurid stories passed down through the generations. Markham described the castle dungeon as the scene of unimaginable horror during medieval times. Here, in cages, on racks, and using thumb screws, breast rippers, and head crushers, witches were compelled to confess their sins against the Church. Many of these same devices were alleged to have been used during the waves of subsequent persecution against the Jews.

Markham couldn't say for certain how many Jews lost their lives in the castle's dungeons, but there was more than adequate evidence from human remains unearthed in a burial pit found in the west wing. The pit, known as the Norbertus Hole, allegedly named in honor of a particularly brutal lord of the castle, contained the bones of a hundred or more torture victims, stretching from modern times back several centuries. And this, Markham pointed out, was before Himmler opened his own concentration camp just down the hill.

Horn wasn't aware that there had been a concentration camp anywhere in the area, which didn't surprise Markham. Few among the Allied military, and even among the Nazis themselves, had heard about it. This was how Himmler wanted it. He went to great lengths to keep if off the map. As Markham knew from his research, even the Berlin and Munich archives made scant reference to it.

According to the major, the first camp was built in the pasture directly below the castle and was designated a labor facility. The prisoners simply lived in tents. It wasn't initially paid for out of Reich funds but operated under the aegis of a private philanthropy, the Society for the Protection and Maintenance of German Cultural Monuments, which Himmler incorporated to renovate and improve the castle.

Horn recognized that name from the tourist map at the entrance to Externsteine.

Markham didn't know how many other projects were operating under the umbrella of Himmler's various philanthropies, but the Reichsführer's avowed goal in Wewelsburg was to turn the castle into an SS academy, where senior officers would receive ideological training, and as a stepping-off point for scholars on their archaeological and scientific endeavors. Eventually, however, this relatively modest ambition gave way to a much grander vision. The way Markham described it, Himmler had begun to see the castle as the seat of his private empire, a modern-day Marienberg. It was to become a monastic city for Aryan studies, a kind of Teutonic Mecca.

Markham gave Horn a folder of concentration-camp records to prove just how many prisoners had been brought to the castle for its renovation. An initial labor force of seventy workers was expanded to become a force of several hundred highly skilled men and women from the Sachsenhausen concentration camp in Berlin.

They weren't Jews, Markham said, calling Horn's attention to a particular point he wanted to make. They were Jehovah's Witnesses, members of an American religious movement that had taken root in Germany in the late 1890s. Known throughout Europe as "Bible Students," they were, by and large, well-educated professionals. Himmler had specially selected them for their engineering, building, and clerical skills.

Horn already knew that the Jehovah's Witnesses were unique among those whom the Third Reich persecuted. Unlike Jews, Gypsies, and the many other ethnic and religious groups arrested and sent to the concentration camps, the Jehovah's Witnesses chose their own fates. They had only to swear allegiance to the Führer to be given their freedom. Hundreds and then thousands of Jehovah's Witnesses chose martyrdom rather than swear fealty to Hitler.

According to Markham, Himmler went out of his way to bring Jehovah's Witnesses to the castle, because they were in good health, technically skilled, and, by virtue of their beliefs, compelled not to escape. He selected stonemasons, plumbers, electricians, carpenters, glaziers, bookbinders, librarians, and translators. He handpicked the inmates from camps throughout Germany and Poland according to the skills he needed. Markham noted that a few of them were still in

Wewelsburg, helping out with the British Army's cleanup operation. They were, he said, a remarkable group of people.

Markham continued by explaining that as the war got under way and Himmler's plans for the castle expanded, he didn't restrict himself to Jehovah's Witnesses. He also needed more funding than his philanthropy could provide. The labor force grew to more than four thousand inmates, and a separate, larger concentration camp right in Wewelsburg village was made to house them. Himmler called it Niederhagen, the supposed ancient Aryan name for the forest adjacent to the castle.

Like the earlier facility, Niederhagen didn't initially appear on the Reich registry. Himmler employed a combination of subterfuges that would ensure Reich financing even when the work being done didn't qualify as a war-related expense. All of Himmler's other camps were built in proximity to armaments factories, quarries, brickworks, and defense-connected industries. Not Niederhagen. This was Himmler's personal project.

The major, at this point, didn't expand on why Himmler needed four thousand laborers to renovate a castle that was only a block long. He said only that conditions at Niederhagen were as heinous as those at Dachau and Auschwitz and that more than eight hundred inmates—nearly a quarter of the prison camp population—died in a single year while renovating the castle and quarrying additional stone for an expansion. There were so many bodies needing to be disposed of that Himmler installed a crematorium because the ones in nearby Dortmund and Bielefeld couldn't cope with the volume.

Markham showed Horn photographs. They weren't particularly gruesome, not like those the lieutenant had seen from Dachau and the other camps, but they conveyed the same message. Human life in the Niederhagen camp meant nothing to the Nazi overlords.

It was only after Horn had turned away from the photographs that he directed the conversation to his primary concern. Did Markham know anything about the Crown Jewels? Had the slave laborers at the castle or the townspeople heard of Himmler removing them from Nürnberg? And was there anything that could connect the castle to modern-day Teutonic Knights?

Markham was not surprised by any of the questions. Rather, he was delighted that an MFAA officer other than himself was raising questions of this kind. Most of the inquiries he had received for information on the castle and its occupants were requests for statistics—how much slave labor had been expended in the castle's renovation and what resources had been put into the project.

To understand the place, Markham said, Horn had to see it for himself. It wasn't only about lives lost and Reichsmarks spent; it was what they were building at Wewelsburg that told the larger story.

In answer to Horn's particular questions, there was much to connect the castle with the ancient brotherhood of Teutonic Knights. An entire study room was given to the knightly order, although Markham couldn't tell him what was done with that research or whether modern-day Teutonic Knights studied it.

Markham also noted a connection with the Crown Jewels, which he said were put on display there. The treasures he was referring to, however, were not the ones from Nürnberg. They were replicas, Markham said, complete with jewels. Facsimiles of the crown, scepter, and orb were put in glass display cases in the castle museum, and a copy of the Holy Lance was kept on Himmler's desk. According to rumors, and a mystery to Markham himself, the lance was kept on Himmler's desk alongside a vial of blood. All the major was sure of was that they weren't paperweights.

The facsimile of the Holy Lance, like the ceremonies said to have been conducted in the castle, had been widely speculated upon by the surviving Jehovah's Witnesses. They considered Himmler demonic, like the Beast in the book of Revelation. Their only regret about the Nazis' departure from Wewelsburg was that Himmler's commandos didn't complete their assignment and demolish the entire castle. They had left the north tower.

No one Markham had spoken to could explain precisely how the lance figured into the Reichsführer's belief system or what role it or the Crown Jewels might have played in the ceremonies conducted at the castle. A large part of Himmler's interest in the lance, Markham explained, obviously rested in the object's historical importance and central role in the Christ story. In addition to this, some legends told of Odin, the chief divinity of the Norse pantheon, using a spear to impale himself on a tree to gain enlightenment.

Then there were the runes, which Markham said could be found throughout the castle, as well as on Himmler's china set. The most common rune in evidence was the Tyr, or spear rune, which the Aryan warriors of Thor and Odin were said to have cut into their own flesh so that they might enter Valhalla.

To the seemingly bottomless pit of ancient lore and legend that the Nazis had made their own, Markham now added another. It wasn't only the historical and mythical connections to the Holy Lance that obsessed Himmler but the actual spear shape, the Tyr, which runologists believed to have magical properties, as it connected the heavens and the earth and the mythic gods with man. It was somehow viewed by Himmler and runologists as a channel for energy. Just as the plowman cuts into the earth to grow crops, so the Lord of the Universe pierces man to bring about enlightenment. The ancient legends referred to the place of that enlightenment as the Axis Mundi.

After hearing about the concentration camp and Markham's allusions to ceremonies conducted in the building the inmates had labored to renovate, the glazed images of the runes on the side of his teacup didn't hold the same fascination for Horn that they had when he had first lifted it to his lips. The runes were no longer examples of ancient intellectual history recycled for new eyes, any more than the Holy Lance, in Himmler's hands, was a venerated Christian icon.

Horn's natural instinct was to smash the teacup on the floor. Instead, he quietly put it down and asked how soon he and his driver could tour the castle and review the files and paperwork that remained.

Markham assured Horn that there was no shortage of things to look at. And also plenty he wouldn't want to see.

CHAPTER 18

BLACK CAMELOT

July 29, 1945

Private Dollar expected Horn to deliver his usual scholarly recitation when Major Markham showed them into the castle. Had the lieutenant been inclined to provide a commentary as in Nürnberg and Externsteine, he would surely have noted the care builders had taken to position the fortress on an easily defended rocky outcropping overlooking the valley. Horn might have paused on the arched bridge over the moat and pointed out the fine craftsmanship on the stone buttresses, the decorative filigree carved over the ancient portcullis, and the spectacular tracery on the ornamental rain spouts beneath what had been domed cornices on two of the three towers. Despite the fire that had destroyed the pitched roofs and leaded windows, Himmler's castle was still a masterpiece of late Renaissance art and architecture.

No such lecture from Horn was forthcoming. Knowing who had ordered the restoration and the hapless victims who had lost their lives laboring to bring the dream into reality, Horn was markedly silent. The wrought-iron Death's Head hanging precariously off one of the fire-scorched walls, the runes carved above the guards' station, and the checkerboard pattern of Nazi symbols on the steel-reinforced gates were grim reminders that they were not visiting a historic monument so much as walking in the footsteps of murderers and their victims.

Debris from the firestorm that had engulfed the castle littered the path leading into the triangular cobbled courtyard beyond the main gates. Pieces of charred furniture, heaps of shattered glass from the leaded windows, smashed pottery, burned remnants of wood paneling, torn carpet, typewriters, and piles of water-damaged books and papers cluttered the bailey. Laborers had simply shoveled the debris out the windows into the courtyard.

Markham led them between the mounds of refuse to a wooden door in the west wing to begin the tour. From here, he would guide them through the castle chambers counterclockwise to their ultimate destination, the north tower.

Their first stop, at the bottom of a series of stone steps, was a cavernous room filled with broken and smashed showcases and cabinets, described by Markham as Himmler's private museum. Here the facsimiles of the Holy Roman Empire's crown, orb, and scepter had been displayed.

Every visitor who came to the castle would have been led to this room first, Markham explained. It was Himmler's showpiece. A new exhibition was thought to have been put on display every time the Reichsführer or his bureau chiefs visited the castle. Invariably, the display would include Germanic art borrowed from museums or artifacts that Himmler's team of archaeologists had excavated from ancient grave mounds and pre-Christian village settlements. Most, including the replica Crown Jewels, had been taken away in trucks, but photographs identified many of the items. In the glass cases were urns, iron knives, Roman coins, Bronze Age needles, and plaster casts of runes. Fossils, too. A favorite of the museum, Markham said, was a three-meter-long ichthyosaur, a marine reptile resembling a dolphin that had existed some 90 million years ago.

More debris greeted Horn in the blackened, fire-scorched rooms above. Here, according to the major, Himmler's scholars had their workrooms, which included a photo lab and printing shop, a mimeograph and typing room, and a bookbindery. Nothing could be salvaged here or in the adjacent library, to which Horn and Dollar were shown next.

A camp inmate working as the assistant librarian had told Markham that there had once been as many as twelve thousand volumes in the collection, emphasizing Germanic history, myth, ritual, and a variety of more arcane subjects. A large part of the collection originated in Poland and other occupied nations, but its core volumes had been on loan from German universities and museums. Included in the collection were several valuable medieval codices. The books that had not been taken by the Nazis or burned in the fire were looted for souvenirs by the first team of U.S. soldiers who had been stationed in the meadow at the foot of the castle. All that now survived were the adjustable steel shelves, rare in even the best German libraries.

Markham led them through a doorway into the west tower, Himmler's exclusive personal domain. The Reichsführer had two rooms on the first floor for his offices and a suite of rooms upstairs for his private quarters. As elsewhere in the castle, these rooms had been gutted and all that remained shoveled out the windows.

Markham knew only what the various laborers and cleaning staff had told him about this section of the castle. According to them, Himmler had named his quarters after his patron saint, King Heinrich I, and had outfitted the rooms accordingly. There was a medieval bed, an armchair, a suit of armor, and other furnishings that the Reichsführer had purchased or borrowed from state collections. On a desk beside his fireplace had sat Himmler's replica Holy Lance and the vial of blood.

Their next stop was the dungeon, home of the infamous Norbertus Hole, a deep well with a wrought-iron grill cover. Horn noted the ancient padlock, avoided peering inside, and followed Markham to a side chamber, where the major said his men had found Himmler's safe. The safe had apparently been intact when the invading U.S. soldiers arrived, but by the time the British took over the site, its doors had been blown off their hinges. Except for a few books and papers scattered about the floor, his men had found nothing of consequence.

Markham doubted that the safe had ever contained the missing Crown Jewels Horn sought. Based on what various camp inmates had told him, Himmler had kept in the safe the SS Death's Head rings that were presented to officers after three years of dedicated service. By tradition, when an officer died, his ring was returned to the castle and eventually presented to another officer. Engraved with a skull and cross bones and a row of Germanic runes, they were cast in honor of Thor, the pagan god of thunder, who was said to have possessed a pure silver ring on which his warriors swore allegiance.

How and where the Death's Head presentation ritual was conducted Markham could only guess. Captured SS prisoners either wouldn't say or didn't know. However, Markham suspected that the ceremonies took place in the north tower, as camp inmates were barred from entering the tower when Himmler and his staff met or gathered there. No such restrictions, however, were placed on camp inmates entering the south wing of the castle, where Markham showed Horn next.

The largest and most impressive room in the castle's south wing was called the great hall, which Markham said was used for dining, lectures, and large meetings. From photographs and first-person accounts, Markham knew that this was also where Nazi wedding ceremonies were conducted. According to the camp inmates, Himmler had discouraged his inner circle from participating in Christian ceremonies, including weddings, baptisms, and many other traditional festivities. Christmas was replaced with a Winter Solstice celebration, during which officers and camp staff sang around a bonfire in the courtyard. The day of traditional gift giving was switched to the Summer Solstice celebration.

At the far end of this section of the castle, in the east tower, were rooms reserved exclusively for the Führer's use, although there was no documentary evidence that Hitler had ever been inside them or that he had ever actually visited the castle. The rooms were named and decorated in honor of Frederick the Great, Hitler's idol. But this was all Markham knew about them. A large portion of this section of the castle now formed the rubble in the moat below.

Like Hitler's quarters, the rooms in the eastern wing had also been named in honor of historical figures or noteworthy subjects and had once been decorated with historic accuracy and included swords, blazons, armor, clothing, jewels, and books.

Markham listed the names of a few of the rooms: Henry the Lion, after a Saxon warrior king who defended the pagans from

Charlemagne; King Arthur of the Grail legend; Emperor Frederick Barbarossa; and Christopher Columbus, whom Himmler's scholars determined was of Aryan ancestry. The room that interested Horn honored the Teutonic Knights. The major couldn't shed any light on who had occupied this room and what his studies entailed. He could promise Horn only that he would find out if one of the former labor-camp inmates knew anything.

The major eventually led Horn and Dollar through the ruins to the north tower, the least damaged part of the entire castle. The renovations here had been monumental, as the structure had been dismantled block by block and then reassembled to form a more perfect round tower. The construction of the two existing chambers inside was undertaken with such exacting care that a penknife could not be slipped between the stones, and the placement, dimensions, and proportions of each window, column, and pedestal inside were identical. Even acoustics had been considered: a bell rung in the bottom chamber would echo right up through the floor and could be felt by someone standing on the roof.

They entered the tower though a narrow portal, which had once led into the private chapel of the prince-bishops of Paderborn. Himmler had clearly also used it as some kind of chapel or shrine. No one on site knew what had transpired inside. All Markham could say for certain was that Himmler had planned three chambers in the tower, one on top of the other, but only the lower two had been completed.

Horn stepped into the middle chamber, an enormous, empty circular room with a high-domed ceiling. On the floor, inlaid with white and black marble, was an enormous image of the Black Sun with twelve arms, the sacred sun wheel design that Troche had described to him back in Nürnberg. The only other architectural features were twelve pillars, arranged to circle the room and arched at the top to form a second, inner ring.

Markham speculated on the room's purpose, based on paperwork that his men had found hidden behind a false wall in a nearby monastery. Himmler had commissioned carpenters to build a special table to stand in the center of the room above the sun wheel. It was to be circular and open in the middle so that the design on the floor could be seen by everyone seated around the table. There were also to be twelve armchairs, one for each of his most senior SS officers. Behind each chair, the walls were to be adorned with coats of arms specifically designed and produced by castle craftsmen for particular officers. Identical coats of arms were to be embossed on each armchair's pigskin coverings, beneath which, on the wood-framed back, was to be attached the silver nameplate of each officer. A few of the chairs had been found hidden in a neighboring barn, but as far as Markham knew, Himmler hadn't taken delivery of the table or the coats of arms.

Judging by what Markham said and Horn could see, the Reichsführer clearly had King Arthur and his round table in mind. As Dr. Otto Rahn—the Ahnenerbe medieval scholar who had so impressed Troche in Berlin—would surely have said, this was to be Himmler's Camelot.

Markham, like Troche before him, had provided yet another example of how Himmler had drawn from the legends of the past to build his dream of a new Reich. However, as the major was quick to note, Himmler hadn't necessarily built this room to conduct court business. Such exacting details in the tower's construction were unnecessary for that. Nor was the room meant for dining. The castle kitchens were too far from the chamber for practicality. Below this chamber, what camp inmates called the "Nazi crypt" suggested its purpose.

Horn followed Markham down stone steps into a second round chamber, with another domed ceiling, but darker and more ominous than the one they had left. The only windows were near the ceiling, barely large enough to permit more than scant shafts of light to illuminate the interior.

This chamber, too, lacked furniture. Instead of the columns that ringed the circumference of the upper chamber, twelve granite pedestals stood around a large circular stone basin, or shallow well, sunk into the middle of the floor. Centered in the domed ceiling, directly beneath the inlaid Black Sun on the floor of the chamber above, was another wheel design, with a cross at its center.

Renovating this room, Markham said, had required the most work. The chamber in ancient times had been the castle's cistern. Himmler had had it dredged by several more feet for reasons unclear to the slave laborers who had pickaxed their way through the solid rock on which the tower rested.

Some of those surviving laborers had told Markham that the pedestals were to be bases for large stone urns to contain the ashes of distinguished SS officers who had died serving their country. The basin-shaped structure in the middle of the floor was to be filled with oil, to fuel a perpetual fire, similar to the eternal flame in the Temple of Vesta in the Roman Forum of two thousand years ago.

Markham's theory was that some form of ordination ceremony took place in the chamber to connect the soldiers of the modern Reich with their ancestors.

Horn, after being told about the two things that Himmler was said to have kept on his desk, agreed with the major. What came to his mind, however, chilled him thoroughly.

Ancient legends told of crusader knights of the Holy Roman Empire being drenched or "baptized" with blood from heroic brethren who had fallen in battle. Having undergone such a ceremony, they believed themselves merged with alleged powers that would make them invincible. In the Nazi cult's crypt with its eternal flame and in the Death's Head rings passed from one knight to the next, the fallen soldiers lived eternally in their successors. This had been the promise spelled out in the runes on the sun wheel on the ceiling and on the one inlaid into the floor above them and symbolized by the lance held in the hands of the Roman centurion at the Crucifixion.

Were these two chambers why Himmler was so desperate to destroy the castle that he had dispatched his most elite and dedicated storm troopers to break through American lines just to blow it up?

Markham didn't know. There was, however, still more to see. He led Horn and Dollar out of the subterranean chamber, back into the sunshine, across the arched bridge, then through the village to the Niederhagen concentration camp.

Horn was immediately struck by the camp's proximity to the village center. Most of the concentration camps lay far from population centers, neatly hidden away in the middle of forests. Niederhagen was actually within the village limits. Everyone could have seen or must have known what took place there. The fumes from the crematorium must have wafted through the streets. Yet the townspeople, then as now, went about their business. Their shops were still operating on the medieval cobbled streets. They attended the same church across from the castle.

The barbed-wire fence enclosing the camp remained in place, but the entrance was now surmounted by a massive wooden cross. This wasn't a Nazi addition, the major assured him. It had been erected by freed camp laborers after the U.S. liberators arrived, in commemoration of those who had died while renovating the castle.

Like Dachau, Niederhagen had been built on a uniform grid, where individual buildings and inmate compounds could be easily observed and controlled by guards in machine-gun towers. There were seventeen buildings, not including the camp administration office, guards' barracks, and a parking lot. Just outside the barbed wire, these buildings, like the prisoners' quarters, were surrounded by an outer wooden fence facing the village. The outer fence was obviously not built to keep anyone from escaping; it was to prevent anyone outside from looking in.

The camp was designed not just for efficiency but also as an instrument of psychological terror. This was exemplified, Markham noted, by the electrified wire fence. The voltage was regulated to give the inmates a shock that would stun but not kill them. The Nazis didn't want an inmate to be able to end his or her own life by running into the wire. Matters of life and death were determined solely by the camp commandant.

This same psychology, Markham said, was used in positioning a pigsty just outside the wire fence and in plain view of the inmates. The pigs belonged to the commandant and were fattened with the guards' leftover food rations. The pigs were also slaughtered and barbecued in plain view of the inmates.

The room known as the sickbay was similarly situated. It had two doors. The first led inside to a cage. The second opened into the crematorium.

Markham pointed these things out on the way to the camp laundry, which he and his occupation team were using as a temporary storage center to collect art, artifacts, and Nazi documents that had been found in the castle or were hidden around the village and greater Büren. An entire cache of papers had been found behind a false wall in the former monastery. Another large cache came from a farmer's barn.

The room they entered was crammed full of all manner of objects. There were suits of armor, medieval crossbows, chairs, carpets, books, paintings, picture frames, flags, and even toy soldiers. Near a bust of King Frederick was a tapestry embroidered with an image of the Irminsul, the holy symbol of pagan cosmology. On a table was Himmler's ivory chess set, inlaid with black and white runes on its polished marble board.

It was like a strange kaleidoscope of history in which all of the separate parts had been rearranged.

Most prominent among the larger artifacts was a huge diorama from what presumably had been in the castle museum. It depicted the early Roman era, with a replica of a quaint farmhouse complete with straw roof and dollhouse figures of Aryan men, woman, and children dressed in rustic clothes. Across from the miniature house and figurines was a tiny furnace for smelting iron ore. Miniature horses and sheep grazed in painted green fields beyond. It was a glimpse into a paradise lost, an idyll of Germanic simplicity and abundance.

Next to the diorama, panels from a triptych undoubtedly from the castle dining room or great hall leaned against the wall. One depicted SS troops waging battle and a dead or mortally wounded officer. Another panel showed SS troops tilling the hard-won new land. The last panel was missing but presumably would have shown the new village that resulted from the sacrifice, full of happy and prosperous Aryan families with young children.

Horn paused to look at photo albums. One celebrated the thousand-year anniversary of King Heinrich's death, presided over by Himmler. There was an image of the Reichsführer laying a wreath on the king's grave and another of Himmler standing on a podium reading what Horn presumed to be the eulogy.

Other photographs showed SS officers attending wedding ceremonies. In one, a handsome young Aryan couple stood together in front of the castle fireplace, framed by burning candles and draped with a Nazi flag embroidered with runes.

The largest body of materials Horn examined contained press releases, articles, and research files related to Himmler's corps of scholar-excavators and archaeologists. Even Horn, who had been skeptical of Troche's seemingly fantastic stories, was astonished by the true scope of Himmler's grand research expeditions.

The Reichsführer had dispatched one group to the Middle East to search for evidence of Jesus' Aryan ancestry. Another expedition went to Cappadocia, in Turkey, presumably in search of Saint Longinus's tomb, and a third to Spain, searching for the Holy Grail. The Ahnenerbe had scholars in Finland studying Miron-Aku, a famed psychic who could allegedly commune with the spirits of Germany's Nordic ancestors. A fourth foray trekked through Tibet to investigate claims that early Aryans had conquered a great swath of Asia. Yet another expedition set out to Antarctica.

The most ambitious expedition, to Tibet, was led by scientists who measured human bodies and created face masks of the indigenous population, believing they would find vital indicators of Aryan racial characteristics and could determine the moral and intellectual capacities through phrenology. This program was surely part of the same research studies that had produced the Nazis' Jewish skull collection in France.

Less fantastic than these were the expeditions that led to the creation of Himmler's bunker in Nürnberg: one task force was dispatched to Poland to claim the Viet Stoss altar and one to Austria to retrieve the Holy Lance and the Crown Jewels. A Nazi photograph showed the Cracow altar being dismantled for shipment. Another showed Nürnberg mayor Liebel, trailed by his city council, at the ceremony presenting the Crown Jewels to Hitler.

There was unfortunately nothing of more recent vintage about the Holy Roman Empire treasures. There were no lists of Nazi personnel or ledgers tracing the movement of treasure from one location to another.

It was Dollar, not Horn, who drew the lieutenant's attention to something more revealing.

Throughout their tour of the castle, Dollar hadn't put more than two sentences together. To Horn's surprise, he now rattled on about Himmler's black Camelot, the crypt of horrors, and the Longinus lance. What had triggered his diatribe was a partially draped table-length scale model of what Himmler's castle was to become. Looking at it, Horn no longer wondered how Himmler would have used four thousand slave laborers.

The model showed a straight avenue on a north-south axis carved through the middle of the village. The homes, farmhouses, church, and rest of the village were gone, replaced by concentric rings of enormous buildings containing hermitlike study cells and a large lake. The point of departure for the entire design was the north tower, with three chambers. From the top chamber, with its pointed spire, Himmler would have had a panoramic view of his fantastic corner of the Third Reich's kingdom—his Axis Mundi.

The design mimicked the shape of the Longinus spear. The road leading up to the castle was its shaft. The study cells were its blades. Its tip was the north tower.

CHAPTER 19

THE WHITE HOUSE

July 30, 1945

Early the next day, after a restless night billeted with the British Army, Horn and Dollar returned to Freising. Then, accompanied by Rosenthal, they drove on to the picturesque village of Pullach, south of Munich, where the CIC had appropriated the former home of Martin Bormann. The sprawling three-story mansion on Heillmann Strasse, bordered on one side by a meadow and on the other by a hunting preserve, was part of a larger twenty-five-acre compound of residential homes and gardens that had once belonged to a Jewish industrialist. CIC officers called it the White House, as it was the only home in the compound painted that color and because the name suggested that their regional headquarters were more important than their G-2 counterpart's Munich brownstone.

Rosenthal had been inside several times before while doing favors for his CIC colleagues. The largest and most luxuriously furnished house in the compound, it boasted a spacious marble-floored foyer with a massive marble fireplace, a wood-paneled music room with grand piano and Persian carpet, a dining room that sat twenty, and a library and sun porch that looked out on a lily pond decorated with statuary. The only indication that it had once been Nazi property was a guard station at the Heillmann Strasse entrance, now manned by an MP, and what remained of a stone sculpture of a Reich eagle perched on the lintel over the front door. GIs passing beneath had taken turns chipping away at the eagle, and the bird was now missing most of its feathers and one of its claws.

While Dollar waited in the parking lot, Horn and Rosenthal entered the building and were received by an MP at a desk in the foyer. Clerical and secretarial staff occupied the dining room, which had been transformed into the communications center. In place of a sideboard was a row of teletypes and a phone bank. According to Rosenthal, the downstairs contained cells where the occasional prisoner was debriefed or held over for transit to Camp King, USFET's intelligence and interrogation headquarters in Frankfurt. The second floor primarily housed offices for the senior CIC investigators. The third floor, where Rosenthal led Horn, accommodated a few other offices and the file and records rooms.

After they reached the landing at the top of the stairs, Rosenthal guided Horn down a long hall, rapped on an unmarked door, then entered without waiting for a reply. Robert Gutierrez, the officer who greeted them, was tall and lanky, with a bulbous nose, and wore a uniform devoid of military designation save a U.S. Army insignia on his shoulder straps. For all Horn knew, he could have been a lowly lieutenant like himself. As Rosenthal later told Horn, he was a lieutenant colonel, the senior field officer in charge of covert intelligence operations for all of Bavaria and much of Austria.

Horn wasn't privy to the details of the arrangement between Rosenthal and Gutierrez. It involved the return of intelligence favors Felix had previously done for the officer, along with a case of liquor to be delivered to an address in Munich. As for the official story, if anyone were to ask, Gutierrez was bringing Horn and Rosenthal into the CIC's inner sanctum to have them translate Nazi documents requiring special insights only they could provide. This would not, however, explain the breach of CIC security. Gutierrez would be leaving them alone in the file room, where they were free to read what they wanted and take notes, as long as they didn't remove any documents.

The file room they entered had been a bedroom, likely for one of Bormann's servants or aides. In the place of the bed was a table with a reading light, a stack of ashtrays, and a pad of paper. Long rows of file cabinets lined one wall. The papers Gutierrez thought would be of special interest were already laid out for inspection.

Without so much as a friendly nod from one intelligence officer to another, Gutierrez closed the door behind him and left them alone for the next several hours.

To Horn's and Rosenthal's surprise, the records Gutierrez had pulled from the files were not those of RSHA chief Ernst Kaltenbrunner, whom they assumed to be the focus of much of the CIC's recent investigations. Kaltenbrunner may have contributed important details of the shipments of gold, jewelry, currency, and artwork removed from Berlin and Munich in the last days of the Reich, but the documents set aside for them related primarily to a lesser-known figure, Oberführer Josef Spacil, Himmler's paymaster.

Horn knew the SS officer by reputation only. In the final years of the war, he was the chief of RSHA's Bureau II, the department within the SS that set legal policy, administered funds, and coordinated activities among a wide range of separate SS police and state security agencies. In short, Bureau II paid the salaries and purchased property, uniforms, weapons, and other equipment for more than two hundred thousand personnel who operated the death camps and served with the Gestapo, the SD, and the SS throughout the Reich. As the primary functions of these departments were murder, unlawful deportation, and imprisonment, and they were part of the larger criminal organization operating within the Nazi criminal state, all of their members were subject to arrest and prosecution for war crimes. Bureau II's personnel, however, deserved special attention from prosecutors. They knew not only how the funds were spent but whence the funds were stolen.

Like vultures circling dying prey, Bureau II plundered the banks and treasuries of occupied nations, extorted funds from Jews and others seeking exit permits from Germany, confiscated the property they left behind, and stole vast sums of gold, currency, and other valuables from the death-camp inmates. Under Spacil's administration, hundreds of thousands of wedding rings and dental fillings were melted into gold bars, and diamonds, artwork, antiques, and other valuables were sold or consigned to pawnshops or exchanged abroad for foreign currency.

There was even more to this story, as the CIC had only recently discovered. In order to disguise the origins of its plunder, Bureau II created phony business accounts whose sole purpose was to remove the taint of murder, extortion, and theft. Like an alchemist, it transformed the property of death-camp inmates into gold bars and currency deposited into the central Reichsbank and then, by the stroke of a banker's pen, transferred these assets into these phony business accounts that could then be shifted from one German bank account to another or into private numbered accounts in Geneva.

As Horn and Rosenthal soon learned from reading the Spacil files, Bureau II's magicians also created money from nothing: they had a hugely successful counterfeiting operation. Millions of pounds of British bank notes were produced in a top-secret enclosure in Berlin's Sachsenhausen concentration camp and smuggled overseas to purchase supplies and fund foreign spy and sabotage operations.

The CIC intelligence team had lived up to its reputation. The transcripts of tape-recorded conversations, interviews, notes, and reports of findings on Spacil were perhaps as complete as those kept by the Nazis themselves and far more inclusive than the investigative work done by the G-2. Clearly, the CIC didn't have nearly as many men working for it as did its G-2 counterpart, but it had some of the best, and the best of the best were in special operations, such as the covert team headed by Gutierrez, which sought to expose secret Nazi plans to mount a resistance movement in occupied Germany and to track down the gold and other valuables amassed and laundered to fund it.

Gutierrez and his team didn't just interrogate captured Nazis and follow the paper trail the Germans left behind; they also created dummy CIC-controlled businesses and safe houses to lure former Nazis out of hiding. One file Horn read detailed a black-market brokerage company and currency exchange that the CIC was using to entice suspected criminals into depositing plundered bullion and other assets. Another was a tattoo-removal parlor that specialized in eliminating the mandatory blood-type identifiers that all SS soldiers had tattooed on the underside of their left arm, usually near the armpit. Unsuspecting SS soldiers, running from their Nazi past, came to the underground clinics to have their tattoos removed, only to find themselves marched off to a prison camp.

The files set aside for Rosenthal and Horn concentrated on Spacil's activities in the final days of the Reich, when RSHA personnel packed submarines, planes, trucks, and automobiles with gold, jewels, currency, and artwork and fled the ruins of the Reich. Most headed for the Austrian Alps, others for Chile, Argentina, and Colombia. The reason these and other files were classified was obvious. Anyone studying them—whether they were agents of a foreign government or simply freelancing GIs looking for Nazi plunder—could use the files to find the treasure for themselves. This treasure included not only the vast sums of gold and currency but a fortune in counterfeit British pounds and U.S. dollars, which were reportedly so perfect that bankers themselves couldn't differentiate the counterfeit from the genuine.

Nothing in the subject files concerned the Ahnenerbe, the Teutonic Knights, Mayor Liebel, Nürnberg's city council, Himmler's castle, or the many far-reaching expeditions taken by his scholars. These records focused only on RSHA chief Kaltenbrunner's assigning Oberführer Spacil to remove and hide assets in Reich-controlled accounts in Berlin in the last ten days of the war. Spacil was chosen not only because he knew where the SS kept its laundered assets but also because he had served Himmler faithfully for more than a decade and had firsthand experience in all SS operations.

The Bureau II chief, according to the CIC records, had joined the fledgling SS in 1931, at age twenty-five. After several months of volunteer work, the handsome, blue-eyed, blond-haired Spacil was offered a job as a stenographer for the central financial administration of the SS in Munich. Three years later, he was transferred to Berlin, where he worked as a liaison officer between the SS home office and the Reich treasury. He soon returned to Munich as the finance officer for the Dachau concentration camp. By this time, he had proven himself a capable bureaucratic manager. Under consideration for a more significant role in the SS hierarchy, he was transferred to positions that better acquainted him with the wider scope of Himmler's fiefdom. Most notably, he served time on the Russian front, handling the administrative paperwork that led to the organized plundering of Kiev. Eventually, he was promoted to Standartenführer, the equivalent of a full colonel, brought to Berlin, and given command of Bureau II.

The success of Bureau II's counterfeiting operations and Spacil's skill in disguising the origins of looted assets had convinced Kaltenbrunner and then Himmler that he could be trusted to remove the remaining liquid assets of the SS from Berlin and transport them into hiding in Austria for use by resistance fighters and undercover operatives who would be the nucleus of an underground movement aimed at restoring a new Nazi order in postoccupied Germany. In those final days of the war, Spacil was promoted to Oberführer, a rank equivalent to a brigadier general, given authority to requisition whatever manpower and transportation were needed, and sent on his way.

By the middle of April 1945, the largest shipments of Reich assets from Berlin had already been dispatched to salt mines and other underground repositories in the Alps. Spacil's challenge was more difficult. He had an estimated $25 million in gold, precious metals, diamonds, and paper currency to distribute and safeguard from the Allied occupation forces, retrieve without difficulty, and hide in such a way that no single Nazi operative besides himself would have access to all of the locations. With the Reich ship sinking, few men could be trusted not to succumb to the temptation to filch the Nazi gold for themselves.

Spacil chose the vicinity of Zell am See, a resort village in the Alps, as the distribution point for his operation. He was already familiar with the area, as the SS had offices in nearby Fischhorn Castle, where it operated a top-secret horse-breeding program. Himmler called it a cavalry school, as cited in G-2 intelligence reports. The CIC, however, had learned that its true purpose was not to teach riding skills. Instead, it housed a genetic research lab, where unusually large, fast, strong, and attractive horses were brought from all over Europe for the purpose of breeding a "super" horse capable of performing under difficult climate and terrain conditions.

Fischhorn Castle and the accompanying Zell am See resort village, it turned out, were also preferred destinations for dedicated Nazis on the run from the Allies. Hermann Göring and his family had moved there in April 1945, when Karinhall was overrun by the Soviets, and any number of high-ranking SS bureau chiefs and officers, whom Spacil counted on for help, were already living nearby or hiding in more remote mountain retreats.

In those last frantic days of the Reich, Spacil was traveling nonstop, flying from Germany to Austria and then shuttling back and forth between Fischhorn Castle, his wife's palatial home in Bad Ischl, and his mistress's townhouse in Salzburg. When not in the air, he traveled by convoy: a Mercedes sedan, several jeeps, and a truck loaded with treasure. When the Allied Army neared Fischhorn Castle, he dispensed with the truck and jeeps and couriered gold and other treasures in sacks and lockboxes piled into the trunk and the backseat of his Mercedes. As he dashed back and forth, he met with an assortment of contacts who were intended to become the resistance army—farmers and woodsmen, town clerks, shop owners, and, in several instances, Hitler Youth.

Among the many higher-ranking contacts he met in April 1945 were his immediate superior Ernst Kaltenbrunner and Kaltenbrunner's primary subordinates, Bureau IV Gestapo chief Heinrich Müller and criminal police chief Friedrich Panzinger, both of whom, along with Martin Bormann, were high on G-2's most-wanted list. The CIC reports listed numerous other important contacts, among them Otto Skorzeny, Hitler's favorite commando; Sturmbannführer Schuster, Spacil's own key subordinate; and, more significant to Horn's investigation, Erich Naumann, the intelligence officer who had operated the mobile killing squads in Russia and then transferred to Nürnberg just before the invasion. A communications center in Fischhorn Castle provided the vital link to the Führer's bunker in Berlin, where other members of the Nazi high command had met for the last time.

The discovery of the role that the Oberführer played in the final days of the Reich had come to CIC attention under dramatic circumstances. Spacil was behind the wheel of his Mercedes after having deposited a cache of treasure in Graz, Austria, on May 7, when he drove into Zell am See and discovered, to his surprise, an American sentry leading a long column of captured German soldiers out of the village. The time had finally come, he decided, to drop from sight. Spacil abandoned his vehicle, disguised himself as a sergeant, and joined the 352nd Volksgrenadiers, who were headed on foot to a POW camp in Munich. Along the way, he confided his identity to the division's commander, Captain Gerhardt Schlemmer, whom he asked, as a favor, not to reveal his true rank. Spacil would, with the commander's blessing, henceforth be known as Sergeant Aue.

Captain Schlemmer was not altogether comfortable with the

subterfuge but agreed to go along. It was only later, after they had reached Ebersburg POW camp, that the captain had second thoughts. Spacil had, by this time, intimated to Schlemmer that he had access to a million-dollar cache of gold, which he intended to use, with Schlemmer's help and cooperation, to bribe his way out of military prison. In addition to buying freedom for both of them, Spacil offered Schlemmer part of the treasure to disappear and create another identity for himself, as Spacil intended to do.

Unsure whether to believe Spacil, Schlemmer discussed the proposition with his next in command, Lieutenant Walter Hirschfeld. The lieutenant thought the arrangement was a bad idea. The captain ran the risk of a life sentence should he be caught assisting in Spacil's escape. Hirschfeld also had other, more personal reservations about helping Spacil. Before retreating with the Volksgrenadiers to Austria, Hirschfeld had served on the Russian front with a company of soldiers removing expensive furniture, champagne, fine food, and other luxuries confiscated from the homes of Jews. The company's orders were to deliver the goods to the private villas of Nazi high commanders. Spacil and other SS officers were living like royalty while rank-and-file soldiers such as Hirschfeld were left cold and hungry on the steppes of Russia. He didn't want to see Spacil escape to collect his plundered millions while he and the rest of the Volksgrenadiers, and hundreds of thousands of others who had done the real fighting, languished in POW camps.

With Hirschfeld at his side, Schlemmer revealed Sergeant Aue's true identity to American intelligence officer John Alter. After Alter investigated and was convinced that Sergeant Aue was indeed Josef Spacil, he referred the case to CIC field agent Claus Nacke. Together, Alter and Nacke devised a plan to trick Spacil into revealing the location of one or more of the caches of SS loot. They secretly wired Spacil's tent to record conversations between him, Schlemmer, and Hirschfeld. To keep Spacil talking, the CIC had Schlemmer and Hirschfeld convince the Oberführer that they could arrange for his release by bribing one of the "corrupt American guards" to sell them a certificate of discharge. The document would bear the necessary signature and black thumbprint of a U.S. officer. Once the funds were in place and Spacil had the certificate, all he needed to gain his freedom was to fill in Sergeant Aue's name.

After several weeks together in the POW tent, during which many hours of conversation were recorded, Spacil grew impatient. He said that it was imperative that he go free as soon as possible; otherwise, he would lose touch with his entire network of recently installed field agents. Having received as much information as they thought they could obtain, Schlemmer and Hirschfeld pretended to approach their corrupt American contact, Lieutenant Nacke.

The lieutenant played his role well. Spacil provided Nacke with a signed letter to be given to a forester in Taxenbach, outside Zell am See. Once contact was made and the letter delivered, Nacke was to give the forester a password, "sun," and he would be shown to one of the hiding places of the treasure. If all went well and Spacil obtained his freedom, other funds would be forthcoming to Nacke for the release of Schlemmer and Hirschfeld.

Nacke took command of the operation. Accompanied by Alter and with Volksgrenadier Hirschfeld as their guide, they drove to Taxenbach, deep in the Austrian Alps. After some difficulty, they met with Spacil's contacts, gave the password, and were eventually led to a farmhouse in Rauris, approximately eight miles south of Zell am See. There, under the floorboards of a barn, they were shown nearly a million dollars' worth of gold bullion. After Spacil's local contacts were arrested, the premises were searched and approximately one hundred thousand dollars in paper currency was discovered behind a brick enclosure in the attic.

On June 18, Alter, Nacke, and Hirschfeld loaded this portion of Spacil's fortune—nineteen bags of gold coins and bar, three bags of silver, two boxes of coins, and $117,752 in currency—into a jeep and trailer and headed back to CIC headquarters in Pullach.

But not all happened as planned. During the return trip, Alter lost control of his jeep, sustained a serious injury, and was sent to a Munich hospital. The cause of Alter's inability to maneuver the steering wheel on the mountain roads was quickly revealed. When his shirt and pants were stripped off at the hospital, Alter was found to have on him 220 gold francs, 2,780 gold lira, 850 English pound notes, nine rings, four watches, and a jewel-encrusted cross with diamonds. Not even the American intelligence officers could be trusted with Nazi plunder, it seemed.

The larger story, of course, was how much treasure had been retrieved from a single mission into Austria. The CIC shifted into high gear, using Spacil's contacts and Hirschfeld as an undercover operative to track more loot. The team, later joined by Spacil's former secretary, Gredl Biesecker, was extremely successful. Two hundred thousand dollars in gold bars was found at a second location, and more than $2 million was eventually found sunk in a shallow pond, secreted in attics, or buried on the sides of roads. That didn't, however, account for the estimated $20 million in other assets the CIC suspected was still hidden.

But time was running out. Spacil was impatient and growing more suspicious about the delay of his certificate of discharge. He finally stopped talking altogether and was arrested and locked in a POW prisoner's cage at Camp Oklahoma outside Munich with other top-level SS officers. A full body search revealed that he had three cyanide capsules sewn into his clothing. Eventually, he was moved to the Bischofswiesen prison camp in a castle where the Nazis had once incarcerated several hundred Englishmen deported from the Channel Islands of Jersey and Guernsey. Here, CIC specialists subjected him to intense interrogation.

At first, Spacil professed to know about neither caches of stolen gold and currency nor the names and whereabouts of his former colleagues. His tongue loosened over subsequent interviews when he was confronted with what the CIC had found, and he let slip fascinating and occasionally fantastic tidbits of information. Assembling them into a coherent mosaic was up to Lieutenant Colonel Gutierrez.

The more fantastic information Spacil revealed concerned details of Hitler's last days in Berlin and Himmler's plans for a neo-Nazi resurgence. Spacil claimed that Hitler had not died in his bunker. Under cover of darkness, disguised as a civilian, he was secretly transported out of Berlin in a small plane. A partially cremated body double had been left behind to fool the Russians.

Spacil also told of having been given a wide assortment of valuables besides currency, gold, and jewels to hide on behalf of the Reich. Among the treasures was the last uniform the Führer wore in his bunker, his personal diaries, Eva Braun's jewelry, and an extensive collection of personal correspondence between Braun and Hitler. These he claimed were nearly lost when the plane carrying them had crashed outside Berlin, but they were eventually recovered and taken to Fischhorn Castle by undercover operatives.

Of more immediate interest to Horn and Rosenthal, Spacil claimed to have firsthand information about the concealment of the Crown Jewels. At a meeting with Kaltenbrunner, Gestapo chief Heinrich Müller, and senior RSHA bureau chiefs in Berlin on April 1, Spacil was told that the most valuable treasures of the Holy Roman Empire collection had been removed from the Nürnberg bunker by a Gestapo agent on orders from the Reichsführer, taken to Fischhorn Castle, loaded into Himmler's personal Mercedes, and driven into the southernmost end of Lake Zell.

CHAPTER 20

NAZI PLUNDER

July 30, 1945

Horn and Rosenthal spent the rest of the day reading a wide range of CIC reports detailing follow-up investigations of Nazi officers and suspected covert resistance agents, treasure-hunting expeditions around Fischhorn Castle and Zell am See, and summaries of related interrogations. Investigations into Spacil and his RSHA associates were sure to continue for years to come, but Horn and Rosenthal had already read enough to know why the CIC had not shared its knowledge with the greater intelligence community and why it was unlikely, after the treasure-hunting expeditions were over, that details of their investigations, and perhaps his own investigation into the missing Crown Jewels, would ever be released to the public.

These and other subjects were the main topics of conversation when the two officers returned to Camp Freising later that night and compared notes. There would be no home-cooked meal or relaxing bottle of wine, no chess game, and no Josephine Baker on the Victrola. They spent the evening discussing their findings and ruminating on the larger picture of U.S. intelligence interests in postwar Germany.

The papers they had studied left Rosenthal in an unusually somber mood. Bureau II was the division that had forced his family into giving up its Munich home and bookstore, and the two high-ranking Nazis who had met with Spacil at Fischhorn Castle—Gestapo chief Heinrich Müller and RHSA administrator Oberführer Friedrich Panzinger, still on the run from the Allies—were directly responsible for executing Rosenthal's uncles, aunts, and cousins. There was more, however, that cast a pall over the otherwise spirited Rosenthal. The CIC records raised troublesome issues about how intelligence was gathered and being used in postwar Germany. CIC activities weren't as ethical and upright as the public—and most of the intelligence officers themselves—was being told.

The Spacil investigation, they had learned, was the story of a former high-ranking Nazi criminal, currently held in a special CIC protective camp, who was working with intelligence chiefs to recover Nazi plunder. But this plunder wasn't being returned to the victims whose lives had been destroyed and property confiscated by the Nazis or put into the larger pool of funds to bring about the reconstruction of war-weary Europe. There was clear evidence that it was moved without any apparent USFET oversight into accounts controlled by the CIC to build its own treasury and, presumably, expand its classified spy operations. The vast fortune in counterfeit currency could be heading in the same direction.

The CIC actions didn't approach the criminal behavior of Bureau II's money-laundering schemes, but the same principle applied. Neither Horn nor Rosenthal was truly shocked by these revelations; they had been serving in the G-2 long enough to know that high-level operatives often decided that any means were justified by their ends. Yet the Spacil investigation highlighted the disturbing contradictions between their adoptive nation's words and actions. Their words rang offensively hollow to these two intelligence officers who had dedicated their wartime careers to returning justice to a country where human rights, civil liberties, and freedom of information had languished unregarded for more than a decade. Horn's primary attraction to the MFAA was its high-minded principles of justice and fair play. From what Horn and Rosenthal could see from the Spacil files, the CIC wasn't playing by the same rules.

The first embarrassing discovery was that Spacil, bartering information and Nazi plunder in exchange for his life, was missing from the list of captured Nazis facing criminal prosecution. Not that he wouldn't eventually be prosecuted—he might find himself at the war-crimes tribunals. But as of the date of the last report in the CIC files, he was being treated preferentially as a protected witness. The occupation government and CIC, it seemed, wanted him helping their own intelligence operations, not hanging by a noose.

Walter Hirschfeld was another example of subverted justice. The former SS officer had openly confessed to looting the homes of Jewish residents of Kiev. Because he helped apprehend Spacil, Hirschfeld was given his freedom, a salary, and a position as an undercover CIC operative. According to the summary CIC reports, he subsequently penetrated several resistance operations but had recently been released from duty because he was suspected of blackmailing former Nazis and stealing Reich plunder and, much worse, was implicated in a murder to cover up his duplicitous behavior with the CIC. Hiring former Nazis, despite what short-term gain might result, was tantamount to inviting corruption into the intelligence ranks at all levels. Hirschfeld could no more be trusted than Schmeissner or Fries, operating in offices in Nürnberg's Palace of Justice.

Then there was the matter of intelligence officer John Alter, who had been caught stealing Nazi plunder that he and CIC agent Nacke had recovered. He hadn't been prosecuted, merely transferred out of the CIC. His crimes were obviously not of the same order as those of the criminals who had first amassed the treasures, but no effort was made to hold him accountable. Somehow he had been honorably discharged and had gone home.

Much more startling and disturbing evidence of corruption at various levels of American command emerged in the Spacil files. The efforts to retrieve treasure in and around Fischhorn Castle, which directly bore on Horn's interest in recovering the Crown Jewels, were a prime example.

Lieutenant Colonel Gutierrez, or one of his subordinates, had dispatched an intelligence officer to Austria to see what could be found. In addition to dredging a section of Lake Zell, the intelligence officer was ordered to recover SS files and other Nazi documents known to have been at Fischhorn when the Americans seized the property. Upon his arrival, he found the site picked clean not only of documents but also of practically all its furnishings. These included a large safe, similar to the one in Himmler's castle.

Supervision in and around Fischhorn Castle was abysmally lax. In addition to the theft of files and removal of the safe and other property, GIs were claiming souvenirs at will and gathering at a swimming pool for recreation, including drinking bouts and nude sunbathing with local Austrian girls. Large quantities of Göring's French champagne, Spanish rum, and cigarettes had vanished. One high-ranking occupation officer had even shipped Göring's bed, complete with linen, back to his home in Atlanta.

Of greater interest to Horn, as it surely would be to Mason Hammond, several items missing from the castle had a direct bearing on MFAA recovery and repatriation investigations. The most valuable missing treasure was the painting *Madonna with Child* by revered Flemish artist Hans Memling. Along with it had vanished Göring's Reichsmarshall dagger and jewel-encrusted sword. As the CIC documents revealed, the painting had been logged into evidence but disappeared into the private art collection of an American general. The dagger had been taken and sold by a GI for funds to buy a Texas chicken farm.

The theft of Göring's sword was equally scandalous. According to the documents, the saber had been seized and kept by a third officer who said he had found it by accident in Veldenstein Castle, where Frau Göring had been moved by the Americans on June 11, 1945. The officer confessed to having taken the sword, asserting that it was of no particular significance. Frau Göring, however, gave another story. She claimed the U.S. officer had deceived her into believing that her husband was to be released from prison the following day. In her elation, she had handed over Göring's best uniform, medals, and the sword so that her husband would have something special to wear on his triumphal return home.

Horn and Rosenthal didn't dwell further on the more unseemly aspects of the intelligence the records revealed. There were mistakes, theft, and negligence on both sides. Their more immediate task was to determine how much of the intelligence provided by Spacil was accurate.

Much of what the Oberführer told Captain Schlemmer in the Oklahoma POW camp and later confessed to CIC officers after his arrest made sense. Himmler and Kaltenbrunner had attempted to install a resistance movement based in Austria and appointed Spacil to administer and fund it. If the resistance movement failed to prevent the invasion of Germany, then its members were to infiltrate the occupation government and work to create a revolutionary movement whose ultimate aim was to establish a new Reich order.

It was clear from the records that the resistance movement was much less organized than RSHA's wartime activities and ultimately proved ineffective. However, it had been well funded. Spacil had accomplished the superhuman task of hiding about $25 million in Reich assets in a matter of mere days. The discovery of portions of this treasure in the very spots where Spacil led investigators convinced them that these funds existed and that the Oberführer was telling the truth.

At the same time, Spacil had provided the CIC with apparently false testimony. The most obvious was the Oberführer's detailing of Hitler's final days, which Spacil claimed to have learned at Fischhorn Castle while in radio communication with Hitler and others in the Nazi high command in the Führer's bunker.

In his earliest statements, Spacil claimed that Hitler had been wounded by shrapnel during an aboveground foray to view the invasion of Berlin by the Soviets. This conflicted with Rosenthal's G-2 intelligence. Spacil also claimed that Hitler had not killed himself in the bunker but had been captured by the Soviets and smuggled out of Berlin. Though a possibility, all evidence suggested otherwise. Further, Spacil contradicted himself in a subsequent interrogation when he said that Hitler had escaped Berlin by plane.

In all likelihood, Rosenthal conjectured, Spacil had fabricated the earlier stories to impress Captain Schlemmer at Camp Oklahoma with his importance and influence within the Nazi hierarchy. If Schlemmer was sufficiently impressed, he might then believe that Spacil had access to the gold and currency he claimed to have hidden. Later on, after Spacil was in CIC custody, he might simply have been playing games with interrogators to con them into believing their worst fears: that Hitler was still alive and being held by the Soviets. The Americans wouldn't dare hang the man whose help could lead them to the truth.

Then there was the matter of Hitler's personal effects, which included diaries, correspondence, and Eva Braun's jewelry. According to Spacil, Luftwaffe general Robert Ritter von Greim and test pilot

Hanna Reitsch were ordered to fly to Berlin on a special mission to retrieve these and other unidentified valuables before the Soviets overran the city. The pair were said to have made their harrowing escape at midnight on April 28, taking off in a single-engine monoplane from the wide boulevard in front of the Brandenburg Gate. Their plane was described as lifting into the skies above Berlin amid a hail of gunfire and exploding Soviet shells. Moreover, Spacil intimated that this hadn't been the only plane to escape Berlin in those final hours.

Spacil didn't identify who among the Nazi command had told him these things, but he did provide tantalizing information that the CIC had reason to believe. The Oberführer claimed that another plane carrying some of Hitler's personal possessions and other Reich treasures had crashed outside Munich. He gave the date, presumed time, and location. The pilots had both been killed in the crash and the cargo saved by members of the resistance. Intelligence officers were able to confirm that there had been a plane crash consistent with Spacil's testimony. Its presumed cargo, however, could not be confirmed.

Finally, and most important to Horn's investigation, there was the matter of the Crown Jewels. Spacil claimed knowledge of the treasures from a meeting of Himmler's RSHA bureau chiefs, which was held in Kaltenbrunner's Berlin office on April 1. During the meeting, Gestapo chief Müller notified Kaltenbrunner and RSHA senior staff that the art had been protected. On what Spacil presumed were orders from the Reichsführer, the five most important treasures of the Holy Roman Empire collection had been sealed inside specially built zinc caskets, removed from the Blacksmith's Alley bunker by a reliable Gestapo officer, couriered overland to Fischhorn Castle, placed in the back of Himmler's Mercedes limousine, and then driven into the southernmost section of the lake. Spacil claimed not to know who had been dispatched to Nürnberg to accomplish the task or who could provide further details.

Like Spacil's accounts of other hidden treasures, what he said might be true. The copper containers mentioned by museum director Lutze and the two city councilmen might have been placed inside larger zinc containers to protect them from the elements. Or

Himmler and his adjuncts, or Lutze himself, might have been mistaken about the containers' composition. However, the most important detail—the removal of the treasures in sealed containers—was consistent with the testimony of councilmen Fries and Schmeissner.

Based on what Spacil had told interrogators, the CIC had tried unsuccessfully to locate the Crown Jewels in Lake Zell. The CIC's failure to find Himmler's Mercedes did not prove that Spacil was lying. The lake's cool, placid waters were very deep, making a salvage operation difficult. It might take weeks or months to locate the car with the treasures, if they were inside.

Rosenthal felt that there were enough details in Spacil's account to convince him that the Crown Jewels had indeed come to rest in Lake Zell. "It's only a matter of time, and they'll show up," he said. "Along with Himmler's car and perhaps the Führer's diaries."

Horn still wasn't convinced. Besides the matter of the metal used to construct the containers, several things bothered him.

Least important but still worth considering was why the disposition of the treasures would be openly discussed in a meeting of the RSHA chiefs. If Himmler's motive was to keep the location a secret for a Nazi or neo-Nazi resistance movement, why had it been shared with men who Himmler, by this time in the war, could reasonably expect might one day be grilled by intelligence investigators or stand trial for war crimes? Far better, by Horn's reckoning, to give that information to a covert agent, someone who wouldn't appear on the Allied radar screen, just as Spacil hadn't shared the hidden locations of his gold deposits with fellow high-ranking officers.

There was also the question of actually sinking the Crown Jewels in the lake, a possibility that had nagged at Horn since Rosenthal first brought it to his attention. It was illogical that the treasure would have been sunk in the lake when gold and other Nazi valuables were hidden in easily accessible places, such as beneath the floorboards of a Tyrol lumber mill or under boulders in the Alps.

"How would Nazi operatives have recovered it?" he asked Rosenthal. "How could they be certain that the containers wouldn't leak and water damage the artifacts?"

Rosenthal played devil's advocate by suggesting that Himmler had the copper containers sealed into outer zinc caskets as a double layer of protection. "And besides," Rosenthal added, "the Crown Jewels aren't like the other treasures. They're only important once the resistance movement or a neo-Nazi Reich returns to power."

Rosenthal had a point. The Crown Jewels were not assets that would be traded for currency, used to bribe guards into releasing a POW, or used to purchase food and weapons on the black market. Their intrinsic value was to the man who would be king, the new emperor of the Reich. Such a leader, installed in office, could presumably order the entire lake to be drained or dispatch crews with diving gear to retrieve the Mercedes.

Horn still couldn't convince himself that the treasures were right where Rosenthal had said from the start. His immediate problem, however, was what to do about it. A team of Navy divers was already searching Lake Zell. Further, it would be highly unlikely that Horn, in the nine remaining days of his investigation, would be able to trace the movement of a still-unidentified Gestapo officer traveling from Nürnberg to Zell am See.

Horn decided to return to Nürnberg. The story the two city councilmen told made sense, to a point. No city official, he was certain, would actually have turned over a historic treasure such as the Crown Jewels to an officer whose rank was uncertain and whose name was unknown. Moreover, city officials in Germany were noted for their meticulous attention to bureaucratic detail. Even if Mayor Liebel had specifically asked them not to keep a record of what would be their last fateful rendezvous in the bunker, Fries and Schmeissner would have remembered the date of the transfer. What further turn in the story were they hiding? And whom were they shielding? Spacil himself? Or perhaps, as Troche had said, a clandestine Teutonic brotherhood specifically tasked with protecting Reich symbols of the past and also seeking to safeguard them for the future?

Regardless of what more the councilmen knew, everything Horn had learned to date—from his discussions with Troche, his brief but sickening visit to Himmler's crypt, and the CIC investigative reports—proved the importance of the Holy Roman Empire treasures to Hitler. He had to follow the only lead he had left. As long as Nazis or neo-Nazis still possessed some of these symbols of dynastic succession, the dark cloud of a Fourth Reich would loom.

"I've got an idea," he told Rosenthal. "I'm going to frighten the two Nürnberg councilmen into coming clean."

"How do you propose to do that?"

Horn said he had a plan, a gambit right out of Rosenthal's own chess playbook. He needed to go on the attack. All Felix would have to do was persuade Gutierrez to transfer Oberführer Spacil to Camp King in Frankfurt.

Rosenthal didn't think this was a realistic approach. Gutierrez would never let Horn interrogate Spacil without a direct order from USFET. He was off-limits to anyone but the CIC.

"I'm not going to interrogate him. Not yet, at least. I just want him brought to Frankfurt."

Rosenthal was still doubtful that Horn's request would be taken seriously. Even if the CIC was willing to move the prisoner, the request would have to come from someone with a higher rank than a lieutenant from the MFAA.

"Have Gutierrez take the matter up with Patton," Horn told him. "If the colonel complains too loudly, I'll have Mason Hammond ask what the CIC has done with the two million dollars in Nazi treasure he's dug up in Zell am See. And while you're at it, ask him about the Memling painting. Tell him that the MFAA wants it back. That ought to speed things along."

CHAPTER 21

CAMP KING

August 1–4, 1945

The success of Horn's plan relied on stealth, a flair for the dramatic, and the element of surprise. Thus, on the lieutenant's return to Nürnberg, he didn't tell Günter Troche the purpose of his visit. Essential as the curator was to his investigation, Horn couldn't risk Troche inadvertently tipping museum colleagues to the bold move he was about to make. Just because Mayor Liebel no longer held sway over his city council didn't mean that his loyal foot soldiers were out of contact with one another or that a modern-day order of Teutonic Knights—if indeed such a brotherhood existed—hadn't infiltrated the occupation administration from top to bottom. No civilians were above suspicion.

Putting his trust in Captain Thompson posed a similar risk. The MFAA liaison officer had stubbornly tried to stall his investigation before it began, and only under threat of losing his job on the occupation team had he accompanied the lieutenant to the Palace of Justice to interrogate Schmeissner and Fries. Despite Horn's misgivings, however, he needed the captain's support, or his plan didn't stand a chance.

Horn didn't find Thompson at his usual table in the officers' club bar or at occupation headquarters. To the lieutenant's pleasant surprise, the captain was in the field. Horn found him standing in front of Tiergärtner Tor, in the cobbled square just below Blacksmith's Alley, supervising a work crew putting a slate roof on the Albrecht Dürer house.

"Impressive," Horn said, complimenting the captain's decision to save the historic home. "Major Hammond will be delighted."

Thompson accepted Horn's praise as the lieutenant intended—not as a reminder of Horn's previous advice to repair the master artist's home but because it was the right thing to do. Much of the rest of Nürnberg was being shoveled into landfill, but this structure, a symbol of what was truly good and lasting about the old city, would inspire a new generation.

The captain was pleased to see him. He led Horn through the remains of the half-timbered building to a room in the rear, where another crew was cleaning plaster off architectural wall reliefs and building fixtures. Even if Thompson and his team couldn't restore the house to its prewar state, they had saved as much of the original as could be dug from the debris.

Thompson filled Horn in on other positive developments in the city as well. A crew working in a nearby castle had recovered the heavy framework that supported the Viet Stoss altar panels and gilded figurines stored in the Blacksmith's Alley bunker. The altar, now complete, was ready for repatriation to Poland. More significant in the larger scheme of MFAA interests, the new military governor, Colonel Charles Andrews, had promised to restructure the civilian administration and provide the dollars and military personnel to invigorate the demoralized occupation team. Thompson said that Horn could expect to see other positive changes around the city as well before the tribunals began.

The captain's unexpectedly upbeat disposition made it easier for Horn to explain the favor he wanted. The lieutenant took his opportunity as they stood back on the cobbled square out of earshot of the laborers.

"I would like you to arrest Schmeissner and Fries," Horn said.

It took a moment for Thompson to understand that Horn was perfectly serious. He wanted the captain to sign warrants that very morning.

Predictably, Thompson was appalled by the notion. The two councilmen had already confessed to their participation in the theft. The matter, as far as he was concerned, was over and done with. It was time to move on.

"The point is to scare Fries and Schmeissner into believing that Army intelligence knows more than they do, that the councilmen conspired at every step of the way to hide the Crown Jewels, and that since Himmler and Liebel are dead, Allied command intends to pin the rap on them."

Thompson's manner turned frosty. As Horn would later note to Rosenthal, he looked ready to hightail it back to the officers' club for a drink. That, or have the lieutenant report to the new military governor for a dressing-down.

The plan, Horn went on to explain, required that the councilmen be brought to the bunker for what they would think was a final inspection. In front of coworkers and staff—those who had labored to build and operate the facility—Horn would have them sign a prepared document attesting that five items of the Crown Jewels previously in the vault were missing. After the document was signed and as the councilmen were anticipating dismissal, Thompson would have them arrested and put into the very Palace of Justice jail cells that Schmeissner had been renovating. The next day, one or both would be transferred to a holding cell in Camp King, outside Frankfurt, far from anyone they knew in Nürnberg.

"I want them to believe that G-2 and the CIC have identified them as covert agents for Himmler," Horn said. "Once they are sufficiently frightened for their future, I'll have them taken from their cells for another round of questioning. At that point, I'm going to have one of the Reichsführer's personal henchmen marched past them."

That man, Horn explained, was Josef Spacil, whom Himmler and Kaltenbrunner had put in charge of funding and supervising the resistance movement.

"Shocked and frightened, one or both of them might admit further details of their participation in the larger conspiracy," Horn said. "At the very least, I'll know by the expressions on their faces if Spacil was the officer sent by Himmler to take the Crown Jewels."

Thompson said that he would be signing his own discharge papers if Horn's plan backfired. Andrews would have him on a plane back to Virginia faster than he could pack his things, and nothing the lieutenant or Hammond could say would make a difference.

Horn presented an alternative scenario. If there was a break-through in the investigation, Thompson, as the city's ranking MFAA officer, would be heralded as the one who cracked the case of the missing Crown Jewels. The captain wasn't to forget the hotel full of journalists in the city who would be avid to file a story.

Thompson warmed slightly to Horn's plan, though the idea of his own press interviews wasn't sufficient to win him over.

"You owe me this," Horn said. "I was right about Schmeiss-ner and Fries before, and I'm right about them now. They already admitted that they're more than just card-carrying Nazis. Liebel trusted these men with the keys to the vault containing the most valuable treasure in Germany. And so, I might add, did you."

Even Horn's browbeating wasn't enough to move Thompson. The captain finally capitulated, Horn suspected, because he was ac-tually tired of letting former Nazis set the agenda in the city that he and his team sought to govern—this, and perhaps because of the shifting tides brought on by the arrival of Colonel Andrews. Many of Thompson's colleagues were under investigation by the CID for failing to adequately de-Nazify Nürnberg's civilian workforce. The removal of Governor Fuller was only the first of many dismissals that would result, by the end of the year, in the replacement of virtually the entire occupation team.

In an attempt to save his career, Thompson, it seemed, had de-cided to leave the officers' club dugout, step up to the plate, and swing for a home run. Never mind the fallout that might be caused by the removal of Schmeissner and Fries from office or that the chief justice of the tribunals might temporarily have to share quarters with the secretarial pool. The only place for former Nazis in the Palace of Justice was in the dock.

Horn congratulated him for coming on board. It was now only a matter of filing paperwork and rounding up a few helpers, and they would be ready to put the plan into motion the next day.

Everything proceeded flawlessly.

The following morning, Schmeissner and Fries were not permit-ted access to their offices at the Palace of Justice. While they stood out front haggling with the MP at the gate, Horn and a full military escort arrived with orders from Thompson to take them to the bunker. As expected, they were furious at the surprise interruption of their work. Schmeissner complained the loudest, claiming that his contribution to the occupation effort came before everything else. He had responsibilities to the military government, he protested.

Horn feigned ignorance of Thompson's intentions. The lieutenant said only that he had orders to prepare a final inventory to be sent to Allied command in Frankfurt.

"One last visit," Horn assured them. "Likely, it's just a formality."

Fries was stoic. As Horn would later note in his report, the councilman pursed his thick lips and straightened himself, attempting to effect a military bearing, then looked to his colleague for direction. Schmeissner shrugged and remarked once again that the interruption of their work was an unacceptable inconvenience.

This was but the first of several surprises for the duo. Once inside the bunker, the councilmen were confronted by the witnesses whom Horn had previously interviewed. Among them were the bunker's chief administrative inspector, the collection administrator, and the two female clerks. This was another indicator that something important was taking place, even if the councilmen had no idea what it was.

Having the former staff gather in the vault was mere window dressing. The MFAA didn't need another inventory. The intention was to lead Fries and Schmeissner to believe that new information had been obtained and that Thompson was officially closing the case. Horn explained that he just wanted the principal officials previously connected to the bunker and its operations to verify what items were currently in the vault. In addition to this, each was asked to sign the loyalty oath to the occupation government. Fries and Schmeissner were the last to put their signatures on the document, claiming that it was unnecessary because they had sworn a similar oath to the previous military governor.

"I'm sure it's merely another formality," Horn told them. "Nothing to be concerned about."

That this was something more than just a procedural formality became evident after Schmeissner and Fries had finally affixed their signatures to the documents and were taken outside. Horn took possession of the vault keys and ordered the two men arrested.

Once again, the lieutenant feigned ignorance of Thompson's purpose. He didn't know the charges. The orders came down from Frankfurt. Surely the captain would explain. Perhaps it was only a mix-up.

Thompson was not present to reassure the now frightened councilmen that there was a mix-up. He didn't appear in the bunker that morning or in the Palace of Justice jail where Schmeissner and Fries were taken.

An entire day passed before Horn reappeared, this time to accompany Fries to Frankfurt.

Horn decided to concentrate on Fries first and leave Schmeissner behind in Nürnberg, based on the observation that Fries was the less stable, more sensitive, and perhaps more vulnerable of the pair. At their previous interrogation session and in their last trip to the bunker, Schmeissner had done most of the talking. Fries had either nodded his head in agreement or looked to his colleague for direction. If Fries were alone, without guidance, and fearful of a life sentence or worse for war crimes, he would be more inclined to give up what he knew.

"But why am I to go to Frankfurt?" the councilman protested as Horn led him out of the cell.

Horn was noncommittal, offering his sympathies as one German to another. He had orders to take the councilman to Camp King. That's all he knew. Surely Fries could understand that he, a mere lieutenant, was only following the instructions of his superior.

"It's likely just more paperwork," Horn said, trying not to sound too convincing. Documents would have to be signed. At command level. He was just doing what he had been told.

The councilman's stoic demeanor collapsed as he was put into handcuffs and led to a waiting jeep. He slumped in the backseat beside Horn for the four-hour drive.

Fries peppered Horn with more questions as they left Nürnberg and joined the procession of other military vehicles on the autobahn. How long would his confinement last? Why didn't the authorities give him the courtesy of calling his wife and three children? And, as Horn fully expected, why wasn't Schmeissner being brought to Frankfurt? Horn purposefully avoided any discussion of Schmeissner or the case. He instead made polite conversation about the state of

Germany's fall harvest, wondering aloud if there would be famine when the winter came on.

Horn's commentary was a subject much on the mind of all German nationals, foremost among them farmers who hadn't the fuel to operate heavy equipment in the fields. Even horses weren't available, as the Nazis had moved them to the Eastern Front, and the Soviets had kept them. The subtext of Horn's discourse was intended to unsettle the councilman. If Fries were arrested and sitting in a POW camp when the winter snows fell, he would be unable to care for his family.

Camp King was the perfect setting for the next act. A high-security facility with two rows of barbed wire around its perimeter, it still had the look and feel of a Nazi interrogation center. And as the already frightened councilman would soon discover, he would be in exalted if infamous company. Among its prisoners were Admiral Dönitz, Hitler's chosen successor; Hans Frank, the former Reich minister and governor-general of occupied Poland; Albert Kesselring, the supreme commander of the Nazi offensive in France and western Europe; and Air Marshall Göring. Here, too, were female inmates, including Hanna Reitsch, the test pilot who was the last-known flyer to visit Hitler's bunker and escape Berlin. Soon to join them, thanks to Rosenthal, was Oberführer Josef Spacil.

After passing through the main gates, Fries was taken to the prisoner enclosure, a large cement building with steel doors and barred windows. There, Horn turned the councilman over to guards who had been advised in advance to treat him as if he were a Nazi official soon to be tried for war crimes.

Fries, for the first time in his life, went though the elaborate procedure of being registered, fingerprinted, photographed, and stripped of all his possessions. Guards took his watch, fountain pen, pencils, and wallet. They probed his mouth for a hidden suicide capsule. Then they led him to a dismal solitary cell, fitted with a narrow cot and iron bars on the windows.

As a precaution, Horn left specific orders to keep Fries on suicide watch. There was no telling how the already unstable and petrified bureaucrat would react to his new surroundings. Horn didn't want a death on his hands and knew full well, after the incident with Kaltenbrunner's failed suicide attempt, how a minor oversight such as laces left in a pair of shoes could undo the effort to bring a prisoner to justice.

All the while Horn was with Fries, a CIC officer was driving Josef Spacil from a prison camp in Laufen, on the Austrian border. Arranging the transfer, at short notice, wasn't the hurdle he anticipated. As Spacil's presence in Camp King was for identification purposes and not for questioning, and as long as Spacil's handler, Robert Gutierrez, accompanied him, it was only a matter of logistics—a CIC favor to the G-2, brokered by the resourceful Rosenthal.

The plan was to put Fries and Spacil together the next morning, Friday, August 4. It would climax, Horn imagined, the moment the lieutenant, speaking German, would point to Spacil, accompanied by Gutierrez, and demand of Fries, "Is this the man to whom you turned over the Crown Jewels?"

If Fries was unable to identify Spacil, they would repeat the routine with Schmeissner. Horn hadn't yet decided how much further he was willing to press the matter, but as a last effort, he would question them individually, leading them to believe that they would be held liable for the crimes of former Mayor Liebel, as he was deceased and could no longer be prosecuted. Still, it was a long shot. Horn might get lucky; then again, he could be right back where he had started.

The next morning, just after sunrise, Fries was given a meager breakfast, which he barely touched, then was brought to the interrogation room and questioned by a G-2 captain about Himmler's plans for a Bavaria-based resistance movement. His interrogator had to convince Fries that Army intelligence knew he was a covert agent assigned to help overthrow the Allied occupation and lead a neo-Nazi resurgence. The officer didn't refer to the bunker and vault at all. That role was for Horn, who promptly appeared thirty minutes later, after Fries had been left alone for ten minutes to think over what had been said.

Horn entered the room with a pen and paper. He noted that Fries was even paler than he had been earlier and showed fatigue from the night spent in a solitary cell. After dismissing the captain, Horn told Fries that he had been asked to help the councilman prepare a formal statement that would be introduced at the upcoming tribunals in Nürnberg.

"The Crown Jewels are among a larger aggregate of valuables

and gold bars that Reichsführer Himmler ordered hidden and U.S. intelligence is in the process of recovering," Horn explained. The lieutenant went on to outline a scenario: gold bullion to finance the neo-Nazi insurgency and the Crown Jewels to provide symbols of the Fourth Reich.

After letting his words sink in, Horn opened the door he hoped Fries would step through. He allowed that the removal of the jewels from the bunker did not necessarily make Fries a criminal, since at the time, he was under Nazi jurisdiction and following the orders of Mayor Liebel.

"You were doing what you were told and knew nothing of the conspiracy to finance a neo-Nazi movement in Austria," he began. "If, however, you have withheld any knowledge of the location of the crown regalia, you will be guilty of conspiring with a subversive movement. The punishment for such action is death by hanging. All that is now being asked of you is to sign an affidavit confirming what you have previously said about the missing jewels."

Fries grew paler. But he understood what was being asked of him and the potential consequences should he lie under oath. Horn placed a sheet of paper in front of him and dictated, in English, what the councilman was to write: "I, Johann Wilhelm Konrad Fries, city councilor of Nürnberg, hereby swear . . ."

As Fries wrote, Horn noticed a strange graphological drama unfolding in front of him. The councilman's pen slowed at the word *swear.* There was a slight tremor in his hand as he started to write *by God Almighty.*

Already shaking at the word *God*, Fries found *Almighty* torturous to spell. His pen laboriously climbed up the *A*, made the peak of the *A*, and dropped down on the other side as though in exhaustion. The *l* that followed was worse. In the middle, he stopped.

The councilman's hesitation had nothing to do with writing in the English language. Horn knew in that instant that his instincts had been right. The councilman had held something back.

The lieutenant waited a few moments and then pressed Fries to continue writing. "I don't have all day."

Fries moved his pen aside and looked up. His face was damp with sweat. "If you should find the missing Crown Jewels, what will you do with them?" he croaked.

As calmly as possible, Horn told him that naturally, they would be restituted to their legal owner, the city of Nürnberg or Vienna. It was a decision for the Allied government and the German courts.

"In that case," he said, "I know where they are, and I will take you there."

Horn glanced at his watch. In another thirty seconds, Spacil would be brought into the room to spring a trap that was no longer needed and might, in fact, give Fries pause for concern or, worse still, make him change his mind.

Horn picked up the phone and told Gutierrez in the adjoining room that his help in the interrogation room would not be necessary. Then he turned to Fries and asked, "Where are the jewels?"

Himmler's men had not come to claim the treasures at all. This was only the story that Liebel had coached Fries and Schmeissner to tell the occupation army. Julius Lincke, on orders from Liebel, had packed the missing Crown Jewels into the copper containers. Fries and Schmeissner had then put them in inconspicuous duffel bags and taken them by bicycle to a second bunker. They were hidden, the councilman said, under an elementary school adjacent to Nürnberg's Pannier Plaza.

CHAPTER 22

THE CROWN JEWELS

August 5–6, 1945

Horn's hunt for the missing treasures was all but over. His investigation, however, was far from complete. The devil was in the details.

Konrad Fries claimed that he and his fellow city councilmen—on orders from Mayor Liebel—had removed the Crown Jewels from the bunker on March 31 to protect them from the invading U.S. Army and the inevitable occupation. He acted, he said, "for Mayor Liebel, for the city of Nürnberg, and for Germany."

The councilman's explanation could be true. Fries had done what he believed to be his patriotic duty, however confused or misguided his loyalties. Horn's challenge was to reconcile Fries's account with the larger and more complex conspiracy that unfolded the next day, April 1, in Berlin, when plans commenced to fund and mobilize a covert resistance movement aimed at creating a new Reich order in occupied Germany. Regardless of what lies, exaggerations, and disinformation Josef Spacil had shared with his CIC handlers, it was clear that the missing Crown Jewels had been safeguarded for a revitalized Nazi order, that senior RSHA staff knew that they had been packed into metal containers, and that they had been recently removed from the bunker.

Horn drew several conclusions. The security of the treasures doubtless concerned the senior RSHA bureau chiefs, and Kaltenbrunner or Himmler had taken steps to safeguard them. Further, Himmler or Kaltenbrunner, and possibly Müller and Spacil himself, must have had direct contact with Mayor Liebel or his Nürnberg councilmen. The question still facing Horn was why RSHA's senior staff were led to believe that the treasure had been sunk into Lake Zell and not removed to a new hiding place in Nürnberg.

Logic pointed to Troche's theory. Himmler didn't leave the task of protecting the treasure to his own officers—men who, if they didn't commit suicide first, would eventually be arrested or hunted down as war criminals. He entrusted the task to covert agents, quite possibly a modern-day Teutonic brotherhood under the direction of Liebel, whose hidden mission was to bring about the Fourth Reich. The infiltration by Liebel's former city councilmen of the highest levels of the city's civilian occupation team could be viewed as the first step to resurrect the Nazi regime in a new guise. The Crown Jewels would be revealed when a new leader was ready to assume the Reich throne.

Horn considered the possible complicity of the city councilmen in the larger, more complex Nazi plot as he accompanied Fries back to Nürnberg. He didn't discuss the subject with Fries for the same reason he hadn't confronted the councilman with Spacil. His most important task was to return the missing Crown Jewels to the vault treasury. If all went well and the treasures were found, Horn would return them safely to the vault the next day. Only after he accomplished this would he delve deeper into the motives of the principal players behind the theft. The councilmen would have to be grilled for exact details, as would Spacil and perhaps Kaltenbrunner himself.

When they arrived back in Nürnberg, Horn returned Fries to a jail cell in the Palace of Justice, checked in on Schmeissner in a nearby cell, then reconnected with Thompson at his occupation headquarters office.

The captain was thrilled with Horn's report. In no time, he found the Pannier bomb shelter on his MFAA map. The facility, he said, dwarfed the Blacksmith's Alley bunker and had upward of fifty rooms, corridors, passages, and stairwells that had sheltered several thousand left homeless after the invasion. It had originally been an emergency facility for elementary schoolchildren, but after the school was closed and most of the city's youth evacuated to the countryside, it had been expanded and reengineered as a shelter for city residents during bombing raids and to house a Nazi communications hub and emergency medical treatment center.

The facility, accessed from the ground floor of the school, had been cleared of refugees and homeless only the month before. As he had with the other underground shelters, Thompson ordered it boarded up and locked. After listening to Horn, the captain dispatched military police to guard the entrance and an additional unit to patrol the entire area until the Crown Jewels were recovered.

Early the next morning, Horn returned to the Palace of Justice and took Fries under military escort to the Pannier Plaza. The site was just east of Blacksmith's Alley. The treasures for which he had crisscrossed Germany had apparently been hidden less than a thousand yards from where his investigation had begun.

Thompson, accompanied by two stonemasons, a metallurgist, and military police carrying lanterns, met Horn and Fries in front of the roofless remains of the schoolhouse. A few minutes later, the team walked though the school's deserted hallways until they came to a wide corridor. The entrance to the subterranean shelter was secured by a sheet of plywood. Guards easily removed the plywood to expose a flight of cement steps that descended into darkness.

The stench of urine and excrement assailed them from below. This wasn't the clean, well-lit, and air-conditioned former beer cellar up the street but a dank and claustrophobic catacomb where thousands of residents had stood or squatted shoulder to shoulder while their homes burned overhead.

Fries led them down several flights of stairs, past a large rectangular room with a switchboard and radio transmitter, and then down another flight of steps to a labyrinth of narrow tunnels that wound under the adjacent plaza. The swinging lanterns, casting shadows on the cement walls, briefly illuminated pipes and electrical lines. In one of the rooms stood rows of sinks and shower stalls. Another contained coal bins and a furnace.

The chamber that Fries led them into next had served as a classroom. There was a large slate blackboard at one end of the cement cubicle and rows of wooden benches. A child's mildew-covered spelling book lay open on the floor; scattered about were torn loose-leaf pages and assorted empty food tins, soiled clothing, blankets, empty liquor bottles, and other debris from those who had sought shelter here.

They walked on through the room to an alcove. "Here," Fries said, pointing to a spot near the ceiling.

Masons had plastered over the walls. The combination of mold from the moisture seeping through the sandstone and soot from lantern smoke had well camouflaged the hiding place. There was no way to know from looking at it that a niche had ever been cut into the wall.

Thompson's laborers went to work cutting away a four-foot-by-four-foot section of the wall and ceiling. Removing the plaster was easy. The two feet of cement behind it required pickaxes. Three and a half sweaty hours later, the team reached the hollowed-out space that contained the treasure. Then it was only a matter of reaching in by hand to clear away loose fill and chunks of sandstone to reveal two stacked pairs of copper containers.

Horn pulled the containers from the niche and set them on the floor. The metallurgist lit his blowtorch to break their seals. The work took hardly any time, and the cases were opened. Inside the containers, wrapped in spun glass and in perfect condition, were the missing items from the Holy Roman Empire collection: orb, scepter, crown, imperial sword, and ceremonial sword. The gleaming treasure of the ancient soldier-kings had now changed hands once again.

An hour later, Horn and Thompson, accompanied by the guards, returned the Crown Jewels to the Blacksmith's Alley vault. The two American officers and Fries signed a document verifying their placement back in the vault.

There was no celebration. Horn was exhausted from his two-and-a-half-week investigation, and Thompson, perhaps reluctant to take credit for an investigation in which he had only marginally participated, offered Horn little more than a handshake and a con-gratulatory toast at the officers' club.

Even if Horn desired to indulge in a well-deserved celebra-tion, the return of the Crown Jewels coincided with the far more monumental news that greeted the officers the next day. Nürnberg's teletype machines were spewing out reports that an Allied plane had dropped an atom bomb on Hiroshima. "Little Boy," as the 9,700-pound experimental weapon was called, detonated above a Japanese parade field. As the officers and the rest of the world would soon learn, 60 percent of Hiroshima was destroyed and some seventy thousand residents obliterated in a mere five seconds.

The overloaded telephone and telegraph lines delayed Horn's call to Mason Hammond with his own news until the next day.

The major was impressed with Horn's work. He hadn't actually believed that the lieutenant would succeed in his mission. "I'll be putting you in for a promotion," Hammond promised.

Horn thanked the major for having given him the opportunity to play a part in the greater MFAA recovery mission and then expanded on the various steps he had taken to secure the return of the treasure. He pointed out the many unanswered questions relating to Himmler's decision to move the Crown Jewels and what must have been a covert resistance operation to protect the Reich symbols for future generations. He all but named the members of what might be a Teutonic brotherhood that had come up in the course of his investigation and expressed his belief that Hitler himself was involved in the decision to safeguard the holy relics for a neo-Nazi resurgence.

At the conclusion of Horn's monologue, he shared with Hammond what had been on his mind since he had written his report in Belgium. He didn't express himself in quite the same way as he had in his Camp Namur report, before Troche showed him the blueprints for the Führer's intended Nürnberg renovations, or after he had seen the Nazi crypt in Himmler's castle—before he had come to understand fully the Third Reich as a feudal monarchy and Hitler as its titular Holy Roman Emperor.

"Hitler intended to crown himself the next Holy Roman Emperor," Horn told Hammond. "It was part of the Führer's vision for Germany and the world. His master plan, if you will. If he couldn't accomplish this goal for himself, he wanted the imperial insignia for his successor."

There was a long and uncomfortable silence on the other end of the line. When Hammond finally spoke, it wasn't to confirm or deny the lieutenant's conclusion. He said only that there were additional files at USFET headquarters, above and beyond those kept by the G-2 or the CIC, which he wanted to share with Horn. It was nothing urgent, but they were something he wanted the lieutenant to read before writing his final report.

"Come by the office, and we will talk about it, and where we'll go from here," Hammond told him.

Horn arranged to meet Hammond in Frankfurt. The lieutenant also asked for a short personal leave, five or six days, before reporting for duty. He didn't specifically reveal his itinerary.

Hammond told him to take his time, reminding him that his travel permit, fuel vouchers, and USFET orders were good for the rest of the month. "Just be careful I don't have to negotiate your release from the Russians," he said.

The major, remembering that Horn's family had been split between occupation zones, had guessed the lieutenant's intentions. He would be exceeding his authority to permit Horn to travel outside U.S.-occupied territory. However, the jeep, fuel vouchers, and driver were available to him for the rest of the month. How he chose to use them was not Hammond's concern.

After bidding Thompson farewell and paying Günter Troche a last visit, Horn loaded up the jeep. Before setting off, he checked to see that the liquor, dry goods, and additional supplies were still in his footlocker. Everything was in its proper place, as Dollar had promised it would be. Satisfied, Horn said they could leave. They would be traveling north toward Bayreuth.

"I've an errand to run," Horn told him, but wouldn't elaborate further. The less his driver knew, the less likely he would be called to task for participating in an unauthorized trip into the Soviet zone.

Dollar didn't ask for more details until they reached the outskirts of Bayreuth and Horn made it clear that he would be leaving Dollar at a hotel for the night and would himself be driving the jeep to his next destination. Dollar, however, was reluctant to give up the keys without an explanation.

"It'll just be for the night," Horn told him. "I'll pick you up tomorrow morning."

As Horn would later describe, Dollar refused to hand over the jeep's keys. The vehicle, he reminded Horn, was temperamental. It had served them well so far, but there was no telling what might happen if he, and not Dollar, was behind the wheel.

Horn was adamant about not involving his driver in the next leg of his journey. By way of an explanation, the lieutenant listed the crimes he intended to commit over the next twenty-four hours. He would be crossing into Soviet territory without authorization from either the Americans or the Russians. He would also technically be stealing the jeep, as he hadn't been authorized to drive it into foreign territory. The footlocker of black-market contraband, chained to the jeep's spare tire, was another breach of military rules, not to mention fraternization with German nationals.

The lieutenant went on to list several other lesser infractions before revealing the more serious crime, which could potentially land him in a Soviet labor camp or at the very least get him court-martialed. "I intend to sneak into the Soviet zone, find my mother and my half-sister, and somehow smuggle them into American-occupied Heidelberg."

"Is that all?" Dollar said, grinning. He drew the jeep's key out of his pocket and dangled it provocatively in front of Horn. He was coming along as the driver, whether the lieutenant wanted him or not.

37

Top: Heinrich Himmler's triangular-shaped castle, in Wewelsburg, in the district of Büren, 1944, where top SS officers received spiritual training in Nazi mysticism and cult practice. The North Tower (still under construction) is to the left, and directly opposite it, in the foreground on the right, are the Reichsführer's personal chambers. The Führer's chambers are in the tower to the far right. Bottom: scale model for the castle expansion showing spear-shaped design, dormitories, study and meditation rooms, library and ceremonial centers. Note that the tip of the spear is the North Tower.

38

Top: entrance gate of Wewelsburg Castle showing Germanic runes. Bottom: castle courtyard showing entrance to the North Tower, once the chapel of the electors of the Holy Roman Empire. Under Himmler, this is alleged to have been where the Nazi high command intended to perform cult and ritual practices.

Left: Nazi crypt under the Wewelsburg North Tower showing the pagan Black Sun design on ceiling, pedestals on the floor for urns where ashes of SS heroes were to be interred, and in the center of the room, a basin where the Nazis' "eternal flame" was to burn. Bottom: Major Sydney Markham with liberated Jehovah's Witness inmates standing in front of the Niederhagen Concentration Camp, which was to provide the work force Himmler intended to use to build his expanded Nazi study and ritual center in Wewelsburg.

44

Top: entrance to the Bernterode
Mine, outside of Nordhausen,
where a Nazi crypt containing
four coffins was discovered.
Right: an empty coffin,
intended for Hitler, was found
in a partitioned bay inside the
Nazi crypt. Bottom: soldiers
loading the casket of Emperor
Frederick the Great for removal
to Marburg, Germany.

Left: SS Oberführer Joseph Spacil,
Himmler's paymaster, believed
to have played a key role in the
disappearance of the Crown
Jewels, was assigned to hide $25
million in plundered gold and
other valuables for a future Fourth
Reich. Bottom: Fischhorn Castle
and the shores around Lake Zell,
in Austria, became the destination
of choice for Air Marshal
Hermann Göring and other Nazis
fleeing the Allied armies.

On April 25, 1946, U.S. soldiers loaded the Viet Stoss Altar and twenty-seven other crates of looted artworks into former foreign minister Joachim von Ribbentrop's private railcar for return from Nürnberg to Cracow, Poland.

On General Eisenhower's orders, the entire collection of Holy Roman Empire treasure was returned to Vienna on January 5, 1946. Left: the Crown Jewels are examined after their arrival in Austria by Monuments, Fine Arts and Archives officers—left to right: Colonel Theo Paul, Andrew Ritchie, Commander Perry B. Cott, and Major Ernest T. DeWald. Bottom: U.S. occupation authorities present the Crown Jewels to the Austrian prime minister.

51

Top: Felix Rosenthal, after his return home to Berkeley, California, in 1946, became a highly respected architect, bibliophile, and U.C. Berkeley lecturer before his retirement in 1983. Right: Walter Horn, photographed on Skellig Michael, off the coast of Ireland, after his retirement from U.C. Berkeley in 1979. Before his death in 1995, at age 87, he traveled to Vienna, Austria, to view the collection of Holy Roman Empire treasures that he had recovered for the Allies, preventing their becoming a symbol for a Fourth Reich.

CHAPTER 23

THE FAUSTIAN BARGAIN

August 7–8, 1945

Leica cameras were the most desirable luxury item still produced in postwar Germany. The camera bodies were made in the American Zone, the lenses in the Soviet, and the shutters in the French. The challenge for manufacturers was overcoming the draconian regulations that prevented parts from being shipped from one occupation zone to another. Interzone passes were virtually unavailable. And yet Leica cameras were produced by the thousands and were being sold in black markets from Berlin to Munich.

Horn would try to enter the Soviet Zone the same way the truck drivers traversed the borders: with a bribe. To increase the likelihood of success, he chose a sufficiently remote checkpoint to avoid drawing attention to himself and Dollar, cross when he could reasonably expect the least traffic, and give the guards an adequate but not exorbitant bribe. Offering too little would invite negotiation and possible delay. Too much would raise suspicions about the purpose of his visit.

After studying his map, Horn selected a suitably isolated border crossing just west of Jena, a rural farming community with no large military or industrial installations. Farmers hauling cheese, not convoys of soldiers, plied its unpaved roads. Rationing the goods in his footlocker—more valuable than cash—was the difficult decision.

Entering the Soviet Zone with his driver, Horn reasoned, would not be nearly as costly as leaving with two additional passengers—his mother, Mathilde, and his half-sister, Friedl. Two bottles of whiskey, a few large tins of sardines, and an assortment of nylon stockings would surely be adequate compensation. These he put into a rucksack, which he could easily hand off to the guards, lessening the risk of their rooting about in the footlocker and finding the larger cache he would surely need on his return trip.

They left the autobahn just after sunset when military traffic had dwindled and pedestrians were few. Thanks to the curfew in place, German nationals were not permitted out of their homes after 6:00 P.M. There would be no lineup at the checkpoint, and if all went well, they would recross the border well after midnight, when there would be even less risk of being detained and possibly arrested.

For the first few miles, they drove east on a dirt road between pastures and isolated farmhouses. There was no evidence of abandoned half-tracks, troop transports, or other war debris. If fighting had ever taken place here, the Soviets had already hauled away what remained for scrap metal, or the villagers had cannibalized the parts for farm equipment.

Eventually, the terrain became rockier, and the pastures gave way to neatly terraced vineyards. The Soviet border station lay just ahead, well positioned between a stand of trees on one side and an old rock wall on the other. As Horn had anticipated, the transit point was nothing more than a makeshift length of timber blocking the road and manned by two guards with lanterns. Their quarters were a tattered tent in the adjacent grove of trees.

Dollar slowed the jeep and left the engine idling when they came to the roadblock. Surprised by the appearance of the two uniformed American soldiers on the otherwise deserted road, one of the guards, whose sole identification was a red star on his cap, raised his rifle to waist level. It was less an aggressive move than a gesture to stop Horn and his driver from advancing. His counterpart emerged from the tent, approached the jeep, and shone the lantern into their faces.

Horn knew a word or two of Russian but didn't need them. A

mere smile, a tilt of the head, an exaggerated show of affection from one Allied soldier to another, was all it took to establish his friendly intentions. No, they weren't lost or on official business, he communicated in body language.

Then, before the guard could ask for his papers, Horn spoke in English, marshaling his finest Camp Ritchie "Yankee-speak," as Rosenthal called it when Horn didn't wish to reveal his German accent. "Just out for a good time," he said.

Horn then looked down at the rucksack at his ankles and with slow deliberation, avoiding any appearance of reaching for a weapon, handed it over to the guard.

"For my Russian comrades," he said with fanfare commensurate with its value.

The guard took it without comment, looked inside, and then said something to his fellow Russian with the rifle.

The two guards examined the booty and without so much as a second thought pulled the barrier from across the road and waved them through.

Dollar eased the jeep ahead, and they were on their way again, soon passing through Jena, a town of bombed-out medieval homes and narrow one-way streets. They could have been anywhere in occupied Germany but for the Red Army flags hanging from the clock tower. A troop of male and female soldiers loitered in front of what remained of an old inn. They paid not the slightest attention as Dollar drove past, maneuvering the jeep between lamp-lit half-timbered homes and a stable.

Eleven years had passed since Horn had seen his half-sister at their father's funeral in Heidelberg and even longer since he had visited her home on the outskirts of Jena. The eldest of the family, Friedl was the first of his father's children to obtain a degree and make her way in the world. The last he had heard, she taught algebra and worked part-time as a bookkeeper.

He found her two-story, weatherworn, wood-frame house with surprisingly little difficulty. A shutter or two were not quite square with the dormers, and the hedge out front was overgrown. No matter. A wheelbarrow full of manure in an adjacent garden was a sure indication that the house was still occupied. Light from the vestibule window suggested someone was home.

The only question now was whether Friedl and his mother still lived there. His half-sister might have sold the house, abandoned the property, or been evicted to make room for Soviet soldiers.

There was no point in dawdling. Dollar parked behind the house to avoid detection from the street, while Horn walked to the porch and peered through the windows. Seeing no one, he rapped quietly on the front door.

Moments later, a woman peeked out from a side window. Horn couldn't see her face clearly enough to confirm her identity, and he had no way of knowing how well she could see him. She had heard his knock or, more likely, already been alerted to someone's presence on the property by the sound of the jeep parking around back.

He couldn't blame her for being wary. Only the Russians had fuel for motor vehicles, and a strictly enforced curfew prevented casual visits from neighbors.

"It's Walter," Horn said quietly.

A moment later, Friedl opened the door. She didn't speak at first but stood still in the doorway, looking him up and down for what seemed like ages.

She wasn't ever what one would call a handsome woman, more Bavarian than the rest of his family, with large round shoulders and wide, rolling hips, and the intervening years hadn't been kind to her. Her strawberry-blond hair had turned gray, her rosy cheeks had gone pale, and her lips, once full and rich, were now chapped and colorless. Her clear blue eyes, however, were the same, and they bore down on Horn as if he were a schoolboy requiring a scolding.

Then, still without addressing him, and characteristic of her cool and unemotional disposition, she abruptly turned and walked to the rear of the foyer to the stairs leading to the second floor. "Mathilde," she called out. "There's someone here to see you."

A moment later, his mother carefully navigated her way down the steps. She didn't hesitate to greet him, the way Friedl had. She instantly quickened her pace when she saw him and then enveloped him in her arms.

Pressing her head to his shoulder, she must have sensed his relief in knowing she was alive and well, as he sensed hers.

Only after they had separated, after Friedl, too, hugged him and they stood together at the foot of the steps, did he redirect his attention to his mother with a more searching eye, looking for telltale signs of hardship and malnourishment.

Remarkably, he found none. A petite woman, with long white hair wrapped in a bun and a Prussian's sharp nose and delicate tapered fingers, she had aged gracefully. It had been a decade since he had last seen her seated in his father's study writing poetry, but she still had a quiet dignity and a gentle bearing.

"An officer, no less," his mother said in German, beaming with pride. "Don't you look sharp."

Horn had put on his dress uniform, not to impress his family but to look important at border crossings.

From behind them came another, Private Dollar, who had entered carrying an armful of PX cans and bottles of schnapps and introduced himself as the other half of the rescue.

Friedl straightened Dollar's perennially crooked tie, then told him, in broken English, to stand up straight in the presence of a woman. She hadn't changed, despite the war.

They repaired to the dining room and talked for the better part of an hour before Horn revealed why he had come. "You'll be far better off in Heidelberg, in the American Zone, where I can protect you."

At first, both Friedl and his mother protested. They hadn't suffered under the occupation, and although the soldiers stationed in Jena had gone on a monthlong looting and raping spree, at times spilling out into the rural countryside, conditions had now improved and showed no signs of deteriorating.

But Horn spelled out the hard facts. "There's no telling what the Russians will do after the fall crops are harvested, winter sets in, and their families back home are starving. After they've taken the food, they'll cut down the trees, and then they'll take the furniture."

Friedl didn't argue. She said only that she wasn't leaving regardless of what happened. Little more could be done to her that she hadn't already experienced. The conviction in her voice told Horn that she had suffered in ways she was unwilling to describe. Her home and her friends were all that now mattered to her. Mathilde, however, would clearly be better off with the rest of the family.

Mathilde consented to go. She had a son and another daughter in Heidelberg, in addition to Walter, who was well positioned to look after them in the American Zone. Choosing what possessions she would bring and what to leave behind was an issue. "Not that I have much left besides memories of better times," she said, hinting obliquely at the hardships she had endured.

She wanted to bring her books. Dollar loaded a few volumes under the jeep's seats, but taking anything more than these, a few dresses, her collection of knitting needles, jewelry, and a photo album was out of the question.

They were ready to leave by midnight, when they would be unlikely to encounter a senior Russian occupation officer at the border. As an afterthought, Horn asked Friedl for a blanket to cover his mother. Mathilde could scrunch down behind the front seats, and with luck, the guards might not even know she was with them. And even if they did, it wasn't likely they would find the smuggling of an elderly woman to be an infraction that merited the attention of the high command. She and Friedl together might pose a problem but not Mathilde alone.

The drive back to the border was without incident. More than that, it was a release of tension in a way that coming hadn't been, when he wasn't sure he would find his mother and, if he did, that she would be in any shape to travel. Mathilde was safe. That's what mattered.

The lieutenant and Dollar encountered the same pair of crossing guards as before. This time, Horn feigned no comradely show of brotherhood with fellow Allied soldiers. He merely stepped to the back of the jeep, opened his footlocker, and let the soldiers take what they would, which was everything they had left. Mathilde, hidden in the back and covered with a blanket, might have slept through the event. Horn later swore to Rosenthal that he had actually heard her snore, but in all likelihood, it was his own rattled nerves when one of the guards shone his lantern across the back of the jeep, smirked at what obviously was a person hidden under the blanket, then proceeded to the unclaimed treasures in the footlocker.

By sunrise, they were driving through a countryside of orchards, pastures, and plowed fields dotted with picturesque stone villages and graceful churches on the route into Heidelberg. Mathilde sat upright in the back, wrapped in the blanket and clutching to her bosom her collection of jewelry—really nothing more than baubles

Horn's father had bought on a trip to Rotterdam but of much sentimental value to her.

They crossed into Heidelberg on a makeshift steel trestle over the Neckar River. The city had survived the war virtually unscathed. Only the old stone bridge, a marvel of Renaissance craftsmanship, surmounted at one end by a bronze monkey, had been blown up. Fleeing German troops had demolished it in an effort to slow the outright road race between competing Allied armies to reach Berlin first. Heidelberg wasn't a military objective, as it was neither an industrial center nor a transport hub. Its university—the oldest in the nation—and the scholars who walked the old bridge, stopping to rub the monkey's nose for good luck on their way to exams, distinguished the city.

Horn mourned the bridge's loss for the memories it evoked. It had been just upriver, on a bitterly cold winter morning, when the Neckar looked frozen solid and he sought to take a shortcut to school, that he had once plunged through the ice and been swept away. A pretty young girl—a Jew—standing at the foot of the bridge had seen it happen. She had raced to his aid, kicked a hole in the ice, and rescued him from death. Horn wondered what had become of his pretty angel, and also of his violin, still clutched in his hand when she pulled him onto the bank and wrapped her coat around him.

The flood of memories increased the nearer he came to his family's modest redbrick house on the hill across from Heidelberg Castle. It wasn't the house where he had been born or the home of his early childhood, which was in a tiny village a few miles upriver. But he had lived in Heidelberg with his Aunt Clara and Uncle Rudolf through his high-school and college years. It was here also, after his father had retired from the pulpit, that he had been reunited with his parents just before his father's death.

No one was yet awake when they pulled up in front of the house. As was the family's tradition, the front door was unlocked, a nod to his father's years in the parsonage, when their home was open to anyone in the community who needed help or comfort.

Horn assisted his mother with her things while Dollar made himself at home in the kitchen with a tin of coffee and a box of saltines. Not much of a celebration for the weary travelers, but it would do.

They were seated around the dining-room table, with Dollar

toasting their triumphal return to American territory, when Rudolf, Walter's older brother, unshaven, unkempt, and dressed in a bathrobe, appeared before them.

As pleased and surprised as Rudolf was to see his mother, whom he greeted with affection, his response to his brother was subdued, more formal. "It's you," Horn remembered him saying, less as a statement of fact than a question. "I never thought I'd see you back in Germany. In uniform, no less."

Horn smiled at him, trying not to spoil the moment for his mother, who delighted in her family, reunited after more than a decade apart.

His relationship with Rudolf had always been difficult, a Jacob and Esau rivalry rather than affectionate brotherhood. In their childhood, they had released tensions with a fistfight or combative words, but as they had matured and gone their separate ways, words left unsaid and actions not taken mattered the most.

Their differences wouldn't be resolved that morning. After years of successfully competing for their mother's and father's affections, for academic and athletic accolades, and for the attention of Heidelberg's female student population, Rudolf was now saddled with an onerous and debilitating burden. A card-carrying Nazi, he had lost his professorship at the university, along with any prospects for employment in the near future. As a German male, he had the added shame and humiliation of contributing to a war that devastated the nation and brought hardship, famine, and death to defenseless women and children. Walter, on the other hand, had returned home the victorious hero, the savior of their mother, the one woman in their lives who mattered the most.

Horn wanted to embrace his brother. Either that or pick a fight. Anything that would erase the lingering suspicion that Rudolf had actively aided and abetted Himmler's corps of scholar-soldiers. To what degree had his brother struck a Faustian bargain?

Heidelberg University, their alma mater, where Rudolf had been a full professor, was the first university in Germany to expel all of its Jewish professors and students. His brother had been on the faculty when the Hitler Youth took over the university's gymnasium, when books were burned in front of the library, and when a mob of Nazi Party terrorists set fire to the city's two synagogues.

How far had he gone to compromise his integrity and the trust of his students? Did he lift a hand to try to stop his Jewish students from being deported to the concentration camps? How long, and under what circumstances, did he continue his research at Externsteine? Had he replaced their father's and grandfather's Lutheran Bible with the one the Nazis used to champion the Aryan Jesus?

These and many other questions were boiling up within him, but before he could ask them, his younger sister Elsbeth appeared in the dining room.

A bright and cheerful young woman, with their mother's good looks and their father's optimism, she had more reason than anyone in the room to bemoan the tragedy of the war and how it had divided the family. Her husband, Erich Maschke, the former chancellor of the University of Leipzig, had been sent to a Soviet labor camp in the Ural Mountains. She hadn't had news of him in more than four months.

The family, now reunited but for Friedl, spent the rest of the day reminiscing about the more distant past. There were innumerable stories of how the children, as young teens, thought they had outwitted their father by sneaking out of the house to meet schoolmates in one of Heidelberg's many beer halls, where they would invariably encounter a parishioner from the church and pay the penalty upon their return. Then there were the many trips to the Roman ruins outside Heidelberg, where their father, a scholar of Tacitus, entertained them with the stories that inspired them to pursue academic careers.

Horn's intelligence-gathering activities, his promotion to the MFAA, and the subject of the Crown Jewels never came up. The closest any of them came to talking about the Nazis and the rise to war was Elsbeth's reminding him of something he had completely forgotten: the day he had burst into the family study while his father was writing his weekly sermon. No one but Elsbeth dared disturb their father on such an occasion.

"You had just finished reading *Mein Kampf*," Elsbeth said. "You were angry as all hell that none of the rest of us would listen to what you had to say."

Horn thanked her for remembering. It was as close to a confession of culpability and regret for what had happened as he would receive.

"Are you going to stay in Germany?" she asked. "The university is about to reopen. They're desperate for professors. You could move back home."

The University of Heidelberg's stately, oak-paneled classrooms, with their stadium seating, still fascinated him. It had been his childhood dream and his father's desire that he would teach there someday.

"I don't know," he demurred, trying to sound noncommittal, so as not to offend his family or denigrate what had once been among the finest schools in Europe.

The truth of the matter was that he had decided, only that morning, while sitting with his family, that he wouldn't remain in Germany once his tour of duty was over. He wouldn't help his friend Felix Rosenthal in the book business or become a professor at Heidelberg University. Despite the tirade he had launched in his father's study after reading *Mein Kampf* and his demands that the family discuss its contents, his father and his siblings hadn't sat down and actually read the book. Neither had his university classmates or his professors. It was the most popular unread book in the nation. He couldn't now imagine setting foot in a German classroom without being reminded of that fact, any more than he could look into the eyes of his brother for very long without thinking of runes on Himmler's teacups.

He had another dream now. It involved a small house—a cottage, really—overlooking the Golden Gate Bridge and students who looked to the future unburdened by bitterness and regret. The America he knew, the country he had come to love, was like a steaming locomotive about to leave the station. He wanted to be onboard.

CHAPTER 24

THE FOURTH REICH

August 9–14, 1945

Horn spent the next six days pretending that the war had never happened. He hiked with his brother and sister to the old Roman ruins, camped overnight at his favorite fishing spot, passed a pleasant afternoon eyeing a pretty art student in the Heidelberg University library, and accompanied his mother to put flowers on his father's grave. He might have stayed longer, but he had an imposing list of things to do before he could submit his written report to Mason Hammond. Josef Spacil needed to be interrogated and, if possible, RSHA chief Ernst Kaltenbrunner. He also wanted to question city councilmen Schmeissner and Fries, as well as Julius Lincke, if he could track him down. Allied intelligence, it seemed, hadn't actually gone looking for him.

Refreshed, ready to tackle what might come, he and Dollar rose early on the morning of August 14, ate breakfast, then drove north to Frankfurt. An hour later, in the USFET parking lot, he thanked Dollar for his help and good company over the last three and a half weeks. USFET's motor pool was notorious for playing musical chairs with their jeeps and drivers. He and Horn might not be paired again.

"I'll see you later, Professor," Dollar said. "Maybe at Berkeley."

"Sure thing, kid," Horn said. "But don't expect me to cut you any slack."

Dollar saluted and said he would look after Horn's empty footlocker and other belongings until after the lieutenant had spoken to Hammond.

Horn presented his identification at the front desk and was escorted to the third floor. To his surprise, everyone he met seemed to know who he was, from the MP at the door to the MFAA secretary at the front desk to several monuments men in Hammond's outer office. They greeted him as a celebrity.

The way Horn remembered it, one of the MFAA officers offered to show him around his museum—the Met in New York—"when all this Nazi business is over." Another invited him for lunch in the officers' club, where they could talk about the art history program at Princeton. A third thought there might be a place for Horn at the University of Pennsylvania when he returned stateside.

For Horn, it was like the old days in Italy, at Bernard Berenson's weekly salons. The unexpected attention shown to him made his head spin, and this was before he had even entered Hammond's inner office.

The news of Horn's successful recovery of the missing Holy Roman Empire Crown Jewels was everywhere, Hammond said, handing the lieutenant a press release and a clipping from *Stars and Stripes,* the newspaper of record for the soldiers in the field. As Horn quickly saw, Colonel Charles Andrews, Nürnberg's new military governor, had alerted journalists to the story the day after Horn left the city, hailing the return of the treasure as a major American victory and a lasting testament to the good that his occupation team was doing in Nürnberg.

Horn surmised from reading the article and the press release that Andrews had invited the world press, already in Nürnberg to cover the war-crimes tribunals, to tour the Blacksmith's Alley facility and look into the vault. Reporters were shown the entire Holy Roman Empire collection while Thompson detailed its storied history and the investigative work that had led to the recovery of the five most precious treasures. Not once did Horn's name appear in the article or the press release. Nor was any mention made of why Hitler had coveted the treasures and sought to hide them from the occupiers.

Hammond told him that he shouldn't feel slighted by not having his name included in the story. Nürnberg's military government needed to polish its reputation. However, at command headquarters, Hammond had seen to it that the people who mattered knew that Horn was the MFAA officer who had recovered the Crown Jewels.

The major led Horn to a seat in front of his desk. Always the diplomat, he explained that Horn and others like him would be the unsung heroes of the war, which was how it should be. The Crown Jewels had survived centuries of European conflict and destruction before the MFAA stepped onstage, and not by accident. It was because dedicated men like the lieutenant had seen to it that they were preserved. By this, Hammond didn't mean the Nazis. He was referring to monks, museum archivists, and scholars who had come before him and, God willing, would follow in his footsteps.

Horn was commended for doing a spectacular job. He had completed his mission with days to spare.

Hammond then presented Horn with a letter and encouraged him to open it. Inside was a citation from Eisenhower. He was being promoted to captain.

Horn was euphoric, not only for the distinction that came with the higher rank but also for the new pay grade and the help he would be able to give his family. This was indeed a banner month. He couldn't wait to tell Felix and claim the Dietrich photos.

The major didn't give Horn much time to bask in his new status. He wanted to know every last detail about how Horn found the Crown Jewels.

Hammond took a seat across from Horn, while the former lieutenant, now a captain, recounted the odyssey: Rosenthal's first mention of the Lake Zell rumors; the help that Günter Troche had provided in setting up interviews with the bunker operations staff; his suspicions of councilmen Schmeissner and Fries; the trip to Himmler's castle; and finally, his last-ditch decision, "really a calculated gamble," as he described it, to put Fries into the hot seat at the USFET interrogation center. In retrospect, his investigation seemed easy, but it hadn't felt so at the time.

The major marveled at the twists and turns of the story. This surely was a case where the truth was stranger than any fiction the

Allies could have imagined or the Nazis themselves concocted. It was also clear to him why Colonel Andrews and Captain Thompson had jumped the gun in hosting their own press conference and why, intent on bolstering their tarnished image, they hadn't detailed the finer points of the discovery process.

Horn understood the political reality. Not that he liked it. Not that he believed for one instant that it was better to soft-pedal the truth for the sake of appearances. The Nazis were masters at propaganda. He knew firsthand what the consequences could be. Still, he understood why the American occupation government wouldn't go to any great lengths to praise the resourceful work of two expatriate Germans, a POW, and a mixed group of former Nazis of dubious loyalty who deserved the real credit for the Allied recovery of the treasure.

Private Fritz Hüber, a captured German soldier, had revealed the existence of the Nazi bunker, and German-born Horn, a recent U.S. immigrant, wrote the report. Credit for finding the tunnel didn't go to Captain Peterson but to South African James Low, who had joined E Company at great personal risk after his release from a German POW camp. Captain Thompson had been able to open the bunker only with the help of Albert Dreykorn, secretary to Nürnberg's highest-ranking Nazi. Günter Troche and Eberhard Lutze, former card-carrying Nazi Party members, had led Horn to Heinz Schmeissner and Konrad Fries, who might still be Nazis. Felix Rosenthal, another expatriate German, whose family had just barely escaped Dachau, had risked his career to gain access to the CIC files on Josef Spacil, a known war criminal and mass murderer whom the CIC had in protective custody and who wasn't likely to be handed over to the war-crimes tribunals. This wasn't the story the U.S. Army occupation team wanted wired home, though it was the story that ought to have been told.

As far as Horn knew, Colonel Andrews, whom he had never met, hadn't been in the bunker or seen the Crown Jewels until the day of the press conference, and Captain Thompson, who with Andrews took credit for the discovery, had cribbed what he knew about the Crown Jewels and the investigation from Horn. These weren't the kinds of details that journalists could use to polish the image of America's white knights.

As Hammond told him, it was all rather unbelievable. Horn agreed, then pointed out that he still had much work to do before completing his investigation. First, he would interrogate Spacil, since he was already in Frankfurt, and then Kaltenbrunner.

Hammond said that he would do what he could to help, but Kaltenbrunner, as Horn already knew, would be in the dock at the war-crimes tribunal, and there was a line of people ahead of Horn waiting to interrogate him. Spacil was also in high demand. The CIC had barred him from giving testimony outside of ongoing investigations, which included one team still dredging Lake Zell, another scouring the shores for gold and currency, and a third searching for Hitler's diaries. It could be months, maybe even years, before Horn could interrogate him.

This wasn't the news Horn expected. But he understood military priorities, as he did political realities. "There are still Schmeissner and Fries," Horn said. "They are sure to furnish us with more details, such as why the Holy Lance was not included among the items selected for protection."

Horn explained the possibility that with the bombing and Allied invasion, Hitler's talisman had lost its mystic luster and so wasn't included with the items Himmler dispatched into hiding.

In addition to finding the answer to that question, Horn wanted to know whether the Blacksmith's Alley escape hatch actually led into the King's Chapel.

Most important, there was the matter of the Teutonic Knights. Captain Horn wanted to know if anyone besides the city councilmen knew where the missing Crown Jewels had been hidden. If they truly were the only ones aware of the location in the Pannier shelter, then they were his best chance to expose the larger plot, hatched by Himmler, to create a Fourth Reich.

The two councilmen, Hammond assured him, weren't going anywhere. The major had requested that Colonel Andrews keep them in custody pending a trial. He had also asked the CIC to initiate a search for Julius Lincke.

Hammond then brought up another matter. Pending further information, he was having Heinrich Kohlhaussen relieved of his duties at the Germanic Museum. He surely must have known about Mayor Liebel and Himmler's plans. And since Eberhard Lutze was involved with removal of the Stoss altar from Cracow, Hammond didn't think he ought to step into the position. This would leave the occupation government short of museum staff in Nürnberg. Did Horn have anyone to recommend for the Germanic Museum directorship?

Horn had the ideal candidate, someone who had not only helped enormously with his own investigation but would do much to reform the city's cultural institutions. "Günter Troche is your man."

Hammond consented without reservation. The job was his.

Having resolved the most pressing issues, Horn turned to the more complex question: What was to become of the collection in the bunker?

"For the time being, they're being treated as prisoners of war," Hammond said humorously. "No determination has yet been made."

"But surely you've thought about it?"

Restitution, Hammond said, would be decided shortly. Now that the MFAA had secured the missing items, thanks to Horn, Hammond would have something to report in Munich, where discussion would be under way later that month.

Horn volunteered to join him in Munich. After all, he knew more about the recent history of the Crown Jewels than anyone.

The major said that he would consider taking Horn along, but he had something more important in mind for him. There was a missing coin collection. Not just any coin collection but Hitler's collection, which the Führer had intended to install in his "supermuseum" in his hometown of Linz, Austria. Himmler and the Ahnenerbe, Hammond said, had scoured museums and monasteries all over Europe to complete the collection.

"You say it's missing?"

According to Hammond, upward of two thousand coins were deposited in the Altaussee salt mine, but at some point during the Allied invasion, they had vanished.

Horn was familiar with the Altaussee mine. It was like an Aladdin's cave: a vast chamber under an Austrian mountain where Hitler had hidden more than six thousand paintings that were to be the core of his Linz "supermuseum." The collection of artwork, which Hitler intended to build upon as the Reich expanded worldwide, was eventually to be housed in the largest, most lavish building of its kind anywhere. Even in his last hours, the Führer was so obsessed with this dream that while the Reich was being immolated, he sat in his bunker and pored over the blueprints and a three-dimensional mock-up of his museum and the future greater city of Linz.

Altaussee, Hammond said, contained more than just paintings. The coinage stored there was the most complete collection that had ever existed in any one place in the world. Among the most valuable items were examples of ancient Sumerian shell money and imperial Roman gold. The major had had three of his best people working on the case since the previous May, and they hadn't made much progress. He wanted Horn to take over. This time around, he might just get a medal if he successfully completed his mission.

Hammond stood and crossed to the window, giving Horn a chance to think it over. Enticing as it would be to begin a new investigation—as a captain, no less—he still had the interrogations to conduct and his report on the Crown Jewels to write. He also couldn't help but wonder whether Hammond, on orders from Eisenhower, wanted Horn sent to Austria and away from Germany to prevent him from interrogating Spacil and Kaltenbrunner, war criminals whose testimony could potentially embarrass U.S. high command by drawing attention to the alleged covert army of neo-Nazis on the occupation government payroll.

The major, sensing Horn's indecision, provided more incentive. SS major Helmuth von Hummel, last in possession of the coin collection and believed to be in hiding in Austria, was the right-hand man to Martin Bormann, private secretary to Hitler and the highest-ranking unaccounted-for Nazi in postwar Europe. Finding the coins might lead Horn to Hummel, and Hummel might know where to find Bormann.

No further inducement was necessary. While waiting to interrogate Spacil, Horn would get started on the case of the missing coin collection.

Hammond didn't seem content to leave it at that. Still standing at the window, he waved Horn over to join him.

As Horn later described the meeting to Rosenthal, he and the major stood looking down into the courtyard parking lot and reflecting pool in front of Eisenhower's office. In the far distance were the jagged ruins of the Frankfurt skyline and above it the ever-present dust cloud. Hammond asked if Horn noticed anything different.

Horn looked a second and then a third time. Fritz Klimsch's water nymph was missing from the reflecting pool.

Hammond complimented Horn on being so observant. Mamie Eisenhower, the major said, didn't think it was appropriate for her husband to have a bronze statue of a nude woman standing in front of his office window. It might give people the wrong idea.

Horn chuckled. But it was not the missing statue that Hammond wanted Horn to notice. The major was looking at the parking lot.

Horn inspected the cars and their drivers in the rectangle of pavement below the window. USFET's jeeps were parked at the other side of the building, out of sight. Parked here were limousines and town cars, bearing bumper flags, belonging to the top brass.

"I've got some bad news for you," Hammond said. "I'm taking your jeep and driver away from you."

Horn was dumbfounded. Austria, where the missing coins had last been seen, was no place to rely on troop transports and hitched rides. He was still puzzling over the major's judgment when he finally noticed what Hammond was looking at.

Parked immediately beneath the office, in the line of limousines, was a sleek white BMW sports car with a low-slung hood and shiny chrome radiator. A convertible, no less, with its top down. In the backseat were Horn's footlocker and duffel bag.

Hammond said that the previous owner wouldn't be claiming it anytime soon. He would likely be standing trial in Nürnberg. The major thought Horn might like to use it while he was running around Austria looking for the missing coins.

Horn beamed. A captain and head of his own MFAA investigative unit, he was now able to move freely about Germany and Austria. And as a newly single man, with a few extra dollars to spend, his remaining tour of duty, behind the wheel of a sports car, promised enticing adventures.

There were still, however, questions that needed answering. Did Hitler truly see himself as a part of a long line of ordained emperors destined to rule the world? Did he actually think to crown himself the next Holy Roman Emperor?

Horn was fully aware that few of his fellow intelligence officers would believe such a notion. Demented and egomaniacal as the Führer certainly was, his known connection with arcane secret societies was tenuous at best; and however grand his ambitions, he met his challenges with practical and ruthless efficiency. To think that such a man also lived in a delusional world governed by synchronicities, symbols, and medieval superstition was to stretch the boundaries of credulity.

Horn, in the report he planned, would be making a major leap by suggesting that Hitler actually intended to hold a coronation mimicking those of Emperor Charlemagne and his beloved Frederick the Great. It was one thing for Heinrich Himmler to conduct pagan blood ceremonies in the privacy of his castle fortress but quite another for the supreme Reich commander to strut through the halls of his supermuseum wearing a crown and carrying a scepter.

Hammond understood Horn's concerns; he had similar reservations. However, he was convinced that Horn was on the right track. There had been other things the U.S. Army found in the course of its investigations. Most notably, there were discoveries reported by MFAA officer Walker Hancock. The major couldn't show Horn the files when he joined the MFAA, because he didn't have the rank or necessary security clearance. Horn now had both, along with the full confidence of Eisenhower and Patton. In addition, until Horn had reported back from Nürnberg, Hammond couldn't be sure that Horn's investigation and the things Hancock had reported were related.

The files Hammond referred to were those he had mentioned by telephone after Horn returned the missing treasures to Blacksmith's Alley. They didn't amount to evidence in the same way as a confession from Spacil or Kaltenbrunner would have, but Hammond thought, at the very least, Hancock's report would help Horn put his own work into proper perspective.

Hammond left Horn alone in his office with a thick set of files and the promise that their contents would remain confidential until Eisenhower decided how to handle the matter.

Horn, seated at Hammond's desk, opened the top file and spent the rest of that afternoon poring over the details of an MFAA investigation that had begun three months before his own.

The files were classified on a need-to-know basis and would, Horn imagined, remain that way for years to come. It was not so much a question of what the MFAA investigators had found but where and under what circumstances the initial discovery had been made.

As in his own investigation, hidden Nazi bunkers and underground tunnels figured prominently in the story. Allied intelligence, in the last years of the war, had pinpointed a secret Nazi facility carved into the side of a limestone mountain outside the city of Nordhausen, due north of Nürnberg and east of Himmler's castle, now in the Soviet Zone.

Horn, like other devotees of the German novelist and playwright Goethe, knew the mountainous and mysterious region. This was where Faust, the legendary German university professor and physician, had a nocturnal meeting with Mephistopheles on his quest for all human knowledge.

The Allied military's interest was in a massive, top-secret, fifteen-mile-long underground facility, a subterranean city, where the Nazis were producing their so-called wonder weapons, the V-1 and V-2 rockets they launched on London. Allied planes had carpet-bombed Nordhausen in an unsuccessful effort to shut the facility. In the process, Nordhausen's historic medieval quarter was completely leveled.

The U.S. 104th Infantry Division invaded the area in April, around the same time as Captain Peterson's E Company arrived in Nürnberg. What the 104th discovered was a nightmare. In addition to the rocket-manufacturing plant, there was an experimental laboratory for futuristic weapons and delivery systems, as well as one of the most gruesome labor and extermination camps the SS had ever operated.

A part of the complex called Mittelbau Dora, built by slave labor, was more than a mile long and as wide as two football fields. A railroad track and an overhead trolley and crane connected fifty or more underground chambers. In addition to hauling materials, the crane served as a gallows to hang laborers who could not meet their work quotas. Intelligence experts determined that nearly one-third of the sixty thousand prisoners who constructed this facility, known simply as Dora, had died from exhaustion, starvation, or hanging.

This much most G-2 intelligence officers already knew. Horn had also heard rumors, unsubstantiated but still pernicious, that the United States had liberated not only the slaves who worked the facility but also the scientists and engineers who operated it. Just as with Spacil—deemed to be a specialist useful for Allied interests—the Nazi scientists and engineers involved with Nordhausen were not being held for war crimes, even though an estimated twenty thousand slave laborers had died in what could be described graciously as a hellhole. The Nordhausen elite were being shipped back to the United States for debriefing as part of Operation Overcast.

The records Horn studied revealed the truth of the rumors. Convinced that German scientists could help America's own post-war weapons and rocket research projects, the Office of Strategic Services, or OSS, a U.S. intelligence agency even more secretive than the CIC, was rounding up the Nazi brain trust that had nearly won Hitler the war. The CIC was tracking the gold, the OSS the intellectual treasure.

At Nordhausen, the OSS had had its pick of the Nazis' most celebrated scientists. But it was a race against time. By the terms of the agreed-upon occupation zones, Nordhausen had to be turned over to the Soviets at the conclusion of the war. Hence the OSS had made a full-scale push to take whatever personnel, equipment, and technical data could be found. In the process of combing through the massive facility and its adjoining hills, the U.S. Army made a different kind of discovery, which was where Mason Hammond and the MFAA came into the picture. Allied command didn't know who else to assign to the investigation, as the discovery, in the Bernterode salt mine, didn't fall comfortably into any particular intelligence division—not the CIC or the OSS or G-2. The subsequent investigation was dubbed, fittingly enough, Operation Body Snatch.

While inspecting the Bernterode mine, a unit of the "Blue Devil" Infantry, from the 350th Ordnance Depot, had turned up a suspicious masonry wall, with the mortar still fresh. The soldiers smashed through the wall and tunneled through six feet of masonry, where they uncovered and broke through an enormous, framed, latticed door. Inexplicably, it was padlocked from the inside.

The soldiers smashed through the door and stumbled into something out of Faust. In front of them loomed a mammoth Nazi crypt and shrine. They found, outlined starkly in their tunneling lights, Germanic runes and other symbols on the walls and ceiling. Everywhere they looked were artifacts, regimental standards, and noble and martial flags. More than two hundred banners, symmetrically arranged, were eventually inventoried, including some that were so ancient that they were mounted on supportive netting for display. A metal chest contained portraits of all of Germany's great leaders, from medieval times to the present. Among a collection of paintings were those by Hitler's favorite artist, Lucas Cranach. The two largest were particularly notable, as they had been looted from the Uffizi in Florence. The first was of Adam and Eve, and the second showed Saint Longinus piercing the side of Jesus. The only thing missing from the subterranean display was an altar worthy of Reich rulership and a collection of artifacts worthy to be displayed on it.

The purpose and significance of the crypt baffled Captain Hancock, who wrote the report. To Horn, however, it bore the unmistakable stamp of the Deutsches Ahnenerbe, just like Himmler's castle and the contents of the Blacksmith's Alley vault. Although there was no evidence identifying the builder of the chamber and it would be highly unlikely that Horn would ever be given permission to interrogate the Nordhausen staff who might know or get permission to enter Soviet territory to inspect the site himself, its purpose was beyond doubt.

The shrine's central passageway led to four bays, each containing a coffin. The body of Frederick Wilhelm I, identified as the "Soldier-King," rested in one bay. King Frederick the Great, Hitler's "patron saint" and the monarch of Germany's First Reich, lay in the stillness of another bay. Field Marshal von Hindenburg, the celebrated general, added to the tableau in the third bay. The fourth coffin, draped with red and black bunting and an enormous Nazi flag, was empty. But the letters written across the coffin lid spelled "Adolf Hitler."

EPILOGUE

Walter Horn traveled through Austria and Germany for the next three months, successfully tracking down Martin Bormann's second in command, discovering the fate of the missing coin collection, and reuniting his stepsister Friedl with the rest of the family in Heidelberg. He continued working for the MFAA until 1948, completing three other major art-related investigations during a period described as the most difficult and important phase of the occupation army's recovery and restitution efforts. Hundreds of thousands of paintings and antiquities still needed to be found, their owners identified, and the art repatriated. The contributions that Horn and the other monuments men made to this postwar effort, however, went generally unrecognized in the press frenzy over the Nürnberg war-crimes trials and the growing Cold War hostilities with the Soviet Union.

Despite his best efforts, Horn was denied permission by the CIC to interrogate Josef Spacil. A long waiting list of other Allied intelligence officers, among them senior members of General Patton's staff, were similarly prevented from debriefing the prisoner. The former Oberführer of RSHA's Bureau II, who oversaw the shipment of billions of dollars of gold looted from the treasuries of occupied nations and the victims of Nazi concentration camps, who personally hid portions of this vast fortune in the Austrian Alps, and who supervised the greatest counterfeiting enterprise of all time, inexplicably evaded prosecution for war crimes. After serving the minimum prison term required of all captured SS personnel, Spacil was released from U.S.

custody in 1948, returned to his native Munich, and later established a successful chain of supermarkets. He died in Munich at age fifty-six, in 1963. Only a small percentage of the gold and other assets he is believed to have hidden has ever been accounted for.

Horn was also thwarted in his efforts to interrogate Ernst Kaltenbrunner, the highest-ranking Nazi to stand trial at the Nürnberg tribunals. Horn and Rosenthal appeared as expert witnesses for the prosecution in the RSHA chief's trial, as they did in the trial of Nürnberg publisher and anti-Semite Julius Streicher. Kaltenbrunner, age forty-three, and Streicher, age sixty-one, were condemned and then hanged in 1946. Deputy Nürnberg Gestapo chief Erich Naumann, Karl Holz's underling, was captured in Austria after fleeing Nürnberg in 1945 and joined his former Nazi colleagues on the gallows in 1951.

Horn succeeded in again interrogating Konrad Fries and Heinz Schmeissner, whom he interviewed in a holding cell in Fürth in August 1945. Fries and Schmeissner steadfastly denied any knowledge of a Nazi conspiracy to hide the Crown Jewels for a Fourth Reich and claimed to have removed the treasures to the Pannier bunker on the orders of Mayor Liebel and no one else. They asserted that they withheld this information from Horn and Thompson for fear that the U.S. occupiers could not be trusted with the treasure's safety. We will likely never know whether they were members or unwitting agents of a Teutonic brotherhood of knights sworn to protect and preserve the Holy Roman Empire treasure.

The two councilmen were charged with obstruction of justice and stood trial in a Fürth military court in September 1945. They were found guilty of giving false testimony to U.S. Army personnel, sentenced to five years in prison, and each fined the equivalent of $2,500 in 1945 dollars. After serving twenty months, they were pardoned, released, and relieved of the fines. Fries became a respected educator and author before his death in Nürnberg, at age eighty-four, in 1983. Schmeissner regained employment with Nürnberg's department of engineering. He died at age ninety-two in 1997.

Julius Lincke, the former city councilman who had helped to build and maintain the Blacksmith's Alley facility and who allegedly assisted Fries and Schmeissner in the removal of the Crown Jewels, reappeared in Nürnberg in May 1947, shortly after the release of his two colleagues. Horn was then occupied with another investigation, Captain Thompson had been transferred from Nürnberg, Colonel Charles Andrews was no longer the military governor, and the American occupation of that city was nearing an end, so Lincke was never charged with any crimes or questioned about his role in the conspiracy. He resumed his career as an architect and engineer and was instrumental in restoring many historic buildings in Nürnberg before his death in that city, at age eighty-two, in 1991.

On the recommendation of Mason Hammond, Günter Troche became the director of the Germanic Museum in 1945, a post he held for five years. Under his management, the museum was completely renovated, and a new wing was built to display the work of German artists who had been persecuted during the Nazi era. In 1951, he moved to San Francisco, resumed his friendship with Horn, and became the director of the Achenbach Foundation for Graphic Arts, where he worked until his retirement in 1970. He died in Stockholm a year later, at age sixty-two.

While actively pursuing his other MFAA investigations in 1945 and early 1946, Horn wrote his report on the missing Crown Jewels, which was incorporated into a forty-five-page brief that USFET used to help determine ownership and arrange for restitution of the contents of the Blacksmith's Alley bunker. At Mason Hammond's request, no mention was made of the CIC treasure-hunting expeditions around Lake Zell or the possible connection between the contents of the Nürnberg bunker and the Nazi crypt at the Bernterode mine outside Nordhausen. These and other politically charged subjects were relegated to a single paragraph in the conclusion to the report, stating that Third Army intelligence had provided ample evidence that the Crown Jewels of the Holy Roman Empire were slated by Himmler and RSHA high command to become the symbols of a future German neo-Nazi resistance movement. How MFAA investigators had reached this conclusion was still classified and would remain so for another two decades.

As the vast majority of art and artifacts stored in the Blacksmith's Alley bunker were easily identified as property of the Germanic Museum, the city of Nürnberg, and the German government, these treasures were returned to their respective homes without difficulty. The Viet Stoss altar and artifacts of the Holy Roman Empire, however, presented more difficult legal and logistical challenges.

Initial plans to return the Stoss altar to Cracow in September 1945 were delayed because of deteriorating relations between the United States and the Soviet Union and U.S. outrage over the Red Army's manipulation of the Polish election process. When a special train with twenty-five U.S. military personnel guarding the Stoss altar finally arrived in Cracow on April 25, 1946, members of the Polish Solidarity Party, seeking independence and stirred by the cherished symbol of the city's former greatness, rioted against the Red Army occupation authorities. A Soviet soldier was shot, and an American GI was taken into Red Army custody. With the help of a young parish priest, Karol Wojtyla, the future Pope John Paul II, the altar was eventually installed safely back into the Basilica of the Virgin Mary, where it remains today.

The decision to repatriate the Holy Roman Empire treasures to Vienna was delayed for an entirely different reason: three strong factions vied for ownership.

Attorney Dr. Hans Liemann, assisted by Mayor Liebel's former secretary, Albert Dreykorn, representing Germany, claimed that the historic artifacts belonged to the city of Nürnberg by virtue of documents signed by Holy Roman Emperor Sigismund, who bestowed the symbols and regalia on the city, where they were kept for coronation ceremonies. Other documents were submitted that described secreting away the treasures in the spring of 1796 against Napoleon's invading army and how, in 1806, Baron von Hugel, Emperor Frances II's envoy from Regensberg, illegally sold them to the Habsburgs, the Austrian imperial family.

On behalf of Austria, Chancellor Karl Renner filed a claim that the Crown Jewels rightfully belonged to the Hofburg treasury, based on the repatriation code previously ratified by the Allied military government. The MFAA was to measure ownership by restitution directives, which stated that all art removed from Austria after March 13, 1938, would be returned.

General Patton, behind the scenes, briefly entered the contest by asserting that the Crown Jewels belonged to the U.S. Army. He dismissed Chancellor Renner's position by arguing that the Austrians were not true allies, like France and England, and hence had no claim on Nazi plunder or war reparations. He pointed out that many of the top Nazi officers, including Hitler, were Austrian by birth, that virtually all of the top Nazi officials had homes in Austria before and during the war, and that the Austrians had not resisted the Nazi occupation but welcomed the annexation of their country. Patton's sudden death in Heidelberg in December 1945 prevented his having any further say in the matter.

Supreme Commander Dwight Eisenhower signed the order returning the Crown Jewels to Austria on December 28, 1945. A week later, thirty-two cases containing the entire Holy Roman Empire collection were loaded into an American Dakota transport plane and flown from the Nürnberg-Fürth Airport to Vienna. There, two days later, American General Mark Clark quietly delivered the treasures to city officials, who placed them in an underground vault at the National Bank of Vienna. Today they are on display in the Kunsthistorisches Museum, where Hitler had first seen them.

Many other investigators have picked up where Captain Horn left off. Nearly everyone who has studied the now declassified CIC and G-2 reports on Josef Spacil and the Austrian-based neo-Nazi insurgency have asked questions similar to those first posed by Horn. Did Hitler himself give orders that the most precious of the Holy Roman Empire treasures be removed from the Blacksmith's Alley bunker? Were they slated to become a rallying point for a Fourth Reich? Did Heinrich Himmler have a dedicated brotherhood of Teutonic Knights who were ordered to hide the Crown Jewels and mislead the American occupation team? When, and on whose orders, were the treasures to be removed from their Pannier bunker hiding place?

Despite several attempts to locate Himmler's Mercedes at the bottom of Lake Zell, no one ever found it. A hand-drawn map created by the CIC, showing several locations where Nazi treasure was allegedly hidden around the lake, is on file at the National Archives in College Park, Maryland. Since the map's publication in 2001, in Kenneth Alford's book *Nazi Plunder,* the city of Zell am See has banned all freelance treasure-hunting expeditions.

Hitler's lost diaries and correspondence with Eva Braun also spurred fevered searches. In 1979, a well-known collector of Nazi memorabilia sold a diary-style manuscript to Germany's leading magazine, *Der Spiegel.* The collector claimed that this notebook, as well as twenty-six other volumes he eventually sold, had been recovered from the crash of the plane carrying Hitler's effects in April 1945, referred to by Josef Spacil. The long-lost diaries, if they ever existed, were not these. Knowledgeable readers could see that they were forgeries, and the fraud was exposed, to *Der Spiegel*'s embarrassment.

Did Hitler keep a diary? Will it surface in the future? Lieutenant Colonel Robert Gutierrez, the senior field officer in charge of covert CIC intelligence operations in Bavaria in 1945, believed that at least one diary does exist. According to Gutierrez, his assistant, Master Sergeant William J. Conner, left Germany with a trove of Hitler's treasures. Conner has been hunted by military collectors and historians in vain for years. What secrets remain with him or his heirs?

Himmler's facsimile Crown Jewels and Holy Lance, supposedly displayed at Wewelsburg castle, are still missing. Copies of four of the Crown Jewels, which may or may not have been the same facsimiles the Reichsführer possessed, did appear. In January 1946, just days after the authentic Crown Jewels were returned to Vienna, items represented as the imperial crown, scepter, and orb—complete with actual rough-cut jewels—were put up for sale in Los Angeles. U.S. Army Colonel Joseph W. Hensel had acquired them on the black market in Munich in 1945 for $15,000, more than $171,000 in 2009 dollars. The subsequent FBI and U.S. Customs investigation threatened to become an international incident. Did the Americans return the real treasures to Vienna or not? Photographs of Hensel's objects were dispatched to Austria. On December 11, 1946, officials opened the vault of the National Bank of Vienna. They took the crown, scepter, and orb to a lab for comparison with the photographs. After lengthy deliberation, experts concluded that the items in the photographs were of remarkably high quality, but they were copies.

Who could have made exact copies of the Crown Jewels, and from what models? Were they originally part of the same collection that included the Reichsführer's facsimile of the Holy Lance and Crown Jewels on display at Wewelsburg Castle? Had it been Himmler's intention, just before the invasion, to fool the invading Allied Army by exchanging the real Crown Jewels for facsimiles? Had RSHA's undercover neo-Nazi operatives, led by Oberführer Spacil, intended but failed to put these facsimile objects in the Nürnberg bunker for the Allies—with the conspirators' help—to find? Had city defense minister Karl Holz unwittingly interfered with the secret plan by ordering the bunker's demolition?

Perhaps the longest-running and most in-depth investigations set in motion by Horn's investigation involved the Holy Lance. Several books, most notably Trevor Ravenscroft's 1972 *The Spear of Destiny* and Colonel Howard Buechner and Captain Wilhelm Bernhard's 1988 *Adolf Hitler and the Secrets of the Holy Lance,* provide widely disparate and generally unreliable accounts of the Nazi plot to steal and safeguard the lance. In Ravenscroft's book, Horn is incorrectly identified as the U.S. officer who first opened the vault and claimed the holy relic for Patton. The Buechner and Bernhard book claims that the Nazis replaced the authentic lance in the Blacksmith's Alley bunker with a facsimile, then secreted the real lance into hiding in Antarctica. A detailed and more scholarly book is currently being written by historians Volker Schier and Corine Schleif at the Arizona Center for Medieval and Renaissance Studies.

A central theme of these books and of numerous television documentaries and Hollywood movies is whether or not the U.S. occupation team recovered the actual foot-long, bladed point wielded at the Crucifixion.

Besides the spear Hitler coveted and obtained, at least three others exist that their owners believe to be from the lance carried by Longinus. The Vatican has in its possession a spear point that it steadfastly refuses to permit investigators to examine. Most historians, as it happens, believe this lance was manufactured during the centuries of the Crusades. Other spear points can be easily dated to later centuries, including one in Armenia, which is venerated and presented for viewing once a year in the Cathedral of Echmiadzin, the church of Armenia's patriarch. Based on its shape and metallurgy, scholars believe it is not from a lance at all but is a spike from a Roman standard that legionnaires carried into battle. Another alleged Holy Lance, embedded with what is believed to be a nail from the Crucifixion, is kept as a treasure in the Cracow Cathedral. It appears to be a medieval facsimile of the one in Vienna.

As for the lance Hitler appropriated, now back on display in Vienna, a 2003 forensic examination, detailed in *Die Heilige Lanze in Wien,* published by the Kunsthistorisches Museum in Vienna, concluded that it was indeed the relic long venerated by Germanic kings. Whether it came from the Roman era in the reign of Tiberius, and whether it could have been at the Crucifixion of Christ, are doubtful.

The more significant question Horn's investigation raised was not whether the lance Hitler brought to Nürnberg was the same that pierced the side of Christ but how Hitler had appropriated the religious and spiritual icon for the creation of a program that had led to the Holocaust. Driven by greed and lust for power, did his Reich, with its Aryan Jesus, completely corrupt the lance's essential message of redemption?

Similar questions can be asked about the accoutrements of the Holy Roman Empire that surrounded the Holy Lance. Are the Crown Jewels merely ancient artifacts of history, or are they timeless symbols of a continuing tribal struggle for world supremacy? Since the story of these artifacts, from the ancient soldier-kings of Germany to Hitler, is crucial to illuminating the greater record of humanity, however troubling their reflections of humanity's darkest impulses and ignorance might be, the discoveries Horn made in his three-week investigation should prompt a critical evaluation of the nature of Third Reich ideology and recast for our own generation the means by which Hitler won the popular support of the German nation and, for a time, appeared invincible.

After his honorable discharge in November 1948, Horn moved back to Point Richmond, where he married Alberta Parker, a pediatrician and faculty member at Berkeley's School of Public Health, with whom he raised three children. He also resumed what became a lifelong friendship with colleague Felix Rosenthal, who, after his honorable discharge in 1946, moved to San Francisco, launched a successful career as an architect and bibliophile, and after retirement in San Jose, died at age ninety-two on October 3, 2009.

Horn went on to chair the Berkeley department of art history and published numerous scholarly articles and books. In the academic community, he is today best known as coauthor, with Ernest Born, of *The Plan of St. Gall*, a three-volume treatise on monastic architecture; and, with coauthors Jenny White Marshall and Grellan Rourke, of *The Forgotten Hermitage of Skellig Michael*, a study of the archaeological remains of a ninth-century hermit's dwelling attached to the monastery of Skellig Michael, off the coast of Ireland. Upon his retirement in 1979, after thirty years of teaching, Horn was hailed by his colleagues as one of Berkeley's most inspirational faculty members.

During Horn's later years, several attempts were made to call public attention to his work with Army intelligence and the MFAA. The most personally gratifying was a 1980 campaign, launched by retired Colonel Charles Kunzelman, for Horn to receive a special Army Commendation Medal for exemplary service to his nation. Alas, this honor was withheld, as the G-2 and related CIC investigations Horn conducted were still classified by the U.S. Army.

In 1983, Horn's life story caught the attention of Doubleday book editor Jacqueline Kennedy Onassis, who had heard about Horn's World War II exploits from her daughter, Caroline, then working at the Metropolitan Museum of Art. The book that was eventually published, *The Nazi's Wife,* by British author Peter Watson, is a thinly veiled fictional account of Horn's pursuit of Martin Bormann and the search for the Altaussee coin collection. Shortly after publication of Watson's book, Alberta Horn, with help from Walter's friends and former Berkeley colleagues, at the behest of editor Onassis, conducted nearly thirty hours of interviews, which Horn anticipated using to write his World War II memoirs. Deteriorating health prevented him from completing the task.

Before his death in 1995, at age eighty-seven, Horn took immense pleasure in visits with his family to Germany and Austria. On a 1991 vacation, he accompanied friends to Vienna to see the Crown Jewels at the Kunsthistorisches Museum. As they walked among the large and well-lit display cases, Horn described the aesthetic and intellectual elements that made the imperial relics unique. How they came to be in the museum, however, was the greater story.

ACKNOWLEDGMENTS

I never met Walter Horn. My knowledge of him comes entirely from students, colleagues, and family members who shared their reminiscences of him with me, permitted me to read from their personal correspondence and consult their archives, or simply joined me in walking in his footsteps through Berkeley or along the beach at Point Richmond.

First and foremost, my thanks go to his widow, Alberta Horn, and their two surviving children, Michael and Rebecca. This book could not have been written without their generosity, encouragement, and trust. Thanks also to Walter and Alberta's neighbor and friend, Grethe Tedrick, who hosted me on research trips and entertained me with her many stories, and to Grethe's son Tom Tedrick, for his personal recollections of Walter, his good humor, and many invaluable insights.

I am also grateful for the help and support of Walter's friend and colleague Felix Rosenthal, whose personal recollections, correspondence, unpublished papers, and reports went a long way to help detail events and provide the background material described in this book. For their help arranging for me to interview Felix, thanks to Felix's brother, Bernard, and to Victoria and Tony Misch.

Many other people here and in Europe have been instrumental in helping me to piece together particular aspects of the story.

Thanks must go to Horn family genealogist Brigitte Harris; Horn's friends and former colleagues Svetlana Alpers and Jennifer White Marshall; Günter Troche's colleagues Ian White and Charles Schlossman; author Peter Watson, who interviewed Walter at length for his book *The Nazi's Wife;* Mason Hammond's daughters Antsiss, Elizabeth, and Florence; military historian Kenneth Alford; archival researcher Mark Ballard; Wewelsburg historian and curator Wulff Brebeck; Nürnberg historian Karl Kunze; city guides Michael E. Gonzales, Bolko Gruell, and Karl Hueser; Nürnberg occupation historian Boyd Dastrup of the U.S. Army Field Artillery School at Fort Sill; Josef Spacil researcher Klaus Gagstädter; U.S. military consultant Kelly DePonte; German military researchers Ralph and Dieter Faber; and Captain James C. Sattgast (ret.), who marched into Nürnberg with the 45th Thunderbirds.

For her editorial assistance and her careful reading of the manuscript, I am grateful to Olive DePonte. No less thanks must go to Hildegard Perlman for her help translating German books and documents; Marisa Bourgoin and Wendy Hurlock Baker, who provided much help in searching the Walter Horn papers at the Smithsonian Institution's Archives of American Art; Walter Gebhardt for his help locating his colleague Günter Troche's records at the Germanic Museum; Stephen Bye, who kindly lent me assistance at the U.S. Army War College at Carlisle, Pennsylvania; Paul Nowacek, who saved me many hours of work at the National Archives in College Park; and Michael Gonzales, at the 45th Infantry Division library and headquarters in Oklahoma City.

Three scholars I have not had the pleasure of meeting but whose research has influenced my own should also be acknowledged: Stephen Brockmann, at the Carnegie Mellon University, author of *Nuremberg: The Imaginary Capital;* Susannah Heschel, at Dartmouth College, author of *The Aryan Jesus;* and Lynn Nicholas, in Washington, D.C., author of *The Rape of Europa.* Appreciation also goes to author and filmmaker Robert Edsel, whose book *Rescuing da Vinci* and work with the Monuments Men Foundation for the Preservation of Art have done much to raise public awareness of the contributions of Mason Hammond, Walter Horn, and their MFAA colleagues.

I owe a debt of gratitude to agent Richard Morris, at Janklow and Nesbit, and editor Roger Labrie, at Simon and Schuster, who saw the project through from concept to completion. Their confidence, editorial eye, and publishing acumen are much appreciated.

Thanks also, on a personal note, to those who have been supportive since I first discussed this project with them: Dayton and Karen Brown, David Cyrille, Robert and Teresa Freaso, Cathy Haenlein, George and Joan Rockwell Gifford, Wilder and Gabriele Knight, Todd Miller, and Ellie Short.

Finally, thanks and love to my wife, Nancy, as always, for her support, patience, and fine judgment.

NOTES

Unless otherwise indicated, all documents cited at the National Archives can be found in the Ardelia Hall Monuments, Fine Arts and Archives Collection, and in the Records of U.S. Occupation Headquarters, World War II, Record Group 260. All documents cited at the Smithsonian Institution are in the Walter Horn Collection at the Archives of American Art in Washington, D.C. The Felix Rosenthal papers, which include both personal and military records, have been made available to me by Felix and his brother, Bernard Rosenthal. The vast majority of other documents cited—which include Walter Horn's diaries, address books, correspondence, personal papers, military records, and the extensive oral history conducted at the behest of Jacqueline Kennedy Onassis in the early 1980s—have been generously made available to me by his widow, Alberta Horn. All interviews cited are my own, conducted in the United States and Germany.

The following abbreviations and acronyms have been used:

CIC	Counter Intelligence Corps
CID	Criminal Investigation Division
CIR	Consolidated Interrogation Report
CMH	U.S. Army Center of Military History, Washington, D.C.
EL	Eisenhower Library, Abilene, Kansas
FB	Donovan Research Library, Fort Benning, Georgia
FR	Felix Rosenthal

FRP   Felix Rosenthal Papers, Berkeley, California

G-2   Intelligence Staff at Corps and Division Level

GM   Getty Museum Research Institute, Los Angeles

JT   John Thompson

LC   Library of Congress, Washington, D.C.

MFAA   Monuments, Fine Arts, and Archives

MGLS   Military Government Liaison and Security Office

MH   Mason Hammond

MHI   U.S. Army Military History Institute, Carlisle Barracks, Pennsylvania

NA   National Archives, College Park, Maryland

OMGB   Office of Military Government, Bavaria

OMGN   Office of Military Government, Nürnberg

OMGUS   Office of Military Government, U.S. Zone

RSHA   Reich Security Main Office

SI   Smithsonian Institution, Archives of American Art, Washington, D.C.

SN   Stadtarchiv Nürnberg, Nürnberg

UH   University of Heidelberg

USFET   United States Forces Eastern Theater

WHA   Walter Horn Archive, Point Richmond, California

WH   Walter Horn

ZCL   Zurich Central Library

CHAPTER 1: BLACKSMITH'S ALLEY

WH's G-2 military status in Namur, Belgium: correspondence from Captain Joseph Sylvester to Headquarters, American Military Intelligence, February 19, 1945, at NA. WH's intelligence work for the Mobile Field Interrogation Unit: CIR report by First Lieutenant Gerhard Liedholz to MFAA, September 19, 1945, at WHA. WH's interrogation orders and Patton's concerns with chemical/biological weapons: WH, "Interrogation about Gas Warfare," undated report, in WHA. Hüber family genealogy, "names directory of Nürnberg," at SN. Dialogue and details of the Hüber interrogation and Camp Namur are drawn from WH's oral history, tapes 4 and 8, at WHA; WH, "The Finding of the Crown Jewels: A Sketch of Monuments and Fine Arts Activities in World War II," lecture delivered by WH on October 4, 1965, at WHA; WH, "Recovery of the Crown Jewels of the Holy Roman Empire," undated and unpublished article, at WHA; and WH, "Recovery of Missing Crown Jewels," lecture delivered at Berkeley, March 23, 1983, at WHA. In addition to these primary sources, I have relied on a lengthy unpublished report by Sergeant Robert Armstrong, who interviewed WH in 1946 in anticipation of filing a press release in connection with USFET's Blacksmith's Alley restitution efforts: Robert Armstrong, "The German Crown Jewels: A Modern Detective Story," report for U.S. Army Group CC, APO 742, 1946, at WHA.

CHAPTER 2: MONUMENTS MEN
Camp Freising: FR's "Camp Freising," unpublished and untitled essay, at FRP and correspondence from FR to Bernard Rosenthal, May 29, 1945, at FRP. WH's conversations with FR regarding Bormann and Kaltenbrunner and details of WH and FR's interacting in Camp Freising are drawn from my interview with FR in May 2009 and WH's oral history, tape 4, at WHA. Third Army G-2 Intelligence Unit activities and role played by WH and FR: FR's "Spring of 1946," unpublished and undated essay in FRP. Interrogation of Kempa: "Hitler's Last Days: Statement of Erich Kempa," at EL. WH's intelligence-gathering activities and attitudes on MFAA: untitled and undated Berkeley lecture notes about WH's WWII activities, at WHA. WH at British Museum: John Goldsmith, ed., *The Gymnasium of the Mind: The Journals of Roger Hinks, 1933–1963,* Michael Russell, London, 1984, pp. 6–9. MFAA activities and discoveries made in Austria and Germany: Lynn Nicholas, *The Rape of Europa,* Vintage Books, New York, 1995, pp. 327–369; Thomas Carr Howe, *Salt Mines and Castles,* Bobbs-Merrill, New York, 1946, pp. 243–259; Janet Flanner, "Annals of Crime: The Beautiful Spoils," *New Yorker Magazine,* March 8, 1947; and Renwick Kennedy, "To the Victor the Spoils," *Christian Century,* July 31, 1946. Dialogue and conversation between WH and MH are drawn from WH's oral history, tape 4, 5, and 9, at WHA; correspondence from MH to U.S. Group Control Council, Reparation, Deliveries and Restitution Division, MFAA, August 20, 1945, at NA; untitled and undated Kaltenbrunner and Streicher report in WHA; correspondence between MH and WH, August 20, 1945, at NA; interview with Antsiss and Elizabeth Hammond in January 2007 and June 2008; and correspondence from WH to Peter Watson, April 25, 1984, and January 9, 1986. MH's knowledge of Allied looting: "The War and Art Treasures in Germany," *College Art Journal,* March 1946, pp. 205–218. MH and Rorimer: James Rorimer and Gilbert Rabin, *Survival: The Salvage and Protection of Art in War,* Abelard Press, New York, 1950, pp. 147–150. Theft of artwork and corruption by U.S. mili-

tary personnel and occupation government officials: Dr. Erica Hanfstaengl and Evelyn Tucker reports in MFAA and CID summary reports, February 16, 1949, at NA; Evelyn Tucker interview of Captain LaVient, July 22, 1948, at NA; and Interim Reports of Colonel James Wood and Sinclair Robinson, "Büdingen Affair," June 29, 1946, at NA. MH background, attitude, and responsibilities: MH, "The War and Art Treasures in Germany," *College Art Journal*, March 1946. Discovery of Viet Stoss altar: report from USFET to CG III Army, September 10, 1945, at NA; and Frank Waters, "Famed Polish Altar Piece Found Cached under Nuremberg Rubble," *Stars and Stripes,* June 13, 1945. Pandora's box and sensitive nature of MFAA intelligence work: classified report NND 750168 by the American Commission for the Protection and Salvage of Artistic and Historical Monuments in War Areas, October 11, 1944, at NA; and memorandum by Lieutenant S. L. Faison to OSS Art Looting Investigation Unit, September 17, 1945, at WHA. WH's travel orders: correspondence from MH to USFET, July 16, 1945, at NA.

CHAPTER 3: CAMP RITCHIE BOYS

Dialogue and conversations between WH and FR at Camp Freising are drawn from WH's oral history, tape 4, at WHA; correspondence from FR to Bernard Rosenthal, May 29, 1945, at FRP; my interviews with FR in May 2009; and FR's "The Questionnaire," undated essay, in FRP. Private Dollar: WH photograph album and notes by WH, at WHA. WH's views on acceptable behavior of servicemen: undated lecture to Berkeley students, at WHA; Emil Ludwig, "Fourteen Rules for the Occupation Officer in Germany," G-2 report, 1945, at NA; and FR, "Guide for U.S. Servicemen," 1944, at NA. Anne Binkley background and WH's relationship with her: interview with Alberta Horn, February 2008; photographs of Binkley and correspondence, at WHA; WH's oral history tapes 4, 5; and interview with FR and Bernard Rosenthal in May 2009. FR's experience in Munich and coming to the United States: interview with Bernard and FR in May 2009 and Bernard Rosenthal, "An Enemy Alien in Berkeley: Reminiscences of the War Years by a Slightly Bemused Thirty Niner," *Book Club of California Quarterly*, Summer 2000. FR's study of Hitler's suicide: FR, "Hitler's Socks: When They Met the Eyes, They Made History," unpublished report, June 2000, at FRP. Background discussions on MFAA relations with G-2 and CIC: Lord Methuen and Charles Woolley, *Normandy Diary*, Robert Hale, London, 1952, pp. 2–40, at WHA; Stratton Hammon, "When the Second Lieutenant Bearded General Eisenhower," *Military Affairs,* October 1983. G-2 and CIC reports on the covert Nazi insurgency and Himmler's participation in it: OSS report, May 15, 1945, at NA; and "Survey of Conditions in Austria," Joint Intelligence Collection Agency, May 27, 1945, at NA.

CHAPTER 4: INVASION OF NÜRNBERG

Captain Peterson's mission into Nürnberg: Paul Peterson, "The Operations of Company E, 180th Infantry in Battle of Nuremberg, Germany, 17–20 April 1945," infantry report, at FB. Additional background and details of Nürnberg invasion: *History of the 180th Infantry Regiment* and *History of the 157th Infantry Regiment*, Army and Navy Publishing Co., Baton Rouge, La., 1946, at CMH; and *USA, Report of Operations: The Seventh United States Army in France and Germany, 1944–1945*, Volume II, at the NA. Account of German activities in April 1945 around Nürnberg Castle and art bunker: interview with Karl Kunze in March 2008. Difficulty determining which Army unit discovered bunker: interview with Boyd Dastrup in January 2008 and Walter Herppich, *Das unterirdische Nürnberg*, Hofmann Verlag Nürnberg, Nürnberg, 1987, pp. 57–130. Additional details of the bunker capture and role played by James Low: interview with Major (ret.) James Sattgast (detailed to the Blacksmith's Alley bunker on April 21, 1945), December 2007.

CHAPTER 5: THOR'S HAMMER

WH's arrival in Nürnberg: WH's oral history, tape 5, at WHA; WH, "The Finding of the Crown Jewels: A Sketch of Monuments and Fine Arts Activities in World War II," lecture delivered by WH on October 4, 1965, at WHA; WH, "Recovery of the Crown Jewels of the Holy Roman Empire," undated and unpublished report at WHA; WH, "Recovery of Missing Crown Jewels," lecture delivered at Berkeley, March 23, 1983, at WHA; and Robert Armstrong, "The German Crown Jewels: A Modern Detective Story," report for U.S. Army Group CC, APO 742, 1945, at WHA. The conversation between JT and WH in this chapter has been drawn from the following sources: correspondence from Second Lieutenant Arthur Forces to JT, May 9, 1945, at NA; report from JT to Third ECA Regiment, Nürnberg, July 27, 1945, at NA; correspondence from JT to MFAA regarding Nürnberg city officials, August 13, 1945, at NA; correspondence from JT to MFAA, August 20, 1945, at NA; and correspondence from JT to Military Government Nürnberg, August 25, 1945, at NA. Additional JT background, attitudes, and general situation in Nürnberg: "A General History of Liaison and Security in Nuremberg, May 1, 1945–June 30, 1946," at NA; "File memo" to Education and Religion

Detachment F1B3, Company B, Third ECA Regiment, July 27, 1945, at NA; Edward N. Peterson, *The American Occupation of Germany: Retreat to Victory*, Wayne State University Press, Detroit, 1968, pp. 155–166; Julian Bach, *America's Germany: An Account of the Occupation*, Random House, New York, 1946, pp. 257–258, and Boyd Dastrup, *Crusade in Nuremberg: Military Occupation, 1945–1949*, Greenwood Press, Westport, Conn., 1985, pp. 20–52. Devastation of Nürnberg and effects on the residents: Neil Gregor, *Haunted City: Nuremberg and the Nazi Past*, Yale University Press, New Haven, Conn., 2008, pp. 1–55. Additional details on the condition of Nürnberg in the first months of U.S. military occupation: interview with Karl Kunze, February and March 2008, and Karl Kunze, *Kriegsende in Franken und der Kampf um Nürnberg im April 1945*, Selbstverlag Des Vereins für Geschichte der Stadt Nürnberg, Nürnberg, 1995, pp. 177–310. Details on the status of personnel and problems confronting the U.S. military government in Nürnberg: interview with Boyd Dastrup in January 2008 and "MFAA Field Report," EIB3, report for May 1945, at NA. General background on occupation efforts: Harry Coles and Albert Weinberg, *Civil Affairs: Soldiers Become Governors, Special Studies of the U.S. Army in World War II*, Office of the Chief of Military History, Department of the Army, Washington, D.C., 1964, pp. 12–14, at MHI; Earl Ziemke, *U.S. Army Occupation of Germany 1944–1946*, Center of Military History, U.S. Army, Washington, D.C., 1975, pp. 371–410, at NHI; and Earl Ziemke, "The Formulation and Initial Implementation of U.S. Occupation Police in Germany," in Hans Schmitt, ed., *U.S. Occupation in Europe after World War II*, Regents of Kansas Press, Lawrence, Kan., 1968, pp. 20–30. Delbert Fuller drinking problems and the "snake pit" officers' club: "Historical Report," Det. B-211, June 20, 1946, at NA; *The U.S. Army in the Occupation of Germany, 1944–1946*, Gordon Press, Brooklyn, N.Y., 1995, pp. 401–477, at MHI; and "Report from Army of Occupation, Bavaria and Nuremberg, July–August 1945," at NA. Corruption of civilian administration in Nürnberg: MGLS Report, May 23, 1947, at NA; MGLS Report, October 25, 1947, at NA; CID reports, Bavaria, April–May 1945, at NA; OMGUS, "Fragenbogen, Prosecution Cases File," at NA; OMGN, "Additional List of Removals, September 1, 1945," at NA; and OMGUS, "Report on Denazification, October 20, 1945," at NA.

CHAPTER 6: PANDORA'S BOX

Männleinlaufen, details of Jewish persecution, and Holy Lance festival: Stephen Brockmann, *Nuremberg: The Imaginary Capital*, Camden House, Rochester, N.Y., 2006, pp. 13–28; and Volker Schier and Corine Schleif,

"The Holy Lance As Late Twentieth Century Subcultural Icon," *Cultural Icon* (ed. David Scott), Left Coast Press, Albuquerque, N.Mex., 2008, pp. 1–32. Layout and condition of the Blacksmith's Alley bunker: Peter Heigl, *Der Reichsschatz im Nazibunker,* privately published by Peter Heigl, Nürnberg, 2005, pp. 7–78; *Die Nürnberger Prozesse,* privately published by Peter Heigl, Nürnberg, 2005, pp. 5–12. General background on the bunker's renovation from a beer cellar, its use by the Nazis, and U.S. Army's control of the bunker in 1945: Walter Herppich, *Das unterirdische Nürnberg,* Hofmann Verlag, Nürnberg, 1987, pp. 51–129; Franz Wolff, *Ausflug durch den historischen Weltkrieg-Kunst-Bunker,* Förderverein Nürnberger Felsengänge, Nürnberg, 2004, pp. 3–15. The conversations that took place in the bunker have been derived from the following sources: WH's oral history, tapes 4, 5, at WHA; WH, "The Finding of the Crown Jewels: A Sketch of Monuments and Fine Arts Activities in World War II," lecture delivered by WH on October 4, 1965, at WHA; WH, "Recovery of the Crown Jewels of the Holy Roman Empire," undated and unpublished report at WHA; and my interview with FR in May 2009. Escape passage in bunker and circumstances of the facility's opening by U.S. military government: Franz Wolff, *Ausflug durch den historischen Weltkrieg-Kunst-Bunker,* Förderverein Nürnberger Felsengänge, Nürnberg, 2004, p. 9; interview with Bernhard Seiler in February 2008; interview with Bolko Gruell in February 2008; and correspondence between WH and Wilhelm Schwemmer, 1978, in WHA (in preparation for Wilhelm Schwemmer, *Die Reichskleinodien in Nürnberg 1938–1945,* Korn and Berg, Nürnberg, 1978). Additional background and history of bunker: Hugo Portisch, *Österreich II: Der lange Weg zur Freiheit,* Kremayr and Scheriau, Vienna, 1995 (unnumbered pages), at WHA. General background on Hitler's "Holy Reich": Richard Steigmann-Gall, *The Holy Reich: Nazi Conceptions of Christianity, 1919–1945,* Cambridge University Press, New York, 2003, pp. 13–86; and Susannah Heschel, *The Aryan Jesus: Christian Theologians and the Bible in Nazi Germany,* Princeton University Press, Princeton, N.J., 2008, pp. 1–67.

CHAPTER 7: SPEAR OF DESTINY

Lecture on Holy Lance and Crown Jewels: WH kept no notes on this specific lecture when it was given. I have reconstructed what he likely said based on subsequent lectures given over the course of his career, which can be found at the WHA, SI, and GM. I have also drawn on annotations WH wrote in his personal copy of Friedrich Sprater's *Die Reichskleinodien in der Pfalz,* Im Westmarkverlag, Ludwigshafen am Rhein und Saarbrucken, 1942, which I presume was in his possession or given to him by FR or

Günter Troche around the time WH delivered the lecture. These materials I have supplemented and cross-referenced with other more contemporary studies and published histories of the Holy Lance and the Crown Jewels. Most notable among these books: Hermann Fillitz, *The Crown Jewels and the Ecclesiastical Treasure Chamber,* Kunsthistorisches Museum, Vienna, 1956; and Franz Kirchweger, ed., *Die Heilige Lanze in Wien,* Kunsthistorisches Museum, Vienna, 2005. As there is much information and misinformation that have been published on the Holy Lance, most notably in *The Spear of Destiny,* by Trevor Ravenscroft, Weiser Books, Boston, 1982, readers are urged to consult the scholarship cited above of Corine Schleif, at Arizona State University, and Volker Schier, at the Arizona Center for Medieval and Renaissance Studies. Image of Spear appearing over Nürnberg: report and woodcut of April 14, 1561, by Hans Glas in Wickiana Collection, at ZCL. Anne Catherine Emmerich touching the Holy Lance: Carl Schmoger, *The Life of Anne Catherine Emmerich,* vol. 2, Tan Books, Rockford, Ill., 1976, p. 558.

CHAPTER 8: HIMMLER'S SCHOLARS

WH's conversations with Troche and Troche's contributions to WH investigation: WH, "Appointment of Günter Troche," at WHA; Günter Troche, "Nürnberg MFAA Survey," undated report submitted to MFAA Committee, 1945, at NA; WH's oral history, tapes 4 and 5, at WHA; and my interview with FR in May 2009. WH in Nazi Germany, Italy, and early years at Berkeley: WH's oral history, tapes 1, 4, 5, 7, 9, at WHA. Meeting with Lady Astor and Eleanor Roosevelt and art lectures: Undated handwritten notes by WH in WHA. Troche history in Germany: WH's oral history tape 4, 5, at WHA. Troche in Nürnberg: Correspondence from MFAA Chief Herbert Leonard to WH, July 8, 1948, at NA; interview with Troche colleagues Peter Selz and Charles Schlossman in April 2008; and correspondence with Walter Gebhardt at Germanic Museum, November 9, 2007, and December 10, 2008. WH and Troche on Ahnenerbe looting operations: WH, "Wolfram Sievers and the Ahnenerbe," undated report, at WHA; Hellmut Lehmann-Haupt, MFAA report, "Cultural Looting of the Ahnenerbe," March 1, 1948, at NA; and Heather Pringle, *The Master Plan: Himmler's Scholars and the Holocaust,* Hyperion, New York, 2006, pp. 1–63.

CHAPTER 9: THE ARYAN JESUS

WH's conversation points with Troche have been drawn from WH to Albert Bühler, October 10, 1948, at WHA; Bühler to WH on January 7,

1972; Peter Heigl, *Der Reichsschatz im Nazibunker*, privately published by Peter Heigl, Nürnberg, 2005, pp. 65–79; and my interview with FR in May 2009. Hitler's plan with Mayor Liebel to reconstruct the city and parade grounds, with specific references to Germanic Museum directors: Eberhard Lutze (ed. by Willy Liebel), *Die deutschen Reichsinsignien und Reichskleinodien*, Nürnberg, 1938, and Heinrich Kohlhaussen, *Die Reichskleinodien*, Berlin, 1935. Nazi building projects: *Bauten in der Stadt der Reichsparteitage Nürnberg* (produced in Nürnberg for 1937 Nazi Party rally). See also *Die Reichskleinodien*, Angelsachsen Verlag, Nürnberg, 1939; *Die Deutschen Reichsinsignien und Reichskleinodien*, Nürnberg, 1938; Friedrich Sprater, *Die Reichskleinodien in der Pfalz*, Im Westmarkverlag, Ludwigshafen am Rhein und Saarbrücken, 1942; and Siegfried Zelnhefer, *Die Reichsparteitage der NSDAP in Nürnberg*, Verlag Nürnberg, Nürnberg, 2002. Additional details and background: Stephen Brockmann, *Nuremberg: The Imaginary Capital*, Camden House, Rochester, N.Y., 2006, pp. 1–31; Volker Schier and Corine Schleif, "The Holy Lance As Late Twentieth Century Subcultural Icon," *Cultural Icon* (ed. David Scott) Left Coast Press, Albuquerque, N.Mex., 2008, pp. 1–32; Thornton Sinclair, "The Nazi Party Rally at Nuremberg," *Public Opinion Quarterly*, October 1938; and Joshua Hagen and Robert Ostergren, "Spectacle, Architecture and Place at the Nürnberg Party Rallies: Projecting a Nazi Vision of Past, Present and Future," *Cultural Geographies 2006*, Edward Arnold Publishers, obtained through JUSTOR, 2006. Mystical connections and history of bunker: Hugo Portisch, *Österreich II: Der lange Weg zur Freiheit*, Kremayr and Scheriau, Vienna, 1995, pp. 1–12. German mysticism and ley lines: Ulrich Magin, "An Assortment of Landscape Lines in Germany: Real and Imagined," *The Ley Hunter*, Cheltenham, U.K., 1999. General background on Hitler's and Himmler's interest in mysticism and the occult: Michael Moynihan, ed., and Stephen Flowers, trans., *The Secret King, Karl Maria Wiligut: Himmler's Lord of the Runes*, Dominion Press, Waterbury Center, Vt., 2001, pp. 15–40; Ken Anderson, *Hitler and the Occult*, Prometheus Books, Amherst, N.Y., 1995, pp. 47–125; and Peter Levenda, *Unholy Alliance*, Continuum, New York, 1995, pp. 167–203. Biographical details of Himmler and his reading habits: CIC File CF/444, testimony of Ericke Lorene (Himmler's secretary), November 18, 1946, at NA. General background on the Aryan Jesus: Peter Head, *The Nazi Quest for an Aryan Jesus*, Continuum Publishing Group, London, 2004; Susannah Heschel, *The Aryan Jesus: Christian Theologians and the Bible in Nazi Germany*, Princeton University Press, Princeton, N.J., 2008; and Richard Steigmann-Gall, *The Holy Reich: Nazi Conceptions of Christianity, 1919–1945*, Cambridge University Press, New York, 2003.

Hitler's known reading habits: Timothy Ryback, *Hitler's Private Library*, Alfred A. Knopf, New York, 2008. General background on German blood cults: Caroline Walker Bynum, *Wonderful Blood*, University of Pennsylvania Press, Philadelphia, 2007.

CHAPTER 10: HITLER'S FAIRY-TALE KINGDOM

Spear shape as a model for the reinvented city: This is a controversial subject, which has been speculated on or referred to by several researchers over the past several decades. I do not know whether or not WH was convinced that there was a direct connection between the Holy Lance and the Nazi plans for the renovation and building projects in the city, only that he was aware that there might be. The spear-shaped motif may actually have been derived entirely from the popular Tyr rune employed by Himmler and the Ahnenerbe. Readers are encouraged to examine the circumstantial evidence as presented in *Reichstagung in Nürnberg, 1934*, part of the series of *Reichsparteitage*, or "Reich's Party Day books," and *Der Kongress zu Nürnberg, 1934*, a lengthy commemorative album published in Nürnberg, at LC and SN, and Eberhard Lutze (ed. Willy Liebel), *Die deutschen Reichsinsignien und Reichskleinodien*, Nürnberg, 1938; Heinrich Kohlhaussen, *Die Reichskleinodien*, Berlin, 1935; and *Bauten in der Stadt der Reichsparteitage Nürnberg* (produced in Nürnberg for 1937 Nazi Party rally). Visitors to Nürnberg are encouraged to see the spear-shaped map on permanent display in the entrance hallway of the Documents Center at the Nazi Rally Parade Grounds. WH's guided tour of the city: WH's oral history, tapes 4, 5, at WHA and interview with Karl Kunze in March 2008.

CHAPTER 11: TEUTONIC KNIGHTS

Display of treasure at Saint Catherine's: *Die Reichskleinodien*, Angelsachsen Verlag, Nürnberg, 1939, pp. 1–15; *Die deutschen Reichsinsignien und Reichskleinodien*, Nürnberg, 1938; Peter Heigl, *Der Reichsschatz im Nazibunker*, privately published by Peter Heigl, Nürnberg, 2005, pp. 35–44; Freidrich Sprater, *Die Reichskleinodien in der Pfalz*, im Westmarkverlag, Ludwigshafen am Rhein und Saarbrucken, 1942, pp. 1–16; and Siegfried Zelnhefer, *Die Reichsparteitage der NSDAP in Nürnberg*, Verlag Nürnberg, Nürnberg, 2002, pp. 1–20. General information on Teutonic Knights: Erich Maschke (WH's brother-in-law), *Die deutschen Kriegsgefangenen des Zweiten Weltkrieges, eine Zusammenfassung*, reprinted by Verlag Ernst und Werner Gieseking, Munich, 1974; Charles Woodhouse, *The Military Religious Orders of the Middle Ages: The Hospitallers, the Templars, the Teutonic Knights, and Others*, Society for Promoting Christian Knowledge, New

York, 1879 (available online courtesy of Harvard University); and William Urban, *The Teutonic Knights: A Military History,* Greenhill Books, St. Paul, Minn., 2006. Nürnberg Castle and chapel: Erich Bachmann and Albrecht Miller, *Imperial Castle Nuremberg,* Bayerische Verwaltung Der staatlichen Schlösser, Gärten und Seen, Munich, 1994, pp. 22–36; and Victoria Salley, *The Kaiserburg, Nuremberg,* Prestel Press, Munich, 2002. Notes on conversation between WH and Troche not cited in previous chapter notes: Walter Herppich, *Das unterirdische Nürnberg,* Hofmann Verlag, Nürnberg, 1987, pp. 96–143; and Peter Heigl, *Der Reichsschatz im Nazibunker,* privately published by Peter Heigl, Nürnberg, 2005, pp. 24–79; Walter Herppich, *Das unterirdische Nürnberg,* Hofmann Verlag, Nürnberg, 1987, pp. 96–130. Fries, Schmeissner, and Lincke on U.S. payroll: Wilhelm Schwemmer, *Reichskleinodien in Nürnberg 1938–1945,* Korn and Berg, Nürnberg, 1978, pp. 1–13.

CHAPTER 12: THE ENEMY AT THE GATES

Interviews with individuals connected with the Blacksmith's Alley facility: WH's oral history, tapes 4, 5, at WHA; WH's handwritten notes of interviews, August 1945, MFAA collection, at NA; WH's transcript, "Zweiter Teil des politischen Testamente," April 29, 1945, at WHA; WH, "The Finding of the Crown Jewels: A Sketch of Monuments and Fine Arts Activities in World War II," lecture delivered by WH on October 4, 1965, at WHA; WH, "Recovery of the Crown Jewels of the Holy Roman Empire," undated and unpublished article at WHA; WH, "Recovery of Missing Crown Jewels," lecture delivered at Berkeley, March 23, 1983, at WHA; Robert Armstrong, "The German Crown Jewels: A Modern Detective Story," report for U.S. Army Group CC, APO 742, 1945, at WHA; memorandum of interrogation dated August 3, 1945, at WHA; and Liaison and Protocol Section, OMGUS, G-448 at NA. Bombing Raids on Nürnberg and impact on residents: Neil Gregor, *Haunted City: Nuremberg and the Nazi Past,* Yale University Press, New Haven, Conn., 2009, pp. 1–50; Neil Gregor, "Civilian Moral and Social Dissolution in Nuremberg 1942–1945," *Historical Journal,* 2000.

CHAPTER 13: CHAIN OF COMMAND

Details of the conversation between WH and Dreykorn are drawn from the report by Albert Dreykorn, July 27, 1945, at WHA; CIR report, July 27, 1945, at NA; WH's handwritten notes of interviews, August 1945, MFAA collection, at NA; and WH's "Report on the investigation of the circumstances of disappearance of the Imperial Insignia from the Crown Treasures of the Holy Roman Empire in the Nuremberg Art Cache, and their recovery," August 14, 1945, at WHA. For additional background material on the circumstances of the interview: Peter Heigl, *Der Reichsschatz im Nazibunker,* privately published by Peter Heigl, Nürnberg, 2005, pp. 13–79; Wilhelm Schwemmer, *Die Reichskleinodien in Nürnberg 1938–1945,* Korn and Berg, Nürnberg, 1978, pp. 1–15; Franz Wolff, *Ausflug durch den historischen Weltkrieg-Kunst-Bunker,* Förderverein Nürnberger Felsengänge, Nürnberg, 2004, pp. 3–9; and WH's correspondence with Albert Bühler, October 10, 1948, and January 7, 1972, at WHA.

CHAPTER 14: HIMMLER'S COURIER

Eberhard Lutze's name is sometimes misrepresented in U.S. military documents and published sources as Eberhard Luze. Dialogue and general details of the interrogation have been drawn from WH's handwritten notes of interviews, August 1945, MFAA collection, at NA; and Lutze memorandum, June 20, 1945, at NA. Background on Lutze: Eberhard Lutze, *Die deutschen Reichsinsignien und Reichskleinodien,* Oberburgermeister der Stadt der Reichsparteitage, Nürnberg, 1939, pp. 1–16; and WH's "Report on the investigation of the circumstances of disappearance of the Imperial Insignia from the Crown Treasures of the Holy Roman Empire in the Nuremberg Art Cache, and their recovery," August 14, 1945, at WHA. For additional background material on the circumstances of the interview: WH correspondence with Albert Bühler, October 10, 1948, and January 7, 1972, at WHA; Peter Heigl, *Der Reichsschatz im Nazibunker*, privately published by Peter Heigl, Nürnberg, 2005, pp. 13–79; Wilhelm Schwemmer, *Die Reichskleinodien in Nürnberg 1938–1945*, Korn and Berg, Nürnberg, 1978, pp. 1–15; and Franz Wolff, *Ausflug durch den historischen Weltkrieg-Kunst-Bunker*, Förderverein Nürnberger Felsengänge, Nürnberg, 2004, pp. 3–9.

CHAPTER 15: KEYS TO THE VAULT

WH's interview with Schmeissner and Fries has been drawn from WH's oral history, tapes 4 and 5, at WHA; WH's transcript, "Zweiter Teil des politischen Testmente," April 29, 1945, at WHA; WH's handwritten notes of interviews, August 1945, MFAA collection at NA; WH, "The Finding of the Crown Jewels: A Sketch of Monuments and Fine Arts Activities in World War II," lecture delivered by WH on October 4, 1965, at WHA; WH, "Recovery of the Crown Jewels of the Holy Roman Empire," undated and unpublished article at WHA; WH, "Recovery of Missing Crown Jewels," lecture delivered at Berkeley, March 23, 1983, at WHA; Robert

Armstrong, "The German Crown Jewels: A Modern Detective Story," report for U.S. Army Group CC, APO 742, 1945, at WHA; memorandum of interrogation dated August 3, 1945, at WHA; Liaison and Protocol Section, OMGUS, G-448, at NA; and Peter Heigl, *Der Reichsschatz im Nazibunker,* privately published by Peter Heigl, Nürnberg, 2005, pp. 13–79. WH's attitude toward and relations with JT: Interview with FR, May 2009, and interview with Major (ret.) James Sattgast, December 2007.

CHAPTER 16: HITLER'S HOLY REICH

Jewish skeleton collection: "Jewish Skeleton Collection," Green Book, Vol. 1, Nuremberg Military Tribunal, 1945, at NA. Status of WH's investigation and personal concerns: WH, "The Finding of the Crown Jewels: A Sketch of Monuments and Fine Arts Activities in World War II," lecture delivered by WH on October 4, 1965, at WHA; WH, "Recovery of the Crown Jewels of the Holy Roman Empire," undated and unpublished article, at WHA; Robert Armstrong, "The German Crown Jewels: A Modern Detective Story," report for U.S. Army Group CC, APO 742, 1945, at WHA; "A Nazi Treasure Grab Upset by Army Sleuths," MFAA report, January 1, 1946, at NA. Details of the conversation between WH and FR not cited in other chapters: Memorandum, "Rivalries among Top Nazi Leaders," European Political Report, OSS, Vol. II, N. 12, March 23, 1945, at FRP; memorandum, "German Scorched Earth," VIII U.S. Corps G-2 Periodic Report No. 287, March 31, 1945, at NA; and memorandum "Extension of Death Penalty by Nazis," European Political Report, OSS, Vol. II, No. 12, March 23, 1945, at NA. FR as Hitler specialist: FR, "My Inquiry into Hitler's Love Life," unpublished, undated essay, at FRP; FR, "The Questionnaire," unpublished, undated essay, at FRP. Several published sources claim that Patton didn't visit Nürnberg at this time. Patton himself, however, documented the trip: Patton Papers, manuscript collection, mss HM 63825–63841, Huntington Library, Art Collections and Botanical Gardens, San Marino, Calif. Patton's trip to Nürnberg and connection to MFAA: Memo from JT to Education and Religion Detachment F1B3, Company B, Third ECA Regiement, July 27, 1945, at NA. Patton's Longinus poem: George Patton, *The Poems of General George S. Patton: Lines of Fire,* Edwin Mellen Press, Lewiston, N.Y., 1991, p. 119. Patton and reincarnation: Frederick Ayer, *Before the Colors Fade,* Norman Berg, Dunwoody, Ga., 1971, p. 95.

CHAPTER 17: EXTERNSTEINE

Details of the overnight trip to Externsteine and Büren and details of the conversations between WH and Dollar and WH and Markham are drawn from my interview with FR in May 2009; July 29 travel voucher, at NA; Major S. F. Markham's "Report" with WH's handwritten notes, at WHA; and Markham's handwritten report of MFAA activities and meetings with U.S. occupation zone personnel, at Kreismuseum Wewelsburg Archive, Büren-Wewelsburg. WH family background and connections with Externsteine: correspondence between Professor Eugen Fehrle and the Deutsches Ahnenerbe, January and February 1942, at UH; Deutsches Ahnenerbe correspondence with UH Department of Archaeology, Wolfram Sievers and Wilhelm Teudt file collection, at NA; WH, "Erich's Story," undated essay, at WHA; WH untitled memorandum on Rudolf WH, April 1, 1947, at WHA; and WH's oral history, tape 2, at WHA. For general background on the Horn family's connections to scholarship during the Third Reich: Erich Maschke, *Die deutschen Kriegsgefangenen des Zweiten Weltkrieges, eine Zusammenfassung,* Verlarg Ernst und Werner Gieseking, Munich, 1974; Erich Maschke, *Das Geschlecht der Staufer,* Scientia Verlag, Stuttgart, 1970; Erich Maschke, *Looking East: Germany beyond the Vistula,* Terramare Office, Berlin, 1935; and Michael Burleigh, *Germany Turns Eastwards: A Study of Ostforschung in the Third Reich,* Cambridge University Press, New York, 1988, pp. 57–59. General background and scholarship on Externsteine: Walther Matthes and Rolf Speckner, *Das Relief an den Externsteinen: Ein karolingisches Kunstwerk und sein spiritueller Hintergrund,* Ostfilder, Edition Tertium, 1997, pp. 184–187; and Klaus Junker, "Research under Dictatorship: The German Archaeological Institute 1929–1945," *Antiquity,* vol. 72, 1988, pp. 282–293.

CHAPTER 18: BLACK CAMELOT

WH's meeting and conversation with Markham and visit to Wewelsburg Castle has been drawn from my interview with FR in May 2009; July 29 travel voucher, at NA; Major S. F. Markham's "Report" with WH's handwritten notes, at WHA; and Markham's handwritten report of MFAA activities and meetings with U.S. occupation zone personnel, at Kreismuseum Wewelsburg Archive, Büren-Wewelsburg. For background material discussed in connection with WH's tour of Wewelsburg Castle: Interview with Wulff Brebeck in February 2008; Wulff Brebeck, Karl Hüser, and Kristen John-Stucke, *Wewelsburg 1933–1945: Megalomania and Terror of the SS,* Landschaftsverband Westfalen-Lippe, Münster, 2007, pp. 23–59; and Stephen Cook and Stuart Russell, *Heinrich Himmler's Camelot: The Wewelsburg Ideological Center of the SS, 1934–1945,* Kressmann-Backmeyer, Andrews, N.C., 1999, pp. 3–119. Niederhagen concentration camp: Hans Hesse, ed., *Persecution and Resistance of Jehovah's Witnesses during the Nazi Regime 1933–1945,* Courier Press, Chicago, 2001, pp. 60–71. Ahnenerbe expeditions and materials found at Wewelsburg: "Looted Cultural Materials at the SS School Haus Wewelsburg," undated CIC report, at NA and Hellmut Lehmann-Haupt, MFAA report; "Cultural Looting of the Ahnenerbe," March 1, 1948, at NA.

CHAPTER 19: THE WHITE HOUSE
Josef Spacil's name is sometimes misrepresented in U.S. military documents as Wilhelm Spacil. WH obtaining and reading the records: WH's oral history, tapes 5, 8, 9, at WHA; and my interview with FR in May 2009. Background on Josef Spacil: Kenneth Alford and Theodor Savas, *Nazi Millionaires: The Allied Search for Hidden SS Gold,* Castmate, Havertown, Pa., 2002, pp. 92–136. Bureau II activities: "Annex III Report," August 28, 1945, at NA. Specific Spacil records reviewed by WH and FR: "Brief on Wilhelm Spacil," 290 GBI-CIB, July 23, 1945, at NA; "CIC memorandum on Spacil," July 27, 1945, at NA; "Fuerstenfeldbruck Screening Center Interrogation Reports A and B, Gretl Biesecker," June 13, 1945, at WHA; "Fuerstenfeldbruck Screening Center interrogation report of SS Sturmbandführer Schuster," June 12, 1945, at WHA; "Fuerstenfeldbruck Screening Center Arrest Report of Spacil and Associates by Claus Nacke," June 18, 1945, at NA; "Fuerstenfeldbruck Screening Center Interrogation Report of Recovery of Money and Valuables Turned Over to CIC," U.S. Seventh Army, June 10, 1945, at NA; memorandum, "Arrest of SS Oberführer Spacil and Associates," June 18, 1945, at NA; Interrogation Reports of 307th Counter Intelligence Corps Detachment, "Interrogation Memorandum, Josef Spacil," July 27, 1945, at NA; "CIC, Headquarters Seventh Army Memorandum," June 16, 1945, at NA; CIC, "Spacil Memorandum," July 27, 1945, at NA; CIC, "Wilhelm Spacil Information Regarding the Discovery of Shipment 31," undated, at NA; and CIC, "Memorandum for the Officer in Charge of the Interrogation of Josef Spacil," July 5, 1945, at NA. Fischhorn Castle and CIC corruption: "CIR and interrogation of Erwin Haufler," September 15, 1945, at NA. Hitler's personal property and papers: "Documents and Effects of Hitler and Eva Braun," CIC team 970–33, CIR report, January 20, 1946, at NA. RSHA operations, Kaltenbrunner, and Naumann: CIC, "Kaltenbrunner Intermediate Interrogation Reports 1 and 2," June 28, 1945, at NA.

CHAPTER 20: NAZI PLUNDER
Details of the conversation between WH and FR are drawn from my interview with FR in May 2009; WH's oral history, tape 4, at WHA; unpublished essay, "The Nazi Mind-Set," by FR, at FRP; and correspondence from FR to Bernard FR on May 29, 1945, at FRP. Funds obtained by the CIC and

corruption of CIC personnel: "Brief on Wilhelm Spacil," 290 GBI-CIB, July 23, 1945, at NA; and CIC, "Memorandum on Spacil," July 27, 1945, at NA. For a comprehensive summary of the CIC corruption in regard to the Spacil investigation: Kenneth Alford and Theodor Savas, *Nazi Millionaires: The Allied Search for Hidden SS Gold*, Castmate, Havertown, Pa., 2002, pp. 92–136; and Kenneth Alford, *The Spoils of World War II*, Birch Lane Press, New York, 1994, pp. 259–269. WH's attitude regarding the MFAA and CIC and USFET authority and oversight: "Notes on MFAA and Wiesbaden manifesto," notes and unpublished essay, at WHA.

CHAPTER 21: CAMP KING

WH's conversation with JT has been drawn from WH's handwritten notes of interviews, August 1945, MFAA collection at NA; and my interview with FR in May 2009. Changes taking place in Nürnberg under new occupation administration: MGLS, Report, May 23, 1947, at NA; MGLS Report, October 25, 1947, at NA; John Gimbel, *The American Occupation of Germany: Politics and the Military, 1945–1949*, Stanford University Press, Stanford, Calif., 1968, pp. 50–103; OMGUS reports: "Fragenbogen, Prosecution Cases File," at NA; OMGN, "Additional list of Removals," September 1, 1945, at NA; and OMGUS, "Report on Denazification," October 20, 1945, at NA. WH's step-by-step recovery and interrogation of Fries and his findings: Memo from WH to Office of Military Government for Germany, Economics Division, Restitution Control Branch, MFAA, May 23, 1945, at NA; message No. 686, January 10, 1945, from General Mark W. Clark to USFET, at NA; and Earl Ziemke, *The U.S. Army in the Occupation of Germany, 1944–1946*, Army Historical Series, U.S. Army, Center of Military History, Washington, D.C., pp. 400–410, at MHI. Details of arrest and interrogation of Fries: WH's handwritten notes of interviews, August 1945, MFAA collection, at NA; WH, "Report on the investigation of the circumstances of disappearance of the Imperial Insignia from the crown treasures of the Holy Roman Empire in the Nuremberg Art Cache, and their recovery," August 14, 1945, at WHA; WH, "The Finding of the Crown Jewels: A Sketch of Monuments and Fine Arts Activities in World War II," lecture delivered by WH on October 4, 1965, at WHA; and Robert Armstrong, "The German Crown Jewels: A Modern Detective Story," report for U.S. Army Group CC, APO 742, 1945, at WHA.

CHAPTER 22: THE CROWN JEWELS

Change of circumstances and political situation when WH returned to Nürnberg: MFAA Historical Report, E1B3, for August 1945, at NA. Pan-

nier bunker and recovery of Crown Jewels: Walter Herppich, *Das unterirdische Nürnberg,* Hofmann Verlag Nürnberg, 1987, pp. 96–119. Return of
Crown Jewels and discussion with JT: WH's report to headquarters, Det
F1B3, Third ECA, JT, August 14, 1945, at NA; and correspondence from
Brigadier General William Draper to WH, August 16, 1946, at WHA. The
most comprehensive single collection of documents related to the discovery: "WH's final report to Office of Military Government for Germany,
Economics Division, Restitution Branch," as compiled with related documents by Mary Regan on March 19, 1946, at NA; and Peter Heigl, *Der
Reichsschatz im Nazibunker,* privately published by Peter Heigl, Nürnberg,
2005, pp. 13–79.

CHAPTER 23: THE FAUSTIAN BARGAIN

Production of Leica camera and interzone passes: Giles MacDonogh, *After
the Reich,* Basic Books, New York, 2007, p. 199. Conversations between
WH and Dollar to bring Mathilde Horn from Soviet Zone have been drawn
from WH's oral history, tapes 5 and 7, at WHA; and my interview with
Alberta Horn and Horn family in April and May 2008. WH family background: WH's "Early Memories of My Family," undated essay, in WHA.
WH's childhood loves, saved from drowning, and experiences at University
of Heidelberg: WH's oral history, tapes 1, 2, 6, at WHA; and my interview
with Jenny Marshall in April 2009. Erich Maschke and academic involvement of greater Horn family in Nazi activities: WH, "Erich's Story," undated essay, at WHA. Rudolf Horn: WH untitled memorandum on Rudolf
Horn, April 1, 1947, at WHA. Fighting with brother: WH's oral history,
tape 2, at WHA. The general status and condition of Heidelberg and role
the university played in the Third Reich: Steven Remy, *The Heidelberg Myth:
The Nazification and Denazification of a German University,* Harvard University Press, Cambridge, Mass., 2002. For general background of Horn
family connections to scholarship during the Third Reich: Erich Maschke,
*Die deutschen Kriegsgefangenen des Zweiten Weltkrieges, Eine Zusammenfas-
sung,* Verlarg Ernst und Werner Gieseking, Munich, 1974; Erich Maschke,
Das Geschlecht der Staufer, Scientia Verlag, Stuttgart, 1970; Erich Maschke,
Looking East: Germany beyond the Vistula, Terramare Office, Berlin, 1935;
and Michael Burleigh, *Germany Turns Eastwards: A Study of Ostforschung in
the Third Reich,* Cambridge University Press, New York, 1988, pp. 57–59.

CHAPTER 24: THE FOURTH REICH

Stars and Stripes article: August 13, 1945, *Stars and Stripes Bavarian Edition,* at WHA. Conversations between WH and MH have been drawn

from WH, "Report on the investigation of the circumstances of disappearance of the Imperial Insignia from the crown treasures of the Holy Roman Empire in the Nuremberg Art Cache, and their recovery," August 14, 1945, at NA; "Armstrong Memorandum," August 1945, at NA; correspondence from Brigadier General William Draper to WH, August 16, 1946, at WHA; Liaison and Protocol Section, OMGUS, G-448, at NA; correspondence from MH to U.S. Group Control Council, Reparation, Deliveries and Restitution Division, MFAA, August 20, 1945, at NA; WH report to headquarters, Det F1B3, Third ECA, JT, August 14, 1945, at NA; "Report of the American Commission for the Protection and Salvage of Artistic and Historic Monuments in War Areas," June 30, 1946, at NA; memorandum of August 20, 1945, from MH to WH, at WHA; and Earl Ziemke, *The U.S. Army in the Occupation of Germany, 1944–1946*, Army Historical Series, U.S. Army, Center of Military History, Washington, D.C., pp. 395–410. Missing coin collection assignment: "Theft of Gold Coin Collection," G-5 Report, October 11, 1945; memorandum by Lieutenant S. L. Faison to OSS Art Looting Investigation Unit, September 17, 1945, at WHA; and WH Report, "The Treasure of Kremsmunster," to Captain Edwin Rae, MFAA, May 11, 1946, at WHA. WH congratulated on a job well done and being given a BMW: Correspondence from WH to Peter Watson for *The Nazi's Wife*, April 25, 1984, and January 9, 1986, at WHA. General background on Nordhausen, the OSS, and CIC: Clarence Lasby, *Project Paperclip: German Scientists and the Cold War*, Atheneum, New York, 1971; and Linda Hunt, *Secret Agenda: The US Government, Nazi Scientists and Project Paperclip, 1945–90*, St. Martin's, New York, 1991. Bernterode mine discovery: Walker Hancock's MFAA Reports, May 2, 1945, and May 12, 1945, at NA; CIR by Lt. H. D. Cragon, May 2, 1945, at NA; and Walker Hancock, "Experience of a Monuments Officer in Germany," *College Art Journal*, May 1946, pp. 271–311.

EPILOGUE

Attempts to interview Spacil: "Memorandum for the officer in charge, regarding further interrogation of Oberführer Spacil," CIC report, July 5, 1947, at NA. What became of Spacil: Interview with Kenneth Alford in April 2009, and correspondence with Klaus Gagstädter, May 2009. What became of Fries, Schmeissner, and Lincke: Peter Heigl, *Der Reichsschatz im Nazibunker*, privately published by Peter Heigl, Nürnberg, 2005, pp. 50–78; Peter Heigl, *Die Nürnberger Prozesse*, privately published by Peter Heigl, Nürnberg, 2005, endnotes; interview with Nürnberg historian Bernhard Seiler in February 2008; Hugo Portisch, *Österreich II: Der lange*

Weg zur Freiheit, Kremayr and Scheriau, Vienna, 1995, pp. 1–12. Trials of Fries and Schmeissner: "A Nazi Treasure Grab Upset by Army Sleuths," MFAA report, January 1, 1946, at NA. Return of the Viet Stoss altar: Report from USFET to CG III Army, September 10, 1945, at NA; and Frank Waters, "Famed Polish Altar Piece Found Cached under Nuremberg Rubble," *Stars and Stripes Bavarian Edition,* June 13, 1945, at WHA. Controversy over ownership of Crown Jewels and interest by Generals Patton and Eisenhower: "MFAA meeting notes of repatriation of Crown Jewels," January 9, 1946, at NA; Colonel M. C. Bauer, "Return to Vienna of Crown Jewels and Regalia of the Holy Roman Empire," addressed to USFET, copy to MH, November 13, 1945, at NA; memo by Colonel C. Klise, "Regalia of the Holy Roman Empire," to Director Office of Military Government, U.S. Zone, December 13, 1945, at NA; and "Secret Routine," memo of Office of Military Government for Germany, reference number WX-85965, December 3, 1945, at NA. Legal opinions of ownership of Crown Jewels: Report by Lieutenant Colonel F. H. Kinners for Office of Military Government for Germany, February 13, 1946, at NA; and Otto Bemus, letter to James Garrison, February 12, 1948, at NA. Return of Crown Jewels to Vienna: Report prepared by MFAA for Lieutenant Colonel Ernest T. De Wald, "Return to Vienna of Crown Jewels and Regalia of the Holy Roman Empire," October 29, 1945, at NA. Gutierrez and the Hitler diaries: Interview with Kenneth Alford, April 2009. Hensel affair and replica Crown Jewels: "Investigation of Alleged Grand Larceny of Lt. Colonel Joseph W. Hensel," September 16, 1946, at NA. The replica Crown Jewels that may have been at Wewelsburg: Correspondence with Albert Bühler, October 10, 1948, at WHA; and correspondence from Bühler to WH, January 7, 1972, at WHA. Subsequent investigations of Holy Lance and Crown Jewels: Captain Wilhelm Bernhard and Colonel Howard Buechner, *Adolf Hitler and the Secrets of the Holy Lance,* Thunderbird Press, Metairie, La., 1988; Alec Maclellan, *The Secret of the Spear,* Souvenir Press, London, 2004; Jerry Smith and George Piccard, *Secrets of the Holy Lance,* Adventures Unlimited Press, Kempton, Ill., 2005; and Trevor Ravenscroft, *The Spear of Destiny,* Weiser Books, Boston, 1973. Books by WH: WH and Ernest Born, *The Barns of the Abbey of Beaulieu at Its Granges of Great Coxwell & Beaulieu-St. Leonards,* University of California Press, Berkeley, 1965; WH, Jenny White Marshall, Grellan D. Rourke, *The Forgotten Hermitage of Skellig Michael,* NetLibrary, Dublin, Ohio, 1990; and WH and Ernest Born, *The Plan of St. Gall,* University of California Press, Berkeley, 1979. Attempts made for WH to receive Army decoration: Correspondence from Colonel Charles Kunzelman (ret.) to WH, August

29, 1981, and March 12, 1984, at WHA; and correspondence from Colonel Charles Kunzelman (ret.) to Lieutenant Colonel Vernon Hull, September 29, 1980, at WHA. Jacqueline Kennedy Onassis working with WH: Interview with Peter Watson, April 2009; Peter Watson, *The Nazi's Wife*, Doubleday, Garden City, N.Y., 1985.

INDEX

ABOUT THE
AUTHOR

Sidney D. Kirkpatrick is an award-winning filmmaker and the international bestselling author of five previous books, including *A Cast of Killers* and *Edgar Cayce: An American Prophet*. He lives in Stony Brook, New York.

INSERT PHOTO CREDITS

1. National Archives, WWII photo collection.
2. From *Eigentliche Verbindung der Helthumb und des Keyerlichen Ornatus,* as reprinted in *Die deutschen Reichsinsignien und Reichskleinodien,* Nürnberg, 1938 (author's collection).
3. *Die versteckten Reichskleinodien, Herold, Insignia,* 1713, as reprinted in *Die deutschen Reichsinsignien und Reichskleinodien,* Nürnberg, 1938 (author's collection).
4. By Heinrich Hoffman, from *Hitler weil ihn keiner kennt,* Berlin, 1935 (author's collection).
5. *Süddeutsche Zeitung* photo, with permission.
6 and 7. National Archives, WWII photo collection.
8 and 9. Reprinted from *Die Reichskleinodien,* Angelsachsen Verlag, Nürnberg, 1939 (author's collection).
10. Reprinted from *Die Reichskleinodien in der Pfalz,* Friedrich Sprater, published by Im Westmarkverlag, Ludwigshafen am Rhein und Saarbrücken, 1942 (author's collection).
11. Reprinted from *Die Reichskleinodien,* Angelsachsen Verlag, Nürnberg, 1939 (Party Day Book and commemorative album published by Willy Liebel) (author's collection).
12–14. Reprinted from *Die Reichskleinodien in der Pfalz,* Friedrich Sprater, published by Im Westmarkverlag, Ludwigshafen am Rhein und Saarbrücken, 1942 (author's collection).
15–18. National Archives, WWII photo collection.
19–21. By Sidney D. Kirkpatrick.
22. National Archives, WWII photo collection.
23–25. Walter Horn Collection, courtesy of Alberta Horn (with permission).
26. Felix Rosenthal Collection, courtesy of Barney Rosenthal (with permission).
27. Mason Hammond Collection, courtesy of the family of Mason Hammond (with permission).
28–30. Courtesy of Stadt Nürnberg (with permission).
31–33. National Archives, WWII photo collection.
34. *Süddeutsche Zeitung* photo, with permission.
35. By Sidney D. Kirkpatrick.
36–40. Courtesy of the Kreismuseum Wewelsburg Archive, Büren-Wewelsburg, with permission.
41. By Sidney D. Kirkpatrick.
42. Courtesy of the Kreismuseum Wewelsburg Archive, Büren-Wewelsburg, with permission.
43–51. National Archives, WWII photo collection.
52. Felix Rosenthal Collection, courtesy of Barnard Rosenthal (with permission).
53. Walter Horn Collection, courtesy of Alberta Horn (with permission).